Fearfully, Wonderfully, and Bipolar-ly Made

Fearfully, Wonderfully, and Bipolar-ly Made:

From Shame to Sanctuary

Laura Joy Palma

Writer's Growth Press

ISBN 979-8-9955469-0-0 (paperback)

Published by *Writer's Growth Press*
writersgrowth.com

Cover photograph by Joy Palma, artwork by author

Printed in the United States of America

First Edition

For Dr. Dennis Bogin (1947-2017)

who once told me:

"It is in the structure of myth that the hero always struggles lost in a dark wood, with many hardships, anxieties, and tribulations before she comes into a clearing, into the light…

…before she finds herself."

Author's Note

This book was written during my marriage. I publish it under my maiden name, Laura Joy Palma, having found that the sanctuary I was searching for was never in a name or a household—it was in the One who made me.

Table of Contents

Preface

When I'd struggled long enough brute-forcing my way through daily existence and sufficiently destroyed everything I touched, I accepted a bipolar diagnosis suggested and dismissed fifteen years ago. It is most accurate I diagnosed myself, and upon leaving the doctor's office with my newly confirmed scarlet letter, shelves lined with psychiatric and psychological texts, I asked my psychiatrist at Christian Psychotherapy if she had a book recommendation for managing this mental illness. She had none.

That was seven years ago. Since then and until prioritizing this undertaking, I have been silent. In hiding. It was only when I turned my personal research toward memoirs detailing the experiences of admirable people who shed light on the bipolar experience that I could identify a heartbreaking pattern, repeated again and again through the chronicles of individuals with mood disorders who greatly impacted the world and continue to do so.

We reject a diagnosis. We soar until we ruin our relationships and livelihood, usually in that order. We accept a diagnosis, get treatment, and restart those lives or we reject the label, avoid treatment, and proceed with self-destruction, substance abuse, and death by suicide or another avoidable tragedy.

The cycle, as you'll see, could also be broken were this mental illness as normalized as ADHD (attention-deficit/hyperactivity disorder), for example. Even some of my sixth-grade students can attribute their misbehaviors during class to an attention-deficit disorder. Meanwhile, I'm three times their age and still swallow my pride before admitting to the proclivities of my mischievous neurotransmitters.

I am writing that book I needed to read: the book you put in the hands of someone you suspect might want to consider a diagnosis; the book you put in the hands of someone diagnosed but too afraid of biological branding to accept a label; and the book you put in the hands of someone who wants to change the stigma, for themselves or their loved ones, to clearly see what bipolar is and is not, and perhaps begin to understand the grandeur of the manic-depressive mind absent fear or generalizations.

While chatting with a friend some time ago about our book writing ventures, something she said stuck: "We need people who have been where we are to look to give us hope; they did it, and so can I." That's why I'm writing this book. I wrestled with the fear and shame of being a person with bipolar disorder (BD). I withdrew from friends and family, hoping not to contaminate them with my tempestuous mood swings. I hid in silence initially, and it had a purpose. I sought out the voices of people who had come out, owned their illnesses, and shared transparently about their journeys.

Then, I saw the pattern. Then, I wanted to help people like me break it.

As a career English teacher entrusted with a hundred or so kids to guide each year, it was easy to neglect my own wellness journey and continue putting off this call. Subsequently, I took a sabbatical from teaching to prioritize my overall health by writing this book. I suspect I'll be a better educator for all my students if I am aware of the dynamics of my illness and mitigate triggers with better strategies in place; I'll likely also be better able to identify and support my neurodivergent students.

This book weaves together the stories of real people living with bipolar disorder—both tragic and heartwarming—into a tapestry grounded in clinical research and lived experience. I draw from varied field experts and guides to bipolar living to define and contextualize our shared experience. While it will serve those newly diagnosed, it's fundamentally the story of my journey from shame to sanctuary, and the accounts and memoirs I reference offer readers resources for understanding how bipolar manifests itself uniquely in various individuals.

What I discovered through writing this book—and living the years that followed—is that true sanctuary doesn't come from proper diagnosis, the right medication, or even a loving family who learns to navigate your moods. Those matter deeply, and you'll find guidance for all of them in these pages. However, the sanctuary I was desperately seeking? It came through relationship with God—an anchor that holds even when the storms don't stop. That's what I want you to find.

In essence, I have committed to this book because I've been convicted that hiding in silence only served to further my shame and worsen our plight. Once I saw my own internal monologue narrated by strangers, I wasn't wholly alone or ashamed anymore. My brain chemistry works like those of President Abraham Lincoln, superstar Mariah Carey, and even the ethereal Buzz Aldrin after he came down from the moon, literally and figuratively.

While I cite research and draw from clinical experts throughout, this book is fundamentally about lived experience. My understanding of bipolar disorder deepened page by page as I wrote, and I hope readers will be inspired to continue their own learning journey. I should note that while I cite anything that's not common knowledge, my study of BD became like its own college course. For clarity, I'll define terms, with support from experts, associated with understanding the disorder—terms that have become a part of my everyday life.

My research comforts me in the link suggested between mania and madness and mania and genius. Since the days of Ancient Greece, they've been debating the catalyst responsible for greatness. This isn't new; nevertheless, if we can reframe the conversation surrounding bipolar, normalizing it as a necessary shift in modern culture, then people battling this illness and unwittingly securing their demise could embrace the hope that comes only after acceptance. When we hurl bipolar as an insult toward someone because of a lost temper or empathetic mood swing, we're spotlighting one undisputable factor for why this stigma exists. We characterize bipolar by what's most visible: when we are unstable, be it for lack of treatment or the wrong treatment, not when we are made stable through the right psychological concoction for assimilation.

This book title was born of a desire to unify my sense of identity as both a person of faith and a person with bipolar disorder—two truths that I've learned don't contradict each other. A young girl being raised in a Christian household with a legacy of faith generations deep didn't lend itself well to temper tantrums. Steadied within a controlled, structured home environment of moderation and modesty, I believe my bipolar tendencies were both masked and managed, for better or worse. The hypomania that distinguishes bipolar disorder type II (BDII) from other mental illness is observable as extreme highs and lows, taking alternate turns, and I deeply regret most considered my emotional state solely a reflection of inward spiritual posture.

Within family and church family contexts, I've experienced the body of Christ fail to recognize the danger of finding wholly spiritual solutions for problems of brain chemistry. In different churches and states and decades, I've seen mental illness shamed as habitual sin. No matter how many times grown-ups forced me to apologize for my temper and go to my room to memorize scriptures about being slow to anger, I'd still lose it too quickly the next time. I've filled dozens of journals with prayers lamenting my inability to be like Christ, despite mirroring my mother's daily waking quiet times with God. We were so busy refining my spiritual character, I couldn't see the real thorn in my side, much less name it, get treatment, and give myself a shot at healthy, godly relationships.

In a post-pandemic era where mood disorders like anxiety and depression threaten the resiliency of character in our nation's youth, it's paramount we distribute a reformed message from the church. I found sanctuary in Christ, and I believe you can too—former misconceptions aside. Humanity is oft afraid of what it doesn't understand, so in sharing my story as a Christian living with BD, I'm hoping we'll be better understood; subsequently, we'll be easier to embrace when we're most in need of respite.

By creating a society where it is safe to own this mental illness and get treatment, we can change the narrative and end the cycle of periodic or lifelong destruction, perhaps by recalling an ancient, Aristotelian stance that a degree of madness is needed for true genius. French philosopher Denis Diderot deepened that discussion, saying, "Oh! How near are genius and madness! Men imprison them and chain them, or raise statues to them." I think it's how we view ourselves in response to diagnosis that groups us in Diderot's former or latter.

May those who read these pages find the ability to recite and believe the words of the psalm and praise God for being fearfully, wonderfully, and even bipolar-ly made.

Introduction

Before you read my story, I need to explain something important about how I've chosen to structure it. You'll notice I've intentionally saved the spiritual dimension for the final section of this book. This isn't because faith is unimportant to my story—as I mentioned in the preface, unifying my identity as both a person of faith and a person with bipolar disorder was central to writing this book. Rather, it's because I've learned that the most effective path to healing requires building a solid medical foundation first.

I'm taking you on the same journey I had to take: first accepting the medical reality, then discovering how faith actually enhances rather than replaces proper treatment. In Parts One through Three, I'll show you what bipolar disorder actually is, how to get proper care, and how to advocate for yourself and others—all through a largely secular lens. I establish the clinical foundation first because that's what preserves lives.

Only in Part Four do I fully integrate the spiritual dimension, showing how proper understanding of bipolar disorder actually deepens rather than threatens faith. I save what I consider the best part of my story for last—not because it's less important, but because it's the crown jewel that sits atop a solid foundation of medical understanding.

This structure mirrors my own healing journey. I had to learn to manage my symptoms before I could fully embrace how God had made me, bipolar parts and all. If you're reading this as a person of faith, I ask for your patience as we build that foundation together. If you're reading this as someone skeptical of faith, I invite you to see how spiritual understanding can complement rather than compete with medical care.

My story could not be told chronologically. Rather, I implement a topical guiding framework and share related details from places throughout my timeline.

Part One examines what BD looks and feels like before diagnosis and without proper treatment. It contextualizes individual experiences with keeping secrets, avoiding labels, and seeking out our own forms of medication—often unhealthy and ranging from risky to downright illegal. Furthermore, it dissembles the stigmatization cycle that perpetuates a resistance to diagnosis, and subsequently, to treatment.

Part Two defines BD, clinically and contextually. Alongside celebrity reveals mirrored with my own narrator experience, I'll highlight current trends in public personas showing symptoms of mania, rapid cycling, and severe depression—often culminating in highly publicized suicide, as in the cases of Kurt Cobain, Naomi Judd, and Marilyn Monroe. It answers the questions: When do I get help? How will treatment work? What helps beyond medication? And finally, who am I now?

Part Three serves as a call to action for advocacy. After shining a light on BD, we'll look at who is already carrying the torch to advocate for a change in the societal stigma that keeps people hiding in fear of abandonment if they don't manage their moods appropriately. The double-edged sword of rejection is itself a backhanded compliment; my innate gusto for life and supreme empathy make people gravitate toward me… and provided I stay in an upswing, I don't fear losing their favor.

We need a systemic shift in educational agendas so that kids are as comfortable owning and apologizing for their bipolar misbehaviors as they are for their ADHD ones.

Part Four explores the spiritual dimension of my journey. Having found my footing in advocacy work, I realized that the secular strategies and professional techniques, while essential, weren't addressing the deepest part of my healing. This section reveals what I discovered after years of proper treatment and a supportive marriage: true sanctuary doesn't come from medication, therapy, or even family—though all are essential. It comes through relationship with God, an anchor that holds even when the storms don't stop. And it envisions how the church can become that sanctuary for others walking this path.

Regardless of one's spiritual position, loving yourself is a foundation for healthy relationships. I want to believe what King David wrote is true: I am, in fact, fearfully and wonderfully made. Even motivated to write a book that helps others accept this diagnosis and seek treatment, I don't yet love the bipolar parts of me. Give me a few thousand words, and I'll show you how I learned to believe what King David wrote: I am fearfully, wonderfully, and even bipolar-ly made. Not despite my brain chemistry but including it. That's the sanctuary I found, and it's waiting for you, too.

Part One: Facing Reality—Dark Night of the Soul

Chapter One: Do You Have a Secret?

For about four years, I blogged faithfully. Every Tuesday night. Rain, shine, snow, heat. It was clockwork. I'd settle into my white wicker love seat on that rented front porch in downtown Hampton and write, unscripted, about whatever I was experiencing. I called it *Writer's Growth* simply because I recognized I grow by processing life this way. For two hours a week, I brain dumped publicly, only my mind would unpack analogies and make connections reflecting an intentionality of planning I'd skipped altogether. Life made more sense after a thousand words.

I blogged through my 2015 summer of online dating fiascos and eventually meeting the man I'd dub Charming—and he was. I blogged through the ups and downs of waiting two years for his epic Cinderella proposal at Fort Monroe beach on Labor Day. I blogged through our fairy tale engagement, and undoubtedly, our curious break up the following May. I managed to maintain my blog for five more months after that, but it wasn't the same.

I was keeping secrets now. Nothing made sense, not even after a thousand words.

For someone who had always found comfort in prayer when life felt chaotic, even that felt hollow now. The daily quiet times my mother had modeled since childhood—her morning ritual of Bible study and prayer—suddenly felt impossible to maintain.

When You Can't Tell the Truth

The premise of *Writer's Growth* was full transparency, an authentic lens into a thirty-something looking for love and belonging. On October 9, 2018, I posted, "The things I can't put on the page weigh on me daily, shelved out of reach as I go through the motions, but always there, neglected during Tuesday night writing binges to maintain status quo."[1] Wednesday, I awoke to a comment from one of my readers: "This concerns me. Why write to maintain the status quo but no longer be open about who you are?" Her words simmered for a couple weeks. Then, I took a sabbatical from my blog.

Having concluded I could not publicly write the truth of what really happened to end Charming and me without damaging his reputation or my family name, I'd resigned myself to clever write-arounds. I could only write around the truth for so long before nothing came out.

It is triggering, in fact, simply to write about this stage. These words don't form themselves easily into sentences. I examine past events and try to recollect them accurately for your benefit while at the same time mindful this act of recalling the memories will alter them by mere action alone. Calling off the wedding with Charming was only one in a series of other twisted events that never made it into the annals of my blog.

When You're Afraid to Be Honest

For much of my life, I was keeping a secret I didn't understand until I was formally diagnosed with BD in February 2019.

And in the years since then, living with BD is the secret I've protected above all else. Growing up in a faith community where we prayed for healing and believed God could fix anything, admitting I needed psychiatric medication felt like admitting my faith wasn't strong enough. I don't type these words because I'm ready for the judgment I always feared would come. I'm typing them because I need to love myself—and as a writer, loving myself means losing the gag order and giving myself the freedom to be honest with my readers.

This isn't a unique journey. Kay Redfield Jamison, a psychologist specializing in mood disorders, published a memoir in 1995, *An Unquiet Mind*, where she exposed her own BD. Like me, she struggled from adolescence but was diagnosed and began treatment much later. I found her perspective refreshing because Jamison was an expert in the illness she herself battled, and she similarly had to overcome her fear of being rejected for coming out.

In the preface to a later edition of the book, Jamison writes, "I did not know what the personal and professional repercussions would be once *An Unquiet Mind* was published; I did know that writing such an explicit book while also a professor of psychiatry at a prominent medical school would ratchet up the stakes by a notch or two."[2] If she believed her message was more important than the risk, why not me? Her support was overwhelming, in hindsight.

And, quite frankly, her stakes were much higher than mine.

When You Keep Too Many Secrets

When my nephew hid something that he'd broken as a child in my parents' home for my mother to later discover, I bet he felt badly about what he had done. He may have been avoiding feared consequences. The problem with keeping a secret like that is its weight on the conscience.

Shame remains where forgiveness or reparation might have been though an undesirable reaction was also possible.

One misstep stings. Collect a bunch, and shame festers beneath the secret-keeping, often bubbling over into expressed anger that further isolates us. I'd filled journals with prayers asking God to help me control my temper, to make me more like the gentle, patient person I thought Christians were supposed to be. But the harder I tried to pray my way to emotional stability, the more I seemed to fail.

That's why I'm here. No one wants to live in fear of my angry outbursts.

My temper's trigger isn't my family and friends; it's my own secret den of shame. My short fuse is fueled by self-loathing. I don't want this dysfunction, but it's real. Keeping it a secret, though, has just made me hate a part of myself… and can we really hate just a part of ourselves? Either way, I don't want to settle for anything less than full acceptance of fearfully, wonderfully, and bipolar-ly made me.

I remember when Mariah Carey was hospitalized for a breakdown my senior year of high school. She was a favored female vocalist of mine, so when I read her 2018 interview with *People* magazine coming out about her battle with bipolar, I didn't mind seeing myself in her admissions. Carey had been diagnosed during that hospitalization in 2001, but she had only newly sought treatment. "Until recently I lived in denial and isolation and in constant fear someone would expose me," Carey told *People*. "It was too heavy a burden to carry and I simply couldn't do that anymore."[3] That's where I am. Even if the secret and its collection of secrets will bring judgment, I must unburden myself of them.

Fast forward seven years from that interview, and a BDII diagnosis sneaks its way merely into the final sentence of her Wikipedia page; coming out did not tarnish Mariah Carey's legacy. Moreover, I'm convinced that every day I keep this secret, I tarnish mine a little more and simply set myself up for failure in the mood management game.

Often, we don't understand the big bipolar secret we're really keeping. When I was first diagnosed, I had no idea what BD actually meant beyond the stereotypes I'd absorbed from movies and casual conversations. I quickly learned it's a medical illness characterized by alternating periods of abnormally elevated and depressed moods—but what that looked like in real life, in my life, was something I had to discover through painful trial and error.

There's no blood test or brain scan that can diagnose BD. Instead, doctors consider your symptoms and history against criteria in the DSM-5, the mental health diagnostic manual. [4] Interestingly, the term "bipolar disorder" is relatively new—before 1980, it was called "manic depressive disorder," which is why you might hear older relatives use that language.

Mood episodes provide data for diagnosis. If a person is having a manic episode, she'll experience "a period of abnormally elevated energy and mood that interferes with a person's ability to function" and meet several criteria, according to the same guide to understanding BD. This moodiness, presented as irritability or goal-directed energy, persists daily for a week or requires hospitalization, and comes with symptoms like an inflated sense of self, decreased need for sleep, excessive talking or distractibility, and an increase in high-risk behaviors.[5] This type of an episode is most characteristic of bipolar disorder type I (BDI).

With BDI, a person may or may not experience depression, the other pole of mood episodes. A major depressive episode is more than just being sad. It can be difficult to find the motivation to get out of bed in the morning. A person will suffer from a depressed mood and may show symptoms like a decreased interest in sex or pleasurable activities, decrease or increase in appetite or sleep, feelings of guilt and worthlessness, and thoughts of suicide. These symptoms are severe enough to interfere with daily functioning.[6] I can bubble up two or three dress sizes when depression smacks me down.

While I have experienced triggered manic episodes as the result of taking prescribed antidepressants, what made diagnosis difficult was that I have BD type II (BDII); we often blend in with the overachievers. BDII looks like periods of depression and hypomania. Hypomania has the same symptoms of a manic episode, but it's shorter, lasting days rather than weeks, and it doesn't cause as severe impairment or require hospitalization. I present better publicly than personally in this state. Hypomania can "make you more engaging, so you may become the center of attention…. For some people, hypomania creates periods of high creativity and/productivity that are positive experiences."[7] Unlike BDI, with BDII, a major depressive episode is needed for diagnosis.

As a result, it's common that we're diagnosed with unipolar depression before ultimately resolving to a BD diagnosis with increased data points. With major depressive disorder (MDD), someone emulates the characteristics of a bipolar depressive episode without the tendency to shift to the opposite pole of mania, which is why it's called unipolar depression. Since there is less stigma surrounding depression, I've found people more willing to share openly about having experienced a dark night of the soul than the cryptic manic state.

There are a few more labels to consider that help us diagnosis and treat mood disorders. Cyclothymia is a milder form of BD where a person swings between mild depression and hypomania. This would be a chronic mood pattern, as opposed to a person with BD experiencing a *mixed state*, or mixed episode. In a mixed state, she can show manic and depressive symptoms simultaneously, where mania's energy powers crippling worries instead. When BD symptoms are accompanied by delusions and hallucinations, schizoaffective disorder is the diagnosis.[8] I'd venture there's a notable genetic overlap between BD and schizophrenia. Furthermore, some medications can cause side effects that mimic other types of bipolar, further complicating accurate diagnoses.

There's so much overlap, in fact, that some leading scientists think we've been too divisive in our sub-classifications within BD. Psychiatrists coined the term *"soft" bipolar disorders* to challenge the classical way of dividing manic and depressive symptoms into separate categories. In this framework, people fall somewhere on the *bipolar spectrum*, a useful context for treating mental health problems with similar origins and overlapping symptoms. If a patient has sufficient symptoms but doesn't meet the criteria for BDI, BDII, or cyclothymia, the DSM-5-TR includes another label, bipolar NOS (not otherwise specified) or NEC (not elsewhere classified).[9] These labels fill out the bipolar spectrum.

Looking back, when life was relatively good and I was in a safe, predictable environment, hypomania made me the perfect person to contract as wedding planner with only five days to go. Likewise, hypomania fueled frantic lesson plans like when I decided I needed an educational video that didn't exist for the next week's lesson, and then spend my weekend compiling every allusion to *Of Mice and Men* in popular culture for my students to watch with corresponding guided notes. Life was a never-ending series of mini projects until I divorced at thirty. I thrived in high-stakes environments; when depressed, I struggled to maintain my established, hypomanic pace of life.

After this crash course, you may be wondering what type of BD you or your loved one is working with. That's a good question; it might take a psychiatrist to arrive at a solid diagnosis, but what's most important is that you're observing mood episodes and recognizing that something is off. We'll explore the clinical side of BD more fully in part two.

When You're Done Secret Keeping

There is hope. When you accept you have bipolar, you join the ranks of many acclaimed, successful individuals who have contributed positively to society.

One of the first books I bought not long after diagnosis was *Fast Girl* by Suzy Favor Hamilton, subtitled "A Life Spent Running from Madness." The title encapsulates the self-effacing humor with which she details her double life as Olympian athlete by day and call girl by night. She was raised with the stigma that mental illness equaled crazy, but she had the courage to face, accept, and treat her illness. Moreover, Favor wrote her story to help raise awareness and help people like me understand the disorder we battle daily.[10]

If athlete Favor's book reads like a Netflix limited series drama rated M for mature, then actress Carrie Fisher's memoir would be an HBO comedy airing in prime time. Are you uncomfortable with the word bipolar? Give yourself three chapters with *Wishful Drinking* and you'll be laughing about it along with Fisher. Does the weight of a potential diagnosis position you in need of some comic relief? Her introduction shows how people who were also "f——ed up" made her feel better "because look how much these fellow f——ups managed to accomplish!"[11] I recognized names like Sylvia Plath, Judy Garland, and Dick Cavett among Fisher's bipolar club members.

Maybe it was time to stop asking God to fix me and start wondering if He had made me exactly as I was meant to be—bipolar parts and all.

When It's Gone with Wind

Most of note for me in Fisher's idols was Vivien Leigh, my adolescent actress inspiration. One Halloween, I dressed up in a pink ball gown complete with puffed sleeves and a hoop skirt with banana curls that transformed ten-year-old me into Scarlet O'Hara. Mom and I had watched *Gone with the Wind* together; despite recent cultural objections, it will remain a favorite film because of the actress. I wanted to be her, and I got to be her for just one night.

I saw myself in that iconic role as a little girl, so much so that when it began to snow and I was forced to put on a sweater over my ballgown, I threw a fit just like her and pouted for every photo. In retrospect, the photos are quite authentic, capturing the moody madness beneath the beautiful exterior. Nor did I understand then that Vivien Leigh's life made her character more fact than fiction. She battled depression and mania. There were no pills or clinics to keep her from destroying her professional or personal life. Leigh didn't have a choice.

I do have a choice. And maybe, just maybe, the God who made Vivien Leigh in all her beautiful, troubled complexity had also made me exactly as I was meant to be—passionate, intense, and yes, bipolar. Perhaps this wasn't a flaw to fix but a design to understand.

We have a choice. Anything of greatness begins with one first step. You might not be ready to step out into the light yet, but when you are, you'll find examples of people who've taken different paths through this journey. Academy Award winning actress Catherine Zeta-Jones shared about her BDII diagnosis and treatment with ABC News in 2011, crediting both medical treatment and her faith in helping her find stability and peace with her diagnosis.[12] On the other end of the spectrum, Comedian Russell Brand published an autobiography about his struggles with substance abuse in 2018, absent the peace or stability of the ABC interview.[13]

Singer and actress Demi Lovato was featured in a 2012 MTV documentary called *Stay Strong* about her struggles with addiction, self-harm, body image issues, and depression, and she didn't stop there.[14] Lovato went on to executive-produce another documentary following three individuals with mental illness in 2017.[15] Though she eventually resolved from bipolar to an ADHD diagnosis, her journey developed publicly. She was brave in a way I wanted to be, but she'd not found healing in the church.

While some celebrities with BD have used their platforms to reduce stigma, the real encouragement comes from those who've found sustained healing and integration—not just professional success or great artwork despite their struggles. A common trend I see is that once we accept our diagnoses, one of those gifts we're naturally motivated to give is our *story*. Collectively, our stories can attack that stigma and help people stop avoiding the BD label in favor of future personal and professional success.

There could be a time when the confusion, angst, and fear of having bipolar is gone with the wind. That doesn't happen until we take a first step out of the storm.

Chapter Two: Are You Avoiding a Label?

When Mariah Carey was first diagnosed, she said she didn't want to believe it. Perhaps that's why it took more than a decade to get the help she needed to find the right life balance of medication and faith for BD to become merely a footnote in her myriad accomplishments. Regardless, she isn't the only superstar I've admired since childhood who avoided a bipolar label like I did.

Behind the iconic Princess Leia character I worshipped as a girl was Carrie Fisher, an actress given a diagnosis she would not readily accept. She used her fame as a platform to advocate for a change in the stigma surrounding mental illness. Fisher responded to a reader's question in *The Guardian* about finding peace with bipolar. "You're lucky to have been diagnosed as bipolar and accepted that diagnosis at such a young age," Fisher wrote. "I was told that I was bipolar when I was 24 but was unable to accept that diagnosis until I was 28 when I overdosed and finally got sober. Only then was I able to see nothing else could explain away my behavior."[16]

Fisher wrote that response just a few weeks before she died of cardiac arrest in 2016. I wonder if she ever found true peace. Her bravery in speaking publicly about BD opened doors for conversations I desperately needed, even if her own journey remained unfinished.

Why does so much time pass between showing symptoms and getting help? There's more at play than brain chemistry. I wasn't unique in taking years to get properly diagnosed—research shows there's typically an eight-year gap between when bipolar symptoms first appear and when someone receives an accurate diagnosis.[17]

The delay is often longer for people like me with Bipolar II disorder, especially when symptoms start in childhood. Having a history of anxiety and suicidal thoughts can extend the timeline even further, while more dramatic symptoms like psychosis or hospitalizations tend to speed up the process. Looking back, I can see how my particular combination— BDII with childhood onset, anxiety, and suicidal ideation—set me up for a longer journey to diagnosis. Getting misdiagnosed with depression first, as I did, added even more years to the process. [18]

Explaining Away My Misbehaviors

I was around the same age as Fisher when the disorder was first presented to me. My moods had always been big; I explained it away as being a passionate Italian with an equally hot temper. I cried during movies and TV shows, wrote codependent song lyrics characteristic of the late '90s, and when my brother was in med school, he tried to diagnose me with histrionic personality disorder. It enraged me then, but he wasn't too off in suspecting during adolescence that I had a mood disorder. It was kept at bay by intense religious commitments and a protective, controlled, routine home environment.

Our cultural and religious heritages were equally prized. Until recently when my father took a DNA test to bring in a small percentage of French and Greek, I boasted my 100% Italian American bloodline.

Moreover, with disparate factions of ancestors pursuing protestant faith, we boasted in not being predictably Roman Catholic. Witnessing their fathers and grandfathers on the pulpit in the Pentecostal church, my parents raised us with a personal saving faith in Jesus Christ. My father's passed-down motto was simply, "Others can. You can't." The Ten Commandments were just the beginning of the guidebook where my family was concerned. Any scripture could be recalled to contextualize action as sin, and subsequently, reprove.

Position me in the family order, and there was always a brother to keep an eye on me. The eldest, David, is five years older than me, with P.J. following three years later. I was five when Timmy was born. Across that ten-year spread, we had constant companions. Fiercely competitive, we overlapped in hobbies and activities. For most of my life, P.J. was either at school with me or I was living up to his reputation. And when Timmy turned ten, my father unleashed him as the unofficial chaperone when boyfriends started calling.

Related or not, in the months prior to expressed symptom onset, I suffered my first significant loss of a loved one when my paternal grandfather died of diabetic complications. I also started my menstrual cycle and had my first near-death experience in the Atlantic Ocean. Hypomania started, for me, in fifth grade. That protective home with its routines, religious boundaries, and brothers served well to manage my mood episodes. That changed in college.

The summer before sophomore year, I accrued a series of deaths—several young people, friends and acquaintances. They were tragic accidents and suicides, mostly, though one loss was my fault. A friend from my floor at college lost her fiancé in an accident on the interstate.

An acquaintance from high school wrapped his car around a tree while driving drunk and died. Another boy went to that boy's grave when his girlfriend cheated on him and shot himself, right there. Death had never loomed so sinister.

Seeing young people's lives end too soon, I felt the need to be honest with my parents about something big that was between us. I wrote it down and let them read about losing my virginity the previous summer. In my mother's eyes, this meant I was damaged goods. Referencing a favorite childhood photo she dreamed of recreating on my wedding day, Mom's response was that she had to bury the little girl who came down the stairs in the white dress when she was two years old. Dad could barely look at me for three weeks, but he told me he loved me the night before I went back to Chicago for my second year of college.

Initially, I left this story out, dismissing it as a painful part of my story that wasn't directly related to my bipolar journey. Perhaps I'd hoped to avoid returning to these weeks of most profound shame, but failing my parents with my confession was the domino that pushed me over the depressive ledge. The loss was my innocence. My mother would question why I turned away strong, Christian suiters in the years to come, but did she really need to ask? For my family, some sins were worse than others. Not waiting until my wedding day, whether I regretted it or not, made me unworthy of those suitors.

I would settle because something was quite unsettled in me.

That's when I experienced my first extended low. Going back to Wheaton College wasn't the catalyst for joy I thought it would be. The dining hall was a trigger, always bustling with happy people going about daily life, only that didn't make sense juxtaposed against what I was feeling inside. I began cutting myself, always ten strokes at a time. Seventy times seven, the biblical equation for forgiveness. I told myself I'd stop at 490.

A friend who was pre-med caught me cutting in the middle of the night and called the dean to force an evaluation. I was diagnosed with depression and an eating disorder not otherwise specified and completed an outpatient hospitalization program. For two weeks, I spent the day with struggling patients then returned to my dorm to journal about how sane I was by comparison, blissfully unaware of the lifelong illness I was just meeting for the first time.

Meanwhile, I had been put on an antidepressant. At the time, I thought it worked wonders. Six weeks after starting, my roommate's family took me on a road trip from Arizona to California. Could I top the highs from the helicopter ride over the Grand Canyon? Well, I got a tattoo and slept with a near stranger in Los Angeles, the latter detail something I've never told anyone before. It is still as though it happened to another person, a story someone told me.

In her memoir about life with BD, Suzy Favor Hamilton recounts a similar experience about six weeks after being put on Zoloft to treat a severe depression. "I didn't feel depressed anymore. In fact, I felt great. I didn't want to die. I wanted to live with a capital L," she wrote. "I suddenly had more energy than I could remember having for ages, and it felt amazing, especially after the heavy dullness of the depression. I couldn't wait to get up in the morning…"[19] She described wanting to run half marathons, experiment, and adventure beyond her ordinary life. I hadn't let myself think about Los Angeles, but I could have copied and pasted that paragraph and claimed it as my own explanation of what was happening inside me.

Had I known I had bipolar, I would never have started that course of treatment, and we'll deep dive into that in part two. Because it is often the case that people seek help during a depressive episode, a misdiagnosis of unipolar depression is common, especially if the prescribing doctor has not been privy to family or patient history of manic episodes.

Furthermore, I now know that giving an antidepressant to someone who is bipolar and undiagnosed or misdiagnosed, like Suzy Favor Hamilton, can activate a manic break that finally exposes the illness. Taking prescribed antidepressants triggered Favor's manic episode and its characteristic thrill-seeking behavior and hypersexuality. While there are some patients with BD who receive help from antidepressants, it's impossible to know whether this medication will push someone into a manic episode or increase illness cycling.[20] That's what happened to me at nineteen, but I added the sin to my mounting shames and pretended it never happened. That was one point at which my illness could have been exposed.

I stayed on that antidepressant for several months. Suspecting the back injury that sidelined me from running track was contributing to my feelings of isolation, my therapist encouraged a new hobby. After fall break, I latched onto a football player who would grow up to become a rector in the Anglican church. I fell in love with Jake swiftly, though he had no interest in dating me. I confided in him about my cutting. I imagine Jake felt somewhat responsible for me, but this disclosure also bonded us. There was no physical intimacy, just lots of long talks late at night when we should be sleeping.

I became good friends with his older sister, Claire. We went to all of Jake's football games together. We had a tradition of stealing a street sign from campuses at the away games. Football with Claire and late-night talks with Jake make up much of that fall semester. I was happy if it was a Wheaton football night or if I was with Jake. When I wanted to cut, Jake wanted me to talk with him instead. One night, I fell asleep in Jake's dorm room and had to sneak out before we faced consequences. Another night, we went to downtown Chicago. We cuddled in the windy, winter air. However innocent, Jake crossed a line in no more than hugs, our foreheads touching. Thirty minutes secure in the safety and warmth of his arms tipped the scales. I began to hope he might see me as more than a friend. My attachment to Jake kept me steady.

Over Christmas break sophomore year, I travelled to see Jake in his hometown. The plan was to attend a Christian event with his friends. I had a bigger plan. While there, I told him I loved him. He didn't love me. The darkness returned. I didn't go back to Wheaton in January. I took a half a semester off, a fact I'd all but forgotten until writing this book. I cut my way to forgiveness twice that year. When I did return to Illinois, I took a trip to Nashville to go to the Dove Awards with a producer friend I'd met at a concert at Wheaton.

I fell in love with Music City and made friends easily. The creative vibe mirrored my soul. I used free miles to fly back again the next weekend for Easter break. While finishing up my spring semester at Wheaton, I saw someone close to me experience a manic episode that required hospitalization. When a new friend invited me to come live with her in Nashville for the summer, I wound up staying in the city for a decade. I got a hostess job, recorded a demo, and hoped to take a year off. My dad insisted I finish school, taking a financial hit on my Wheaton tuition fees, and I transferred to Belmont University, switching my education major focus from music to English. Wheaton College had become synonymous with going crazy.

At a Christian college where chapel was mandatory and faith was woven into every class, my emotional struggles felt like spiritual failures. It was a sad, twisted narrative that whispered in the stillness of the night: If I couldn't even maintain stability at a place dedicated to following Christ, what did that say about my relationship with God?

A Pastor's Missed Opportunity

When I was twenty-one, I fell passionately in love with a Mexican American rapper from San Antonio, Texas. All that Latin energy between us kept a lid on the Pandora's box of mood mismanagement I'd mastered. I did not know what attachment disorder was at the time and did not see my pattern of codependency in romantic relationships. Our highs were high, and our lows were low. We'd often break up and get back together an hour later.

One of these break-ups, however, seemed somehow more permanent than the others. I'd just started student teaching and hadn't slept much, excited to make my first lesson plans. Psychosis was, to me, a foreign concept, but I experienced it that night, nevertheless. My thoughts took a catastrophic turn. My inability to imagine waking up the next day without him in my life crippled me. It's been twenty years, but I can still remember the haze of confusion about my head as I drove to his parents' house to try and get him back.

In the peak of all that emotion, I truly believed that I could not live without him. Enter psychosis. In my distorted thinking, I wasn't just losing a boyfriend—I was failing as the youth pastor this church had trusted. How could someone who led worship and taught others about God's peace be falling apart so completely?

Threatening suicide seems like toxic behavior. It's a no-brainer, right? But a person experiencing a manic break isn't accessing her own brain correctly anymore. It was a delusion that I couldn't live without my boyfriend… but in that moment, my thoughts narrated that delusion as gospel truth. Though I didn't have a plan in place to take my life, I couldn't face or accept his desertion. My mental well-being was wrapped up in him, a common characteristic of codependency driven by a fear of abandonment, clinging to him. Imagine a blizzard of thoughts storming at once. My overloaded brain temporarily broke. Enter expression psychotic break.

His parents wouldn't let me inside when I arrived. My boyfriend was talking to me on the phone from inside the house while I sat in my car, racking my brain for a creative solution to get him to change his mind, but equally aware that his parents were preventing me from seeing him. His father was the pastor of the church where I volunteered in a variety of capacities all week long, from leading worship to running the AV team to teaching English classes and acting as interim youth pastor.

My boyfriend's father, my pastor, did not make any attempts to counsel or console. In fact, when I was on his doorstep sobbing, he spat, "I can't believe I'm looking at my youth pastor right now." His words cut deeper than he knew. In that moment, I wasn't just a heartbroken young woman having a breakdown—I was a failed Christian leader whose very existence challenged everything we'd been taught about faith and emotional stability.

There was seething shame there with the unspoken message that as a Christian woman, it was a sin to be so broken you don't want to wake up the next day. He deepened the separation between us by calling the cops. They had to take me in for a psych eval since I'd made a suicide threat. The message was clear: good Christians don't have mental breakdowns. We pray, we trust God, and we maintain our composure. Whatever was happening to me didn't fit the neat theology I'd grown up with.

Sitting in the back seat as two officers took me somewhere I don't remember, I sobered and centered. The blizzard subsided. I had control of my thoughts by the time I was evaluated and presented coherently at the questioning officer's cubicle. I was released ten minutes later. The entire exchange was something of a joke. The department was overextended, and I got the distinct impression they'd been inconvenienced by ferrying me around when another officer deemed me mentally fit. One joked my boyfriend's dad had them handling breakups like crimes. We would end up back together, after all.

It wasn't just a missed opportunity to get diagnosed, though. It was a missed opportunity to reframe the discussion of mental health and Christianity. Being a Christian doesn't make you immune to brain chemistry imbalances. When those imbalances are severe enough, they can completely disrupt normal thought patterns—turning your normally joyful youth pastor into someone who claims she cannot live without your son.

I'm certain my behavior that night scared him. He responded by shunning me, calling the police instead of offering pastoral care. Perhaps he was, like me, afraid of what he didn't understand. I get it.

Reading Terri Cheney's memoir *Manic* years later, I recognized the same pattern. Her childhood poetry was so dark that she wondered why her father tried to get her published instead of getting her therapy. When her depression was at its worst, she knew that even if her father were alive, he wouldn't have helped her because "he simply refused to believe that the disease even existed." [21] He would have told her it was all in her head, rejected psychiatry entirely, and essentially disowned her for being ill.

I recognized that same spirit in my former pastor's response. For many in the faith community, acknowledging psychiatric illness felt like admitting God wasn't powerful enough to heal us—or that our faith wasn't strong enough to sustain us.

That's the tragedy—words like my former pastor's and Terri's father's are exactly why we avoid the bipolar label when symptoms emerge. We'd rather hope we don't mess things up too badly this time than face the judgment that comes with the truth.

What Manic Looks Like

I was twenty-four and teaching high school English in Nashville at an arts magnet school when the same boyfriend cheated on me. The pretty personal trainer at the gym he worked at told me about his infidelity on my birthday. I became obsessed with his cheating. Back then, we had flip phones, and it was relatively new to be able to see photos and messages on his phone by logging into his cell company account on my laptop.

I can still remember a photo of him in just a towel sent to her with a message inviting her over that night. I'm paraphrasing here, but don't doubt that I remember every text message word for word.

I started cutting again. I was still teaching, but I was having trouble sleeping. I'd been taking Ambien for a few years for what I believed to be an insomnia problem, but it stopped working with this cheating trigger. After about a week racking up sleepless nights, obsessed over the details of my boyfriend's cheating, still faking it and making it while teaching English classes, I checked myself into the emergency room on a Friday night. I'd called around and knew it was the only way to get a psychiatrist to prescribe me something to sleep without waiting months for an appointment.

That was one of the longest nights I can remember, unfortunately animated and waiting eight hours in a tiny room with no belt or shoelaces for the psychiatrist to arrive in the morning. I presented well. I usually do. I summed up what brought me there. He said, "It sounds like you might have some bipolar tendencies." He saw no need to admit me. I'd mentioned quetiapine (generic for Seroquel) had worked well for a brother, an antipsychotic that in low doses could be used off-label to treat insomnia. The doctor prescribed that and referred me to a psychiatrist who would monitor my care for the next several years.

Some years ago, I requested a copy of my prescription record from my pharmacy to help me analyze different medications I had been prescribed and their effect on me. I don't remember why my primary care doctor put me on an antidepressant four weeks before this mood episode, but it doesn't surprise me. Antidepressant-induced manic episodes are familiar now.

The word "bipolar" was never mentioned again for a decade. I could believe I had tendencies toward BD, but I still thought insomnia was the problem. If I got proper sleep, I was perfectly fine.

Mood Management Trigger: Taking on Too Much

Was I really perfectly fine, though? By summer of 2009, I no longer cut, I slept regularly, and I married the reformed cheater. That fall, I picked up AP Language and Composition, a coveted course. In retrospect, I think I suffered a bit from imposter syndrome; I was a third-year teacher, and though I'd distinguished myself through taking over the yearbook program, publishing our first literary journal, and leading our school-based tech trainings, I didn't think I had the prerequisite knowledge. I'd grown up in the holistic language movement and didn't study the rules governing grammar until I started teaching. I'd learned to diagram sentences with the girl I tutored after school in college.

The stakes were intimidating. I hadn't taken an AP English exam in high school, but I had two classes of kids with whom I was entrusted the mission of passing that exam… and scoring high enough to secure a college freshman English credit. Meanwhile, I was so geeked out by using digital media in the classroom that I opted to start my graduate degree at the same time. I didn't understand that, while there might be enough time to take classes part-time while teaching, hypomania would be continually activated to maintain both at my perfectionist level.

You see, deadlines affected me differently from procrastinators. My problem was that nothing was ever good enough until the deadline was upon me. At school, I couldn't just assign a worksheet I found. I had to make my own, create a lesson and notes to go with it, and imagine the perfect assessment context to get kids excited to put pen to paper and show mastery of new skills. In grad school, my expectation was straight As and a 4.0. With each new class from Globalization to Portable Media, I was obsessed with applying my coursework in classroom context, showing mastery of my new skills. I'd use grad projects as opportunities to create reliable, authentic units with culminating projects worth students' time.

Now when I think about how big I made all the little things then, a wave of anxiety settles on me. I went above and beyond regularly, exceeding rubric expectations in favor of using even tiny tasks to create something unique, original, and of value. I balanced work, grad school, married life, and church volunteer work, but there was no rest for my soul. Did my professors who noted brilliance in my essays and projects also suspect the lunacy with which it was done? It's easy for me to say this now, deep into writing this book. If you told a twenty-something me that she worked like a crazy person, however, she would have taken it as a compliment. I was unable to leave well enough alone, in a clinically questionable way.

I think it was Christmas break when everything slowed down, and I went dark. At our regular check-in, my psychologist prescribed me Lamictal, a mood-stabilizer, and recommended that I take a leave of absence from teaching to work through symptoms of depression and anxiety. I could focus on my graduate classes, instead. My then-husband had a banking job by then, and we could afford it if I supplemented with a waitressing gig.

I think some combination of the time and the medication worked well to balance me because I made an unexpected change. In February after loving two months of just being a grad student, I discovered my school replacement hadn't worked out and accepted an offer to end leave early and return to the classroom. I was motivated by ensuring those kids passed the AP exam despite my abandonment. Likewise, I felt guilty for having abandoned them for selfish reasons, like my mental health.

I did not understand then that a mind and mood reset was necessary, would occasionally be necessary, for the rest of my life.

Avoiding the Signs, Working through Therapy

I wasn't ready to accept a label back in the hospital with that on-call doctor. Quetiapine worked so well, in fact, I rarely had to face BD at all. I stayed on that antipsychotic medication for ten years, though apart from doctors and my parents, I did not tell people about my med protocol out of fear of being judged. Avoiding major mood episodes, highs or lows, isn't the same as managing daily mood fluctuation. I didn't understand there was a better quality of life in managing beyond medication. And with so much of my continued volunteer work at his church, my father-in-law easily forgot that episode in his driveway at twenty-one.

There were times something else was added or taken away for depression or anxiety, but the low-dose anti-psychotic meant excellent sleep quality and better mood management. My next bout with depression came with quitting teaching as a last-ditch effort to save my marriage. In December of 2012, I spent two weeks in New York visiting my parents. Just being around my mom was enough to boost my spirits, but when I returned to Nashville on Christmas Eve, the depression settled squarely again. I remember telling my husband I didn't feel in love with him anymore. I did not understand it was the depression talking.

My psychiatrist added an anti-depressant to my quetiapine protocol in January. When I turned thirty the next month, I left my husband and went on a three-week quest around the country, seeking wisdom from friends and family that I stayed with along the way. My husband was more like my best friend than a lover, having dated six years before getting married and adding sex to the relationship. I typically joke in answer to why our marriage failed, citing that he liked drugs more than me. I could not, then, have seen how my manic mood swings may have pushed him to use. This depression culminated with serving my husband divorce papers, leaving Nashville to lick my wounds back in my childhood bedroom up north in March 2013.

For a little over a year, I met with Dr. Dennis Bogin after his regular office hours in Syracuse, New York. Sixty minutes at a time on Tuesday nights, we'd talk through my "situational depression," as he dubbed it, while I crocheted purple and pink baby blankets for the coming additions to our family. Our sessions were, to be vulnerable, the highlight of my week; we'd talk, and I'd grow.

Our conversations made me feel the opposite of damaged. It was a unique bond, and not just for me. Since P.J. and his wife were already balancing full-time jobs with my nephew and one Syracuse winter had reminded me why I'd settled south in the first place, starting over in Virginia near my brother's family seemed like the best next step. But that wasn't the end of my relationship with my psychologist. We stayed in touch when I moved to Hampton Roads to help raise the twins. Dr.

Bogin lived just up the street from my parents, and on a visit home a couple of years later, he hosted me for tea in his garden. It was less than a year later that he passed away.

I valued his opinion so much, however, that when I began suspecting I had BD, I reached out to a colleague of his to see if Dr. Bogin had determined I had more than just depression. Sure enough, his diagnosis? I was experiencing a situational depression triggered by leaving my teaching job, my husband, and a decade built in Nashville. He also wrote that my BD was in remission. I don't even know if that's clinically real, but if you're looking for hope, it's that: I could have bipolar and live absent symptoms. Moreover, I had bipolar back then, he knew it, and he still made me feel the opposite of damaged.

Dr. Dennis Bogin gives me hope still. I aim to be in remission, even if the status is only a made-up gift he left behind so I might learn to live again after diagnosis when he wouldn't be alive to keep on guiding me toward the light.

I filled our sessions with laments of my failures, and he'd reframe the past, forcing me to own the accomplishments I abandoned along with my marriage. Is it any wonder that, when my blog was born, I slipped into Tuesday nights to write through life, much the same way we'd talk through it in Dr. Bogin's office?

Upon reflection, my first blog entry in 2015 began by taking up the torch he lit for me. I wrote:

> "I used to be a writer and a poet and a novelist. And a singer.
> And an actress. And a media tech. And a computer repair
> geek. I used to be a little sister and a big sister, a babysitter, a
> housekeeper, a business owner, a gardener, a receptionist at a
> hair salon, an intern at a church, a tutor at a private school, a

certified personal trainer, a model, a Nashvillian. I used to be
so many things. Even a wife."22

And upon further reflection, I see this snapshot of achievements Dr. Bogin curated for my memory also shows the benefits of hypomanic expenditure when well-invested.

To those teachers who described me in recommendation letters as an energizer bunny, capable of anything, I credit that extra energy I was born with; yet, juxtaposed against that accomplishment is a fiery temper for which I cannot wholly blame my Italian blood, one that can resolve to an omnipotent darkness in the worst of seasons. If these highs and lows could be managed, balance acquired, via some combination of lifestyle alterations, medication, and cognitive behavioral therapy (CBT), might I just believe in myself and achieve again?

The Paradox of Mania and Achievement

My blog itself, with its instant connections and woven threads, was a product of hypomania. Somehow, I love the writer in me yet fear what fuels her.

Is it possible to silence the voice that, since diagnosis, tells me my great ideas and goals are just delusions of grandiosity? Maybe even this very book? When I was diagnosed, I obsessively researched my disorder. I found out that people with BD can have "an inflated sense of self-importance or superiority…, overestimating their talents or accomplishments, having an unrealistic belief in one's potential, making grandiose plans or unrealistic goals." [23] Now, I question if my goals are worth pursuing or simply symptoms of psychosis or mania; I question if I should trust my creative mind.

Ask Google to find you celebrities with BD, and she'll answer with an informed intersection of stars ranging from Kurt Cobain to Linda Hamilton. Having committed myself to deep study, I'm not surprised to see Kanye West and Demi Lovato's head shots repping for bipolar. In essence, it is possible to better understand celebrities' out-of-character actions, position myself in empathy, and encourage acceptance and treatment so they can continue to use their *managed* manic superpowers to top the charts.

And for the rest of us commoners battling BD, my hope is simply that we find peace in our homes, jobs, and relationships by managing our disordered parts intentionally. I ignored the signs too long, and I kept such good secrets that my manic episodes just weren't diagnosable. I could see myself going through highs and lows in an unnatural way, but I was raised to evaluate my mood management failures as sin, and so I tried change with prayer and scripture memorization, however futile.

A Recent Bipolar Episode Recapped

My short fuse positioned me in the family as the black sheep; I owned my spiritual shortcoming and gave nary a thought to that mention of bipolar tendencies back at age twenty-four. Splattered upon the backdrop of family gatherings over the years are black streaks from my unpredictable mood swings.

My siblings never said they wanted to keep their children from me, though it seemed that way on more than one occasion.

I suspect we've all—my brothers, their wives, and their young adult children—been tip-toing around my fragile ego where my mental health was concerned. Fortunately, my fiancé helped me face the facts this past

Christmas when I brought him and his daughter home to Syracuse. I'd hoped to overlap with Timmy's family at my parents' place, but my little brother and his wife opted to cut their trip short, a fact eked out moments after our arrival. My brain broke a bit as I tried to process this detail. It didn't compute at all at first.

I thought, "When we'd had just an hour left on our nine-hour road trip, my little brother had packed his four young ones up and no doubt passed us south-bound on 81 so they'd avoid seeing me?" I'd recently injured my back and suffered through a painful, restless overnight car ride despite taking quetiapine to knock me out. My brain was foggy. "My little brother hates me," it concluded.

It didn't compute rightly, even after processing.

I do not know how long things went on this way. Eventually, my father came out. Even in my own confusion, I registered the changes in his facial expressions—bewilderment shifting to something I recognized from my childhood. In line with his upbringing, Dad came out to intervene, but this wasn't the gentle prayer of clasped hands. Seeing Tony's mild-mannered attempts to calm me rejected, my father resorted to physical force like a spanking he might have used to manage my emotional outbursts as a child. He grabbed me by the neck and continued to pray over me. His desperation matched the intensity of my breakdown. I could breathe, but I could no longer spiral in word vomit.

I was at once still and silent. The train of thought halted, at least. Perhaps you could conclude that my dad's approach worked.

But something fundamental shifted in that mudroom. My father, who had spent decades trying to help me control my emotions, had just witnessed his adult daughter completely lose touch with reality. The daughter he'd raised, the teacher he was proud of, the woman he thought he knew—she was gone, replaced by someone he didn't recognize beating herself on his mudroom floor. I never forgot what he did with his hand when he prayed. Seeing me so broken, so far from the person he'd raised, shattered something in his understanding of who I was.

We just haven't really spoken since, not beyond surface conversations. Not because I'm angry about how he responded—I understand he was as terrified and desperate as I was—but because I suspect the image of his daughter in full psychotic break is burned into his memory just as his reaction is burned into mine. How do you face each other again after witnessing such raw brokenness, such complete loss of control? How do you rebuild a relationship when the person you thought you knew disappears right in front of you?

When I called my brother Timmy later that day, he was sweet and kind in his vagueness and evasively loving, as always, citing baby feedings and church schedules as fillers for what we can't talk about in this family. I could find no fault with him save wanting to protect me from being hurt by the truth everyone else seems to know but not say: *I'm not so perfect after all. Let's be honest. I have a mood disorder.*

My oldest brother's wife, on the other hand, has had more experience navigating tricky conversations with me. Cari explained calmly how my little brother wanted to protect his children's image of their auntie by getting on the road before we pulled in the driveway. I learned through the grapevine that Timmy's wife thinks visits to my parents' house trigger me. Anywhere else is fine, but she doesn't trust me not to have a temper tantrum if we're visiting Syracuse. The truth? My baby brother didn't want my nieces and nephews to think less of me if I did.

And I had, so he probably made the right call.

Cari just barely scratched the surface of my temper crisis, albeit my fragile ego could not have handled more last Christmas. I'm grateful for her honesty and, given time to reflect, it seems to me all these decades of tip-toing have only created an absurd trolley problem that screws me on either track.

In one of Dr. Bogin's final emails to me before his passing, the excerpt chosen for my book dedication, he wrote, "It is in the structure of myth that the hero always struggles lost in a dark wood, with many hardships, anxieties, and tribulations before she comes into a clearing, into the light... before she finds herself."

He was talking about me, only I've not emerged as a hero just yet. Last Christmas, I was still struggling, lost in a dark wood, and that day would be one of several hardships that leveled me properly this year. I had to question myself: Was I capable of becoming someone who could be trusted to tame her bipolar ways and foster healthy family relationships, at home and abroad?

If I'm no longer avoiding a label, maybe my family can stop tip-toing and start having conversations with me instead of about me, absent fear of me flying off the handle. Only by contextualizing behaviors within the proper framework of a BDII diagnosis can I own shortcomings, apologize for misbehaviors, and strategize a plan to make sure my siblings can trust me to maintain proper decorum standards at any location.

I'm ready to step into the clearing and find myself, as Dr. Bogin foreshadowed, and that means seeing myself as I am, bipolar tendencies and all.

Are you ready to stop avoiding and face this label with me? If you find yourself resonating with my experiences, whether you're the one in need of the prayer or the one doing the praying, then you're one step closer to accepting the truth and getting the help you or your loved one needs to live a fulfilled life with this disorder.

Chapter Three: Have You Sought Out Your Own Medication?

I got very good at managing my moods without knowing what I was managing. In Christian circles, we often praised self-control and 'dying to self' as spiritual disciplines. I got very good at managing my moods in ways that looked holy—fasting when I was manic, retreating into 'quiet times' when depressed, throwing myself into ministry when I needed distraction.

For years, I found ways to cope that worked well enough to keep me functioning—and keep me from getting help. Within the framework of this book, if we're avoiding a label (as explored in the previous chapter), likely because we're afraid of enduring ignorance and intolerance (as will be explored in the subsequent chapter), we've also found ways of self-medicating that got us this far.

While it varies, the average onset age of BD is twenty-one years, though symptoms can begin much earlier. [24] Up until my junior year of college, I never had a problem falling asleep. I maintained creative outlets like daily journaling, writing songs and poetry, and working varied jobs that kept me too busy to color too far outside the lines of morality. And though I devoured life with a forceful religiosity, looking back, I see the hypomania characteristic of BDII becoming problematic in early adolescence, with adult-adjacent appetites no doubt cultivated from reading my oldest brother's high school required books before I was yet a tween.

Escalating Behaviors, Creative Coping Methods

Prayer and Bible study had always been my first line of defense against overwhelming emotions. When those weren't enough, I found other ways to cope—some healthy, some not so much.

The predictable routines and near obsessive-compulsive order running my childhood home paired with the omnipotent Ten Commandments protected me from getting into more trouble than I did; nevertheless, my mother will attest that with the early onset of puberty, I began looking for love in all the wrong places. My coming-of-age story starts here. I began intentionally collecting secrets and obsessions in fifth grade, shortly after my first period.

At ten, I was tall and developed, hips and bosom drawing the attention of older boys. That, I couldn't hide; my fixation on weight, however, was a private matter. That year, I began cutting calories, buying only skim milk for lunch and switching to Diet Coke for soda. After school, I began lifting weights daily in our unfinished basement. There, the makeshift exercise room was equipped with a tiny tube TV, on which I began watching *Guiding Light*.

These secretive, self-disciplined habits would subsist for fifteen years, until the soap opera went off the air. Some behaviors would escalate.

By sixth grade, Mom went back to teaching full-time and I was able to get by skipping breakfast, a meal I still avoid as part of my intermittent fasting lifestyle. By seventh grade, I earned babysitting money, and there was no age requirement to prevent a thirteen-year-old me from buying diet pills. God only knows what damage taking stimulants did to my developing brain. To my moods? By eighth grade, I'd discovered that purging was an excellent way to get rid of the temptations in Mom's kitchen I hadn't declined in the evenings.

Years later, I learned there's actually a strong connection between BD and eating disorders, especially bulimia and BDII. Research shows that people with bipolar are much more likely to struggle with eating disorders, particularly binge eating behaviors. [25] Looking back, this makes complete sense—both were ways I tried to control my intense emotions.

My relationship with food was complicated—I'd alternate between starvation and purging, with eating feeling euphoric when I finally allowed it. A dietician later called it a 'punishment/reward' cycle.

Exercise became non-negotiable. I averaged six days a week for years. When I was injured and couldn't work out regularly, I felt like I was crawling out of my skin. I called it burning off 'extra energy,' not understanding that the routine was the only thing keeping me stable. Without it, I couldn't find calm.

Whether it was eating a quart of blueberries in one sitting or exercising until exhaustion, I was chasing something—some feeling that would quiet the intensity inside my head. My highs were all natural until my mid-twenties.

Riding the All-Natural Highs

I started modeling at the age of four, adding piano lessons at five, then dance at six, softball at seven, AWANA at eight, and the flute at nine. I maintained perfect marks in elementary, save for math, where my teacher always noted on my report card that I socialized during class… until they moved me to an advanced class where I was challenged and much quieter. I kept a flashlight under my pillow and read well after lights out until sleep seized me.

In middle school, my parents had unwittingly picked up on my preoccupation with body image and shifted their support of my performing outlet from modelling to the stage. In addition to playing softball and basketball, I had leads in the school plays and took part in community theater productions in the winter and summer months. The classroom, the field, the court, the stage, whether I was accompanying the school choir on the piano or belting out a solo… these were my highs, and I rode them well. All that extra energy went into perfection and ambition, striving to be the best.

But if I'm being honest, the version of me no one saw at school was home on Friday nights, in the deafening quiet of her bedroom, calling friends in the school phone directory, desperately hoping to make plans for a playdate. I loved school and all my activities. I didn't like it when everything went still at the end of a busy week. I had trouble coming down and resting solo, my brothers playing up the street with friends in a neighborhood with no other little girls.

On afternoons when I couldn't find a friend to come over, I'd feel so unlovable I'd cry and lament my lonesome state. This was remedied by retreating into any of my older brother's required reading books, pilfered from his backpack, and finishing it in one sitting before stowing my flashlight away. My emotions were out of proportion to situations, wired to catastrophize life's minor hiccups. It did teach me a good secret, though: If you're looking for safe options to medicate during a manic state, devour a book. It's likely not to incur bad consequences.

Staying busy is a coping strategy that can be particularly effective in managing hypomanic symptoms characteristic of BDII, provided this schedule prioritizes time for sleep and self-reflection. In my teenage years, I unearthed other healthy coping strategies to fill post-school hours like journaling, writing poetry and songs, and running track. My allegiance to Young Life, our local Christian youth outreach, kept many of my urges at bay. Between Young Life club nights at our house, Bible studies before school, and leading worship at church, I was spread appropriately thin enough to sleep quite soundly.

In youth group, we called this kind of intensity 'being on fire for God.' The rush I felt during worship services, mission trips, or late-night prayer sessions seemed spiritual—and maybe it was. But looking back, I wonder how much of my religious fervor was actually hypomania in disguise.

Manically in Love with Love

Perhaps the greatest, deepest, most profound way that I self-medicated over the decades was by being in love. I kept secret logs of crushes and "boyfriends" in my diary starting at age five. From Kindergarten, I had a crush on a boy named Travis, up until fourth grade when he was clearly in love with our student teacher, Ms. Silva, like all the other boys. My attention shifted to another more worthy. At nine, I wrote a song for my pastor's son, Austin, and I attempted to sing it to him outside the fellowship hall after services one Sunday. I'm not sure he heard much before running away giggling, nor did I get to give him the ring in my pocket that had been given to me by an older boy at school.

Growing up hearing that God had "the one" planned for me, my intense romantic attachments felt almost prophetic. Surely this overwhelming, consuming love was how you knew someone was "God's will" for your life?

I'd dare to say that for a solid three decades of my life, I either thought I was in love with someone, had a boyfriend, or was being pursued by a member of the opposite sex.

The attention was the ultimate high at first, with notes passed between class and phone calls to look forward to after homework and snacks. My brain was occupied with my love interest from the moment I awoke until the moment I fell asleep, even drafting poems about him during Ms. LaCava's seventh grade English class. My larger-than-life emotions found a niche falling in love.

The summer before high school, however, those hesitant, stolen kisses evolved. I'd often spend time at my friend Brittany's after school. She lived near an elementary school playground and within walking distance of the mall. Spending the night at Brittany's was a level of independence I didn't often experience. One time, her older brother escorted us to the playground after dark. The thrill was unmatched, swinging as high as we could, trying to reach the moon… unmatched until her brother kissed me under the stars.

He was five years my senior, though remembering him fondly as a good friend of my brother for many years to come, it still doesn't creep me out. He was shy and cute in a smart, nerdy way. Yet, innocent intentions aside, there was an urgency in his kisses that loosened something mature. It was a brief dalliance which my parents discovered and ended forcefully, but not before a few make out sessions made me aware of an incredible heightening of emotions and a physical response in my body, a thrill worth seeking again.

Until high school, being in love with love didn't conflict with my religious upbringing. I navigated the typical late nineties books like *The Bride Wore White: 7 Secrets to Sexual Purity* and *I Kissed Dating Goodbye*. When I was thirteen, I received my purity ring I would wear on my left ring finger until it was replaced by a wedding band. My parents were right to restrict my independence. I couldn't trust myself not to go further than I intended in the heat of the moment. I believed each beau would be my husband, and within such an impassioned state, the thrill of the high would overpower spiritual objections.

This created a fractured identity. Externally, I was the poster child for Young Life. My Bible was well-worn and marked through from sword drills, scripture memorization, Bible studies, and quiet times. Like my mother modeled, I started every morning with prayer, scripture reading, and journaling.

Yet, the theme that runs through forty-plus journals is this: I genuinely regretted those impulses. I was sorry. I repented. I committed not to repeat the same sins again.

But I did repeat them.

Over time, my inability to keep promises to myself created a compartmentalized space in my brain. When no one of merit was aware of my transgression, I could pray, ask forgiveness, and then stow the sin away in the back of my mind where, if I denied its existence long enough, I could almost convince myself I hadn't erred so tragically. Some of my worst hypomanic tailspins won't be uncovered until you've absorbed these pages.

Love was the most intoxicating high I'd found, but that would escalate as I got older.

Leveling Up… and Down

My junior year of college, I was a transfer living off campus in Nashville. I rented a house near Belmont University with a girlfriend of mine. She kept a bottle of International Delight French Vanilla creamer in the fridge and began every day with a cup of coffee. She also kept a bottle of peppermint schnapps in the freezer and took a shot before bed if she was having trouble sleeping.

I picked up those habits; I still drink two cups of coffee a day with flavored creamer, which is probably more than I need, but we can identify something as a coping strategy when we'll defend it even when it doesn't make sense anymore. When I turned twenty-one, I moved into my own apartment in Brentwood, a ten-minute commute to campus. I was in school full-time, balanced work shifts at Best Buy and Gold's Gym, and engaged in church activities. The shot of liquor at bedtime stopped working.

I'd lay down and turn off the lights, telling my body that it was time to go to sleep, but my brain was still wide awake. Imagine a racetrack. The lights go out and the spectators leave, but all the cars are still making laps. I'd try to isolate a racecar at a time, resolving anxieties in hopes of finding sleep. Frequently, I'd get up instead and work on the new song I was writing on the piano or journal on my apartment balcony. When I started student teaching, I'd stay up all night lesson planning and not really feel like I needed sleep at all. I didn't register these as red flags back then.

At my annual physical senior year, my doctor told me that I needed to get more regular sleep. He put me on Ambien, and I added it to my schnapps routine. That worked for a few more years until my ex-husband cheated on me as explored in chapter two, an ER psych mentioned I had bipolar tendencies, and I compartmentalized that detail to proceed through life with my insomnia diagnosis in hand—much preferable to the crazy lady equivalent of a scarlet letter I did not need to add to my shames.

Clinically, there is a high comorbidity of BD and substance abuse. I did not realize my illness predisposed me to develop an addictive-type personality. Research shows a strong association between people with BD and alcohol and nicotine dependence and abuse of or dependence on prescription or illicit drugs.[26] While I was oblivious to my addictive tendencies, I'd only just begun relying on substances to help me manage my moods.

By college graduation, I'd found coffee, sleeping pills, and alcohol. When I got my own classroom teaching subjects outside my discipline, I needed more. At the end of a good school day, my mind was still racing. I felt stressed. Annoyed. Irritated. A Spanish teacher took me for a drive after school one day and gave me my first clove cigarette. I'd never smoked before, but he assured me it would calm me down, and it did.

That post-school drive became a daily routine. Then I added one on lunch break. One after school. One before school. One while grading. Until eventually, I smoked a clove whenever I was driving or working alone. I'd obsessively grade papers, reading every word and leaving more feedback than my students would ever digest, secretly chain smoking my weekend away.

When they stopped selling cloves in the States in 2009, I imported them from Indonesia for several years. At thirty-five, I switched to vaping. Each time I told myself I'd quit, but I couldn't function without something to quiet the noise in my head.

Discovering the Psychedelic Mary Jane

The excitement of the school day somehow put my nerves on edge, and that increased with every new batch of minds to mold. My planning period and lunch block were stacked back-to-back, so I had this two-hour chunk of student-free time. If I didn't have a meeting, I'd pack up my laptop and kids' papers and drive off campus to a nearby church playground to smoke a clove while I worked. It was vacant during the week. I'm not sure I could have made it through a full day of work without losing my temper had I not maintained this practice.

I was twenty-two the first time I tried marijuana. An old high school friend staying with me for the summer convinced me it would relieve the back pain from my college track injury. It was fun to try back then, but I didn't care for it.

By my third year of teaching, I started smoking marijuana to help fall asleep when I was worried about school stuff. By my fifth year, I stashed my bowl and green at the church playground every morning before work. During my planning period, I'd smoke a bowl and burn a couple of cloves while I knocked out my epic to-do list. I felt productive and focused. Whatever demotivating effect weed was known for didn't happen to me.

The guilt was overwhelming. Here I was, someone who had led worship and taught Sunday school, using an illegal substance to quiet the chaos in my head. It felt like the ultimate spiritual failure—until I realized that nothing I'd tried from the "approved" Christian toolkit had worked either. But the fact I felt like a better teacher—more able to stay calm in the face of interruptions or distractions—that outweighed the guilt. Smoking brought me down to everyone else's level. I was still incredibly driven and high functioning. I just needed something to take the edge off the constant intensity. Marijuana enabled others to better cope with me, my gift to them, worth any legal repercussions.

There was one department meeting when I behaved incredibly unprofessionally. I'd spent the summer developing a universal MLA guide that we'd use across the grade levels, trying to create uniformity in citing sources. One of the teachers wanted to do things a different way. I flipped. I lost my temper. I stormed out of the meeting.

Our librarian was the only colleague to pull me aside and suggest I had something extra going on. I'm sure Ms. Watson, like many of my friends and students, knew I had BD before I did. She introduced me to strategies from Al Anon and was a safe place for me to question my sanity. She was my sweet, steady voice of reason in that season.

Damage was done, though, in relationships with my other colleagues. I didn't understand my outburst, and I certainly didn't know how to apologize without revealing I wasn't so perfect after all.

To my English team from back at the arts magnet school, here's a long overdue apology. I'm sorry I lost my temper that day and so many other times. I now know that whether I can control my temper or not, I can always apologize for my outbursts. Teaching inspires me. When I get too deeply focused on one goal, my hypomania takes the reins. I can accomplish great things like all the educational videos I created to help my students develop a good relationship with reading and writing. I can also completely lose my sense of reality and professionality.

Life has sufficient regrets; withholding an apology needn't be one of them.

Beyond Our Self-Medicating

For years, I'd found ways to cope that worked well enough—until they didn't. I'd managed my moods through exercise, relationships, substances, and sheer willpower. But there's only so much successful management you can do without actually understanding what you're managing.

I wasn't ready to accept that I needed help beyond what I could create for myself. That would have to change.

Years later, I would learn the hard way that none of my coping strategies—whether it was losing myself in worship music, marathon prayer sessions, or yes, even marijuana—could fix what was happening in my brain. I wasn't ready to accept that yet either. Admitting my spiritual disciplines weren't enough felt like admitting God wasn't enough.

Chapter Four: Are You Afraid of Ignorance and Intolerance?

When something's off physically, we're quick to complain of ailments and find solutions to remedy them. Constipated? Try a higher fiber diet and increase your water intake. Exhausted? Get a good night's sleep. Broke a bone? Undergo surgery and rehab to get it back in line. Why is it, then, when symptoms of bipolar begin to wreak havoc, we opt to ignore the red flags and deny the illness instead?

My first guess at this answer, based on my experience and those I've met along the way, is that we're afraid of the ignorance and intolerance we'll experience from those around us and even our baffled selves. I didn't ask to have BD, but there's nothing I can do to change it. Some will identify with this admission: my fear of the bipolar label is greater than my belief in the peace and freedom that's possible after acceptance.

The Crazy, Bipolar Insult

Bipolar is often an insult hurled at someone whose moods swing noticeably in a specific situation. I was on the receiving end of that stinging remark on more than one occasion. It infuriated me, hitting much too close to home. I remember learning about various illnesses in health class, but I absorbed the impression that mental illnesses were the kind to make you feel ashamed.

I attributed my epic moods to my Italian heritage and dismissed any potential truth to those hurled insults. Looking back, I wonder if part of me was also protecting something deeper—the sense that I was made with intention, even if I couldn't understand the full design yet.

That was until things got serious with Antonio Ramos. If I was determined to be a wife and a mother, I had to face the "crazy" underneath my mood swings. A passionate Chicago-born Latino of Puerto Rican and Mexican heritage, Tony was no stranger to fiery tempers positioned to strike, only he believes that blaming our blood is just a means of excusing an abiding toxic behavior. If we were going to last, I had to tame my temper.

As per both our track records, we'd fallen for each other fast and hard. To complicate emotions further, Tony had a daughter just starting seventh grade to fall in love with, too. On our first family date to Fort Monroe beach—my sanctuary place, where I felt closest to peace—I laid it on Tony that my summer of soul searching convinced me I was going to get married by my forty-first birthday, a sheer impossibility of just six months.

I had, after all, written a song on my ukulele that summer walking the shore asking God for a husband and child. Tony was looking for someone to round out his little family; much to my surprise, he wasn't entirely opposed. Tony laughed, then said, "How about getting engaged by your birthday?"

I was all in. I believed Tony and Calista were a direct answer to prayers.

Careful, Your Bipolar is Showing

It was probably only about a month into this new relationship when I started showing symptoms of hypomania; most often, that presented to his daughter Calista in little bursts of anger about forgotten chores or tasks done poorly. I'd constantly remind her to put her things away. Living alone for a decade, I was unaware how accustomed I was to a picked up, orderly house. It might not be fingerprint-test ready, but clutter has no place in this productive mind.

And at her birthday party, I couldn't hide my disgust when Calista began throwing wrapping paper and ribbons about that I'd shoved in a trash bag, saying, "This is the way we do things here."

I couldn't see a twelve-year-old simply bucking at a presence of maternal order that's been absent her life thus far. Her lack of manners enraged me. I stormed over and told Tony to ask Calista to clean up the mess, but the damage was already done here, too. Tony's mother, Betty, had witnessed my hushed mini-meltdown and questioned him about my mental state later that night. He had, in return, told her that I had BD.

That further enraged me. I probably held it against him until I started writing this book and could forgive myself for needing to keep the secret in the first place.

When I'd had serious relationships before, I hadn't known about my diagnosis. I figured parents typically loved me, I was wife and mother material, and I had complete confidence meeting the potential in-laws in the past. But Betty knew that I had bipolar before she fell in love with me, and whether or not she judged me, I was uncomfortable at family gatherings moving forward.

It was humbling to see how my internal storms could spill over despite every effort to conceal and contain. In quieter moments, I found myself wondering if there was a purpose even in this struggle—if somehow, learning to manage these intensities might prepare me to help others weather their own emotional tempests. God's providence assured me.

In October, about a week after Calista's birthday party, I injured my back and began a fruitless medical battle trying to fix it. I'd never lived for months at a time in pain. I found it difficult to maintain control of my emotions. Sleepless nights and physical pain exacerbate BD symptoms. I felt like I was fighting a losing battle. I was in and out of the emergency room with strange nerve issues. I am now aware of my capacity for addiction and don't want another one to add to my touted concoction. I refused to take pain medication for more than a couple days.

It got worse. My primary care doctor dropped me, dismissing my pain as a bipolar delusion, instructing me to call my psychiatrist, and citing in my record that I had a history of narcotics abuse. My new doctor giggled with me over this detail, maybe to make me feel better. Narcotics abuse is stereotypical of BD patients, but by the grace of God I never took a drug other than as prescribed and stopped at the gateway entrance, marijuana. I've read enough memoirs of others with BD to know things could have been much worse for me.

Holding Marriage Hostage

Tony observed more episodes than the one in my parents' mudroom last Christmas before I knew that getting my temper under control wasn't something I could do on my own. The day before my birthday, Tony's brother lost a battle with colon cancer, and marriage was not up for discussion. I had yet to keep my promise not to lose my temper again. This death was the catalyst for our household growth, however. Tony's grief was greater than I could help him through. In arguments, he'd hurl it at me that I needed therapy. When his brother died, I found a therapist and began seeing Renee once a week in March 2024. Tony and Calista started counseling the following month.

I began an intense work of self-discovery. I continued to listen to my favorite Christian authors, but a little at a time, I added secular voices to my podcast roster.

If the key to taming my bipolar hadn't been found in Christian literature, had I been ignoring a wealth of information that could help me rewire my brain for a promising future? I began binging podcasts from mental health and wellness and relationship experts like Jay Shetty, Lewis Howes, and Matthew Hussey. Tony listened, too, so he saw the intentional growth in real time. He was so inspired by my immediate behavioral changes that he proposed on the fourth of April at Olive Garden.

The next week, I started a long-term English sub position at our local high school. The more excited I became about our curriculum, the more difficult it became to leave school at school. We'd worked hard to get Calista on the A/B honor roll third quarter, but her grades dropped with my return to work. Scheduling conflicts reduced my counseling sessions at first to every other week, but there was one whole-month gap during which I regressed significantly. I behaved badly at a family gathering, and Tony decided to hold our wedding hostage until I made things right with his sisters and mother.

The difference this time? I had the tools to make peace.

Love and Acceptance vs. Fear of Rejection

Tony and I got married on Fort Monroe Beach on the nineteenth of June at sunset. He knew full well that I had BD when he chose to marry me. He'd seen the worst outbursts of my life and still made me his wife. Standing there as the waves whispered behind us, I felt an overwhelming sense of being chosen. And not despite my struggles, but as someone worthy of love in her entirety. That day, I got a sweet taste of divine intervention: Tony agreed to attempt to love me the way my heavenly Father does, without condition.

For so many years, I was afraid of being rejected, either because someone knew about my illness or because I'd likely behave badly enough to push them away. It turns out, having BD does not make me unlovable or unworthy of a family. That said, having BD does mean that I must manage my moods *better* to love that family well.

I started writing this book several years ago, but at that time, the support of my mother drove most of my big decisions. She worried that publishing a book about having bipolar would ruin my livelihood. With the internet, a quick search of me would yield a bipolar label and block me from getting a position, for example. Furthermore, being honest about using marijuana would surely tank future teaching jobs. I closed the Word document and didn't pick it up again until I was engaged. Tony believed that reviving my book was a necessary part of my healing journey.

My husband has taught me many things in our relationship, and one is what love looks like when it's extended with acceptance. Writing the last chapter about seeking my own forms of medication was cathartic, in a sense, as I was able to forgive myself for each shared transgression. A BD diagnosis might simply block me from jobs I would not want, jobs where I would not be supported or nurtured. Rejection and acceptance are both possible responses when our nature is exposed. Coming out means accepting the possibility of rejection… and the possibility of acceptance like I found with my husband and now our daughter.

Mom's right: ignorance and intolerance exist even within educational institutions committed to promote mental health awareness amongst its student body. I admitted to one principal that I had been diagnosed, and what had been a strong working relationship for half a decade devolved to the point where I resigned. I didn't want to please someone who couldn't recognize all that extra bipolar energy was what made me a rock-star educator who he could count on to deliver. He's the perfect example of what I might face, and I already faced it.

While being a rock-star educator, I got diagnosed with BD and run through a gamut of medications. Understand, there is no one-size-fits-all medication solution for individuals with BD. There is no cure, either, just assistive aides. Starting, stopping, and switching medications presents its own set of observed symptoms. Even after accepting a diagnosis and getting treatment, I remember being on edge at work hoping to manage my moods despite new side effects or sleepless nights from medicines that didn't work. Fear of people knowing I had bipolar was palpable at times.

Might it have been easier if my boss had an open-door policy to work and wellness? It's scary coming out to people important to us. I practice on people I'll never see again.

At this point, I've told five strangers about the book I'm working on. Five for five, the person or a loved one is battling BD. Five for five, they'll be looking for my book when it comes out. I care more about what those five individuals think of themselves and their bipolar loved ones than I do about judgment. For decades, I practiced a discipline of outward perfectionism that amounted to praise and accomplishments sufficient to ignore the debilitating effects of my illness. This did not amount to freedom of mind, heart, or soul.

Contrary to the traditional mantras of my maiden name like "Palmas don't like change" and "Palmas never give anything up," Tony says he married me because of my ability to self-reflect, identify shortcomings, and change them. I had to change the way I saw change. I had to change the way I saw change. It turns out a Palma can learn to give things up— including the belief she's too broken to grow. In our house, when growth mindset dictates protocols, things function well.

The secret to making relationships work when you have BD? Be willing to give things up… and get ready to change.

COVID-19 Reframes Mental Illness

The cultural landscape around mental illness has shifted dramatically since 2018, when Mariah Carey's brave disclosure inspired but didn't embolden me. The pandemic changed everything—in the first year alone, global anxiety and depression increased by twenty-five percent, [27] and by 2023, ninety percent of U.S. adults believed the country was facing a mental health crisis. [28] Some researchers even suggested people were at a greater risk of developing mental illnesses after having COVID-19.[29]

By 2021, when I returned to teaching, I could see this shift everywhere. The sixth graders in my classroom were different—social anxiety was at an all-time high, and I had students in every class battling mood disorders. Mental health conversations that used to be whispered were now happening openly in schools.

And in the years since, I found that one of my manic superpowers is being able to establish that kind of empathetic relationship with my students where they feel safe enough to tell me when they're not okay. There's something sacred about holding space for another person's pain. It was almost as if my struggles were preparing me for these moments of ministry.

Intolerance and ignorance aren't to be feared—they are to be expected. The societal connotation of "mania" is overwhelmingly negative, yet it powers the very creativity that society consumes as entertainment. Van Gogh, Michelangelo, Beethoven—all possibly manic depressive, yet revered for their gifts to the world.

There's a paradox here: Can we truly be intolerant of BD while basking in the manic grandeur of Beethoven's Fifth Symphony? Can we shame Mel Gibson for his mood swings while making Braveheart our favorite movie?

Writing this book is my small attempt to bridge that gap. I'm not trying to be the next Carrie Fisher or change the world overnight. I'm just one person who got tired of hiding and decided to tell the truth about what it's really like to live with this diagnosis. Maybe that's enough to start.

We Have More Power than You Think

We are the BD community. I don't know you yet, but I'm letting you get to know me. If the purpose of this book was my own healing, I'd have written this in another of my journals. I want you to consider BD in a fresh, new way. Set aside your fear of what others might think and start talking about your own mental health journey.

What changed since my childhood about ADHD was an increase in awareness and diagnosis that led to a higher percentage of students in school securing skills for those deficits, therefore being connected with other students like them through special education services, establishing a record of support for success with ADHD, and ultimately helping to normalize the disorder.

From a clinical perspective, BDII shares much with ADHD, particularly in women. In fact, I was first diagnosed with ADHD combined type with anxiety in 2017, a year and a half before my BD diagnosis. There are no concrete, objective tests like MRIs to measure bipolarity like ADHD; some symptoms of the disorder and illness are so similar that misdiagnosis is common. The two can even coexist in the same person, and dopamine plays a role in both.

We'll explore the scientific side more in part two, but to close out our chapters in the darkness, let me propose this: diagnoses aside, there exists a spectrum of dysfunction in mood regulation. Whether you or someone you know is experiencing ADHD, BD, depression, anxiety, or a combination matters far less than the shared reality of knowing what it's like to not trust yourself to behave correctly.

We have the power to normalize BD by getting ourselves and our loved ones the help needed to receive *and* accept the diagnosis necessary to secure treatment, change our lives, and kill the stigma. In this way, we use our *managed* manic superpowers to change the conversation around BD and resolve society toward a more positive connotation of illness. When you start talking openly about mental illness, you might be surprised how many of us just weren't ready to accept the label and join the conversation yet.

Are you ready now?

The next section of this book explores the new life awaiting us after acceptance when we get to step into the light. There, we discover, we're made with intention—even in our struggles. By accepting this lens, this label, we start to see everything clearly… including the Creator's unique design for balance in the human body, mind, and soul.

Part Two: Accepting It—Step into the Light

Chapter Five: What is This Thing Called Bipolar Disorder?

Last year, I began attending a writer's night at the local library. The first time, a colorful intersection of people was already settled in with notepads or laptops chatting when I arrived a few minutes late. I recognized one as a senior at the high school where I substitute sometimes.

We began with a round of introductions. Share my name and a little about my current writing project, I was told. My name came simply, and I attempted to write an oral blurb on the spot for this book. There were a few seconds of uncomfortable silence when I stopped speaking where doubt snuck in. I was exposed.

See, when I share the title of my book, I'm facing a dual rejection possibility: rejection of my ideas or the chemical imbalance that supplied them.

Out of the silence, a middle-aged woman yet to be introduced spoke. She loved the concept. Like every other time I've shared about this book to date, it struck a personal chord.

"My father was manic depressive. My mother could never admit it," she began. "Maybe if she'd read your book, he wouldn't have blown his brains out."

In that moment, I felt something bigger than coincidence at work—as if my vulnerability had opened a door I hadn't even known existed.

Was God orchestrating my chaos, even in that choice to join that group on that night? I haven't run into her on any other evenings.

Just another night at the local library writer's group, right? It bolstered my commitment to this project, just hours after my mother mentioned my aunt didn't believe I had BD. That's not the point. My aunt's disbelief was based on withheld information. A paternal aunt I see a few times a decade would not have access to the internal battle narrated in these pages that I fought so desperately to protect—my secret, personal struggle.

And I'm not the only one. Other siblings have experienced periods of depression, psychotic breaks, and required daily medication to function, but we've never readily owned diagnoses. Our biblical view was shaped partly at Wheaton College, but fundamentalist underpinnings enslaved us early on to an unfounded notion that mental illness was merely an outward manifestation of a shameful, sinful soul at odds with God. I'll unpack this further in chapter fourteen.

Finding Myself in Other People's Stories

Not everyone has an accurate picture of BD, nor an awareness about how symptoms present in BDI, BDII, or another variant. When I accepted my diagnosis in 2019, it was just the beginning of accepting the illness. To do that, I needed to shatter my misconceptions of bipolar.

I ordered ten books, and I devoured them, one by one. I read celebrity accounts like Suzy Favor Hamilton's *Fast Girl* and Carrie Fisher's *Wishful Drinking*. I read memoirs like Andy Behrman's *Electroboy* and Terri Cheney's *Manic*. Reading those stories, getting an inside look at what bipolar looked like in other people's lives, it was impossible to not to see myself in those books. Give yourself a few thousand pages reading about mania, and the word itself begins to normalize.

With a foundation in memoirs, my research turned clinical. I wanted to understand how my bipolar brain worked. I was too bored to finish two of the denser manuals, sifting through them like textbook homework with perfunctory annotations and color-coded tabs. Then Kay Redfield Jamison's *An Unquiet Mind* broke through the mundane. I listened to the audiobook then sat down and read it again, pen in hand, the ideas for what would become my book fashioning themselves in the margins. As a psychologist and leading member in her field who also lives with BD, Jamison was the perfect person to show me how my unquiet mind functioned.

One of the last reads of my initial Amazon bipolar book binge was researcher and psychiatrist Nassir Ghaemi's *A First-Rate Madness.* Ghaemi establishes a link between mental illness and the ability to lead well, denoting the role that depression and mania each play by examining eight leaders with mental illness who were effective during states of crisis and eight "normal" leaders who were ineffective in such instances.

Some of these stories seemed familiar to me. The more I read, the more I became convinced I'd already studied mania before. It was one of those times I was sure God kept me up all night just to discover something amazing about the human mind, crafted by Him, worthy of discovery.

Writing Under the Influence of Mania

Had I done a research paper about bipolar in a psych class in college? Ghaemi published his book in 2011. I was reading it in 2019. I searched my laptop for the word "mania" and was first reminded of positive connotations from my educational experience, like for sports fans and gaming in the classroom. There was one Word document, however, published in October 2009, entitled "Mania—Madness or Revelation," written just a few months after wedding my ex-husband. When I read the words, it all came back.

I wasn't taking any classes. I was between undergrad and grad school.

So, why had I written a six-page research paper MLA style with full parenthetical citations and works cited page?

Because I had an idea on a Friday night that there was a link between mania and creativity. That, and since I didn't have to go to work the next day, I opted to ride out my manic creativity to stay up and write that paper instead, just for me. In the introduction, I went back to the Roman ancient goddess Mania, who governed the underworld, and her Greek counterpart of the same name, the goddess of madness and insanity, to establish a potential origin for the negative connotation of the term mania.

Citing sources with long-dead hyperlinks, I tracked the developmental response to mental illness from ancient times when those with mental problems were punished by gods to the 1300s when the earliest hospitals for the mentally ill were created to lock patients away. It wasn't until the 1700s that scientists began to consider the medical associations of mental illness, and not until the 1900s that drugs emerged to "fix" mental illness.

I concluded my introduction by asking: "But, is mania a condition that needs to be fixed?"[30] Oh, I was so naïve, bless my heart.

It had been a couple of years since an ER doctor mentioned I might have bipolar tendencies, which included a tendency toward mania. Even then, unwilling to accept a label, I was willing to associate myself with the creative energy dominating the bipolar upswing. After establishing a historical context, I offered definitions using reference materials accessed through Grolier. If mental illness was a disorder of the brain that disrupted a person's thinking, feeling, moods, and ability to relate to others, I wondered if that disruption couldn't have positive and negative outcomes, particularly in the form of mania.

Was I aware that I was under the influence of mania when I wrote that little manuscript? Ironically, no. Admittedly, I was leaning into its creative potential, but flirting with mania was a far cry from accepting my mood management issues were more than spiritual shortcomings. That research paper exists as a perfect example of the unique capabilities of a mind operating in overdrive. When my extra energy is well directed, I can accomplish daunting tasks. Still, for all my academic brilliance, I was tragically unaware of how emotionally stupid I was. Had I left my new husband alone in bed to follow this madness vs. revelation idea to conclusion, just because I'd had an epiphany? How many other nights had he lost my attention because I'd lost myself in another larger-than-life project that was urgent only in my mind?

I didn't understand how my unique brain functioned back then.

How My Thermostat is Broken

How, then, does a brain with a mood disorder function? What exactly is a mood disorder?

I'm going to borrow an analogy presented in *Bipolar Disorder: A Guide for You & Your Loved Ones* by Dr. Francis Mark Mondimore. "Our mood is essentially our emotional temperature," he writes, "a whole set of feelings that expresses our sense of emotional comfort or discomfort."[31] In short, humans experience good and bad moods as varied states of being in response to outside triggers like getting a promotion or manuscript rejection. An autonomous system is activated. Our temperatures rise with good moods and fall with bad ones; an internal thermostat brings us back to baseline.

In response to a positive stimulus, a set of positive feelings governs our attitudes and mindsets. More than simply being happy, when we're in a good mood, we feel energetic, sleep well, and experience a favorable disposition when interacting with others. The future looks promising. As Mondimore puts it, "When we're in a good mood, the world seems a wonderful place to live in; it feels good to be alive."[32] I'm sure you can relate.

A bad mood looks like the opposite. In response to a negative stimulus, a set of negative feelings governs our attitudes and mindsets. More than simply being sad, when we're in a depressed mood, our energy is low, we struggle with sleeping too much or too little, and our tempers or inclinations to self-doubt rise quickly, leading us to isolate. In this state, it's tough to think about the future. When thinking about the future, we're plagued by pessimistic thoughts and committing to even small tasks seems intimidating.[33] You don't need a scientist to define this state and can likely relate to it, as well.

One needn't acquire a mood diagnosis to experience these two states of being. We all have good and bad moods. People without mood disorders are not only more naturally equipped to regulate emotional temperatures, but their temperatures typically change in response to stimulus. A person with BD, like me, might explain that her moods control her, not the other way around. When my husband's excited about a new job, he doesn't remain in an elevated state. If he loses a job, he doesn't remain in a depressed state. Tony's able to regulate his emotional temperature in a way that is automatic. I lack this regulatory control, pre-programmed to bring me back to homeostasis.

You're Sounding a Little Manic Right Now

In part one, we qualified mania and hypomania as periods of atypical elation with a decreased need for sleep, an inflated self-image, and ideas of grandiosity. To underscore the similarity between mania and hypomania and unify my audience, further references in this section to the word "mania" may include both states, using "hypomania" only when the distinction is necessary, as in diagnosis qualifications, for example. People with BDI and BDII experience mania to differing degrees and for different amounts of time. The separation between them overemphasizes the types of BD and based on my experiences in mood disorder support groups, this is relevant to people everywhere on the spectrum.

If you or someone you know has been labeled with BD, a degree of mania factored in to produce that diagnosis. In a manic state, a person might feel she can do anything but be plagued by expressions of aggression and irritability. She's more likely to take risks. People might observe a shift in speech patterns, like speaking quickly, animated in a rant about something of apparent import.

For a person with a passionate, Italian temperament, it might just look like a *really* good mood. I publicly presented as a joyful young woman, content in her life and her relationship with God. Acquaintances would have described me as a perpetual optimist in my youth. My mother would have described me as a bright, cheerful, resilient young lady. Until the onset of adulthood (when my illness fully activated) and I experienced a series of losses (resulting in my first depression), my baseline emotion was happy. Quite frankly, I miss that version of me.

It's to be expected, I suppose. Did you know that the symptoms of BD tend to worsen as a person ages? Many coping strategies from my twenties stopped being effective in masking my dysfunction. Understanding the way we navigate the world with bipolar can help us find coping strategies that serve us well in this current season. For example, had I understood that I was experiencing a bipolar depression that would pass, I might not have left my first husband at thirty out of a desire to find my own pulse. These pervasive states of being can be managed.

Now that I know what I'm up against, my husband can hold me accountable for my moods. Recently, I bombarded him after work about my attempts to build a following on social media. I'm not sure how long I rambled before Tony interrupted with what's become a welcomed expression in our house: "Laura Joy, you're sounding a little manic right now." In a sense, Tony's developed a quick check-in with my emotional temperature, prompting that regulation response. I can slow my train of thought and take control back, on purpose.

If losing something triggers panic, Tony can label that state of being and remind me to be rational and objective about locating or replacing it.

I'm fortunate to have found a human willing to partner with me as we better learn to navigate this bipolar world, bit by bit, every day.

Ancient Greece Weighs in on the Bipolar Conversation

When I was first diagnosed, I felt like I was the only person in the world experiencing this strange connection between creativity and chaos. But as I dove deeper into research, I discovered something fascinating: people have been trying to understand this link for thousands of years.

If you've ever heard the phrase, "No great genius has ever existed without some touch of madness," that was Socrates—and he was talking about something I knew intimately. I learned that Hippocrates, the father of medicine, had already identified our brain as "the organ of mental functions, mental disturbances and mental disorders" and was classifying these into mania and melancholia long before we had modern psychiatry.

The more I read, the more amazed I became. An article called "Bipolarity from Ancient to Modern Times" showed me that ancient Greece had developed four different meanings of mania: a reaction of rage, a biological disease, a divine state, and a kind of temperament. The greatest philosophers had been making sense of these extreme mood states as indicators of mental illness—and sometimes as gifts.

This led me down a rabbit hole about the Greek goddess Mania, who Gnostics considered the divine spirit in man. I wrote about this in my research paper, fascinated by Socrates' belief that our greatest blessings come through mania, and that madness from the deity was superior to human sanity. Plato even distinguished between two kinds of mania—one caused by mental strain, the other divinely inspired.

I was grasping at straws to support a feeling I couldn't quite prove: mania could be a blessing. I'm not a historian, philosopher, or psychiatrist, but I do have BD, and I'm aware of an increased connectedness I experience in manic states that's difficult to explain. While riding its high, it's as though I'm at one with God and the universe. I see signs and inspiration in a single rosebud or cloud outline. Since grade school, I've tried to capture these mini epiphanies in poetry, song lyrics, and blog posts.

With that decreased need for sleep and inflated sense of self, it's possible for people with BD to accomplish far more than seems humanly possible. Hyperactivity can have embarrassing consequences, but so does all risk-taking. I dreamed big from childhood, and with my mother cheering me on, I regularly pushed my limits and found new achievements to add to my resume. I navigated the world with a bipolar brain; creativity bubbled up from somewhere, I just couldn't identify the source until I finally got diagnosed.

Like Aristotle and other philosophers observed two millennia past, I believe there is a link between madness and genius, between mania and brilliance—but mostly because I've experienced it.

The Progressive Identity of Bipolar Disorder

After learning about the ancient Greeks, I became curious about how we got from their observations to my modern diagnosis. What I discovered was a fascinating evolution that helped me understand I wasn't alone in this experience.

It turns out that Aretaeus of Cappadocia was the first person to explicitly connect mania and melancholy, recognizing them as two sides of the same illness. He believed they had the same cause—a disturbance in brain function—and that mania was actually a worsening of melancholia. [34] Without our modern terminology, Aretaeus had essentially conceived of BD in the first century AD.

As I traced the timeline, I found that later researchers continued to observe this cycling pattern. Wilhelm Griesinger, one of the founders of German scientific psychiatry, described the disease in 1845 as "a circle of both types with regular changes." [35] He even identified rapid cycling and seasonal patterns—something that made me think of my own winter struggles.

The real breakthrough came in the mid-1800s when Jean-Pierre Falret named the disorder "folie circulaire" or circular insanity, describing it as "a continuous cycle of depression, mania and free intervals of varying length." [36] This sparked the debate that eventually led to Emil Kraepelin's classification of manic-depressive insanity in the 1890s, which later evolved into our modern understanding of unipolar (depression only) and bipolar (manic-depression) disorders. [37]

But here's what really caught my attention: while Falret was making these connections in France, Italian psychiatrist Cesare Lombroso was cementing that ancient link between genius and madness. He concluded that you couldn't have genius without insanity. This sparked a debate that continues today—with Francis Galton arguing the opposite, that sanity equals genius.[38]

When I discovered Nassir Ghaemi's book *A First-Rate Madness*, I was enthralled by what he dubbed the "Inverse Law of Sanity". Ghaemi takes Lombroso's side, proposing that during times of crisis, we're actually better off being led by mentally ill leaders than "normal" ones.

He identifies four elements of mania and depression that make for better crisis leadership: realism, resilience, empathy, and creativity. "Depression makes leaders more realistic and empathic, and mania makes them more creative and resilient," he writes.[39]

This shook my commitment to believing mental illness was wholly bad. Ghaemi examines eight great leaders with mental illness—from William Tecumseh Sherman to Martin Luther King Jr.—and contrasts them with mentally healthy leaders who failed during similar crises.

The accounts encouraged my soul, one by one. MLK Jr. suffered from depression and attempted suicide; Gandhi followed a similar melancholy road. Had the darkness inside powered them to fix the darkness outside? Ghaemi was showing that depression fosters empathy, and I knew this to be true from my own experience. My students sense that I understand struggle—they know they can come to me, know that I care. It's put me in the position of literally talking someone down from a ledge.

Reading this history helped me understand that my diagnosis wasn't a modern invention or personal failing—it was part of a human experience that brilliant minds have been trying to understand for millennia.

The Creative Poet Bipolar Stereotype

If my empathy comes from the depressed pole, I was beginning to suspect that creativity comes from the manic one. Nassir Ghaemi explains that mania puts people at an advantage for the type of divergent thinking required to find and solve problems. He credits the rapid flight of ideas symptomatic of mania: "One's thoughts seem to literally fly in many different directions; they may or may not make sense, but they certainly get around." The hyperactivity that accompanies mania can result in getting things done since people "think quickly, talk rapidly, and need little sleep; they write much; they draw, plan, propose, implement."[40]

That definitely tracks for me. But I didn't fully connect creativity to my diagnosis until my husband's sister made an observation that stopped me in my tracks. When I came out to her shortly before our wedding, her response was simply, "Yeah, I already knew. All the bipolar people I know are super creative." I laughed with her in relief she hadn't judged me harshly—but her casual comment made me ask some serious questions.

Are we all creative, or is it just me? Is there actually a stereotype for bipolar people? And if so, where did it come from?

The image of the tortured artist immediately surfaced in my mind. A great mind with a depth of emotions and a connection to the source of life, propelled to transfer imaginings onto canvas or paper. Ernest Hemingway and Vincent Van Gogh came to mind as real examples, Shakespeare's musing poets from literature. I had to know: was there actually a link between creativity and BD, or was my sister-in-law just being kind?

When I dug into the research, I was amazed by what I found. Mondimore highlights studies where researchers performed psychobiographical surveys of creative individuals and discovered "a striking and inordinate number of accomplished artists, writers, and musicians have suffered from bipolar disorder." [41] But how much more than the general population? Most studies concluded nearly ten times more—between thirty and fifty percent of creative individuals will have BD. Striking and inordinate, indeed.

Even more fascinating was a study by Kay Redfield Jamison, the author who had helped me understand my unquiet mind. She analyzed autobiographical and biographical materials as well as medical records of major British and Irish poets of the eighteenth century, concluding that a third suffered from BD and more than half from some form of mood disorder.[42]

So, my sister-in-law's casual observation was actually backed by solid research. There really is a link between creativity and BD.

This discovery led me to a chicken-or-egg question that I realized didn't actually matter: whether my creativity predisposed me to develop BD or BD powers my creativity is of little consequence. What I knew for certain was this—if there were a pill to "fix" me completely, I would not take it. I'll never surrender my creativity.

And that's when I realized something important: only 20,000 words into writing this book, it sure sounds like I am starting to accept the bipolar parts of me, just as I'd predicted in the introduction.

A Look at the Bright Side of Bipolar

Jamison also explored the relationship between creativity and bipolar from personal experience in *Exuberance: The Passion for Life,* published two decades after her *An Unquiet Mind* memoir. "Exuberant behavior and emotions—whether displayed in love, manifested in laughter and play, or kindled by music, dance, and celebration—have in common high mood and energy," she wrote. "They act on the same reward centers in the brain as food, sex, and addictive drugs, and they create states of mental and physical playfulness."[43] Where Ghaemi uses this as support for the effectiveness of inspired leadership to proffer hope and energy in times of crisis, I've seen it play out on a smaller scale, in my classroom.

I did not know that I had BD when I was teaching in Nashville in my twenties. I thrived the first couple of years, enthralled with teaching English at the arts magnet school. We attracted Music City's most talented and creative students, many of them children to parents in the industry. I incorporated the arts into my English curriculum. It was a natural fit for them and me. My classroom was a stage. I was always performing and encouraged my kids to do the same. It kept students engaged. My playful manner made English class fun; inspired leadership powered my curriculum and empowered my students.

Why did students like coming to my class? According to Jamison's reasoning, my high mood and energy acted on the same reward centers in students' brains as food, sex, and addictive drugs. Okay, this is a loose application of Jamison's premise, but it's still effective. States of mental and physical playfulness promote a positive learning environment. Though my grounding principles were established at an arts magnet, I continued to incorporate music, drama, visual arts, and other outlets of creative expression into my curriculum at my other teaching posts.

When I set up my classroom at a high school in Hampton, Virginia after my divorce, the general population was equally receptive to my dramatic curriculum. A few years later, I moved down the street to the district's gifted center and adapted my curriculum for sixth grade students; I fit right in there, too. It worked the same way across states, grades, and class levels. Exuberant behavior and creativity are some of the bright sides of living with bipolar. Students who loved my class were probably unaware it was my mental illness that had endeared me to them, all these years.

Another bright side of mania is seeing connectivity in everything, powered not so much by critical thinking as by broad thinking. Psychologists call it "integrative complexity". Ghaemi unpacks this when examining the life of General Sherman, saying, "Creative people see farther and wider; their cognitive peripheral vision is clearer; they make connections between seemingly disparate things that many of us miss."[44] For me, this schema manifested as bigger picture education. How could I get all students engaged in English class, not just the students who were naturally more interested in the subject?

In 2007 in Nashville, I developed what I called the "educational workroom" model. Building Perceptions Ink. was formed. (In the logo, spray paint turned the "c" of "Inc" into a "k" for wordplay.) The company slogan was: "There's only one world, but how do you see it?" Its promise was to help students build and share their perception of the world by taking command of language, putting it to work for them. I was the manager of the company, my students completed employee training, and each class formed a department and competed against and within for awards like department or employee of the quarter. Instead of the typical back to school activities, we had orientation. I put students in teams the first day. They filled out applications and were interviewed by a panel of their peers.

It wasn't just the first few weeks of school, either. My syllabus transformed into an employee handbook, quizzes into benchmarks, classwork to daily tasks, homework to workouts, grades to pay, etc. I fully fleshed out the business model analogy. Students could choose to apply for management positions like assistant manager, workroom monitor, and bookkeeper to take on leadership roles in class. Most of the time, my substitutes were simply legal supervision; my management teams were equipped to operate classes normally in the event of my absence. Teachers might leave busy work, but bosses would lose money on a free day; showing up to work without me still meant earning their pay. It was a framework for teaching and learning English that engaged young minds—and produced pass rates that pleased everyone else.

Creativity, exuberance, and integrative complexity are familiar friends to many in the BD community. As we come to terms with accepting our diagnoses, it's important to remember that the catalyst for our potential trauma or backlash is also responsible for our greatest contributions to mankind.

Why Some People Fight the Diagnosis

After I finally accepted my bipolar diagnosis, I became curious about why it had taken so long—not just for me, but for so many people. The statistics haunted me: women wait an average of eight years between symptom onset and getting help. Eight years. I started wondering what forces were working against accurate diagnosis.

As I dove into research and talked with my therapist, I discovered I wasn't alone in facing resistance to the very idea of BD. The pushback came from several directions, and I'd experienced most of them firsthand.

I grew up hearing echoes of what Terri Cheney describes in her memoir *Manic*—her father's dismissive "It's all in your head," delivered "without the slightest tinge of irony." [45] This "just try harder" mentality treats bipolar symptoms as character flaws: lack of self-discipline, poor self-control, moodiness that could be managed if I just applied myself more. The underlying message was clear: I was born with the same emotional regulation as everyone else, and if I'd just try harder, I could be better-behaved too.

My family had a long history of sleep and mood problems. Siblings and I have taken medications since adulthood, experienced periods that now I recognize as mania, depression, and psychosis. But we preferred not to use psychiatric labels. Early on, Mom credited our high IQs with potential for overload during psychotic episodes—and honestly, I liked that explanation better than considering myself mentally ill.

Then there was the religious resistance I faced, the "get right with God" approach. Remember my former pastor's reaction to my suicide attempt? "I can't believe I'm looking at my youth pastor," he'd said with such disappointment. The message was unmistakable: get right with God, and my crisis would resolve. Good Christians don't have psychotic breaks.

But this created a painful contradiction. When I was a student at Wheaton College, I watched several peers living exemplary Christian lives who still struggled with mental illness while deep in study of God's Word—like Martin Luther beating himself for his inability to live without sin. It made me wonder: this far out from the Garden of Eden, doesn't mental illness point not to a broken relationship with God, but to a broken relationship with ourselves?

When I asked my therapist about this pattern, she confirmed it's not limited to Christianity. Many moral and religious cultures make diagnosis difficult because symptoms are treated solely as reflections of spiritual deficits. The dilemma has an origin: religions categorize sin clearly, repentance requires commitment not to sin again, and the bipolar mind in crisis struggles to hold tightly to commitments made in stable periods.

Then there was a more insidious form of resistance—the "I prefer you manic" factor. I had one "friend" who you'll meet in chapter six who enjoyed my company most when I was hypomanic without the depressive crashes. He preferred me when I was medicated into a full-blown manic episode, when I could be encouraged to dance on tabletops. When I finally got proper diagnosis and medication that stabilized me toward a more depressed baseline, he kept insisting I didn't need medication. He missed "the old me." Some people suppress our diagnoses because it keeps us dependent on them, giving them control when we're not thinking clearly. Without an accurate bipolar diagnosis, people also started playing what I call the alternative diagnosis game. I might seek help during a depressive episode only to find the prescribed antidepressants triggered new, more severe symptoms—the underlying bipolar condition still undiagnosed. Others suggested narcissistic or borderline personality disorders, even OCD, because of the overlap in behaviors. But I've come to believe these alternative suggestions often indicate unchecked bipolar and the self-centered, sometimes codependent coping strategies we develop to hide our disorder from the world.

Here's what I learned: personality disorders don't require medication—they can be treated with cognitive behavioral therapy alone. CBT is also highly effective for OCD symptoms, especially when paired with medication for obsessive thoughts. While I practice CBT and believe it can improve the amount of time I spend stable, my research has shown me no conclusive support that I'll ever achieve natural brain balance without medication. I haven't found a natural sleep rhythm without medication since I turned twenty-one.

The real cost hit me hard: if I never embraced the illness inside, I'd never know what changes to make to better navigate my mood patterns. It's possible to have healthy relationships, stable work, and longer periods between episodes. But that only begins when we stop suppressing the truth and start learning to live in harmony with others—and with ourselves. All those years of fighting the diagnosis, all those alternative explanations, all that resistance—it only delayed the help I desperately needed.

And I wasn't the only one paying the price for that delay.

Chapter Six: When Did I Hit My Breaking Point?

When do you get help? Some people never do, in large part due to the opposing schools of thought suppressing a bipolar diagnosis. Others will seek treatment for depression but not accept a label for the greater mood management rollercoaster in play. Often, individuals with BD self-medicate so well that opportunities for diagnosis are missed. I've even seen it possible for someone to be largely successful in navigating BD without receiving a diagnosis or medication, provided family members take ownership of helping them remain stable. It's common to observe codependency in the closest relationships of an undiagnosed BD patient, as we'll see play out in my own story.

When We've Suffered Enough

It is most common that we get help when we are at our wit's end. I discovered this truth not just in my own journey, but in every memoir I devoured after my diagnosis.

When I was desperately trying to understand what was happening to me, I found unexpected comfort in learning that even Abraham Lincoln and Winston Churchill had struggled with what sounded remarkably like bipolar symptoms. Lincoln faced what doctors called being "within an inch of being a perfect lunatic for life," [46] while Churchill named his depression "The Black Dog."[47] These weren't just historical footnotes to me—they were lifelines. If these giants of history could struggle with mental illness and still accomplish great things, maybe there was hope for me too. Perhaps even our darkest moments were being woven into a larger tapestry of purpose.

But it was the contemporary memoirs that really saved me. Let's recall those voices I mentioned earlier that I devoured when I first accepted my BD label. Carrie Fisher started seeing a psychologist at fifteen but wasn't diagnosed with bipolar until twenty-four. Despite recognizing her symptoms, she refused medication and dove into drugs instead. One overdose later, she completed a twelve-step program. Without substances masking her symptoms, Fisher could finally see and accept her bipolar diagnosis. [48] Armed with wit and humor, her memoir helped me understand my own journey.

Professor Kay Redfield Jamison became my favorite bipolar voice. She battled symptoms for years before seeking treatment, with her first major depressive episode hitting during her senior year of high school. Even with her growing expertise in psychology, she continued struggling without help until "within three months of becoming a professor, I was ravingly psychotic."[49] Her description of increasingly feverish behavior at work, her marriage falling apart, spending herself into a financial black hole—it was like she was explaining my own 2010 breakdown when I was newly married, teaching AP Lang, and pursuing my master's degree.

The pattern was clear: we all waited until we'd suffered enough.

Others weren't so fortunate in their timing. Olympian Suzy Favor Hamilton endured very public tragedies before getting help—suspected postpartum depression, a friend's death, suddenly quitting her job, real estate failures. Her first call to a doctor came only after admitting to a suicide plan. [50] Worse yet, he misdiagnosed her with depression and prescribed antidepressants that induced mania, as I explored in part one.

Terri Cheney's story particularly haunted me. At thirty-eight, she left Los Angeles for Santa Fe after her father's death, planning to make it a permanent vacation—meaning she planned to die. The trip triggered mania: four-day spurts without eating or sleeping, nonstop talking, reckless behavior. [51] She'd chosen Christmas Eve for her suicide attempt, laid out a black cashmere dress, saved up over three hundred pills. But she was locked out of her house when she went to buy tequila. The locksmith who came to help her raped her with a broken bottle. She still intended to take the pills at midnight but woke up in the hospital instead. "I didn't want this life that I'd been given back," she wrote, "but it was a gift nonetheless." [52]

The word "gift" stopped me cold. Even in her deepest despair, Terri recognized something sacred in being given another chance. It made me wonder if survival itself was a form of grace—an invitation to discover what our lives were truly meant for.

Reading all these stories, I kept asking myself: Do we have to wait until we lose it all to get help? What finally triggers that timeline of acceptance? I was beginning to suspect that sometimes what looks like rock bottom is actually solid ground—the place where we finally stop running and start listening.

For me, the answers were somehow simpler and more complex than I expected.

What Triggered My Acceptance Timeline

By the time I completed my fourteen months of therapy with Dr. Dennis Bogin in Syracuse in 2014, I found I was quite happy again in Virginia. I loved my job at the high school and was promoted quickly to head of the English department. My work producing the school yearbook gave me a creative outlet and authentic relationships with returning staffers. My brother had shared his family with me. I had a full life again. I maintained a weekly blog, through which I reconnected with a friend from college. We began dating, and the legacy of Charming was born in my blog as I wrote through our romance.

It was a long-distance relationship between Hampton and D.C. Charming would come visit me one weekend, and I'd visit him the next. We traded weekends for a couple of years this way, racking up two friend groups, two churches, and two routines. For the sake of saving money on hotels, we stayed together, but not *together* together. We were committed to honor God by waiting until marriage for sex.

We never did normal things like paying bills, buying clothes, cleaning house, or grocery shopping; Charming planned epic adventures, keeping our time together filled with natural highs and a lot of laughter.

It felt to me like Charming dragged his heels at every turn, having experienced one broken marriage and protecting himself rightfully from jumping into another one with me. There was something holding him back. He told me he loved me after nine months. A year later, he wisely asked me to do counseling together before he would consider getting married. He was stationed in Norfolk for a couple of months, so when I got back from taking a group of my students to Italy, we spent the summer of 2017 trying to figure out what was wrong with me.

Charming wasn't wrong that something wasn't right with me. He'd seen my temper flare in the past, and he knew it wasn't normal where I'd go in my mind at the threat of us breaking up. He was also aware that I'd taken quetiapine for a decade to treat my insomnia, a drug not approved for use during pregnancy. We wanted to start a family immediately.

Charming had enough front row seats to my basket case meltdowns to likely suspect insomnia didn't explain it all. In August, our therapist gave me a battery of tests, and I was diagnosed with ADHD combined type with anxiety. The first thing my nurse practitioner did was take me off quetiapine and prescribe me Adderall.

I wrote about these things in my blog, as well. It was an awakening to see myself in the diagnosis. I was quite happy in the first couple of weeks. I blogged to understand and accept myself. I wasn't ashamed of ADHD. Something from mid-August was almost prophetic about my relationship with Charming, though, and worth sharing now in hindsight. "Maybe after all I've learned about myself this summer, after all he's learned about me," I wrote, "I need him to be a thousand percent sure that I am the woman he wants to build a life and legacy as much as he's needed that certainty himself."[53] I feared, deep down, that my disordered mind made me less lovable.

Then Labor Day, Charming proposed, and I was made whole.

September also meant back to school. I had trouble sleeping and began feeling anxiety. Well, what did my nurse practitioner do? Leslie said, "Laura Joy, are you sure you don't have bipolar?" I fired Leslie. I liked my ADHD diagnosis better. My psychologist wanted me to be seen by a psychiatrist at his practice instead of this nurse practitioner, anyway, so I used that as my excuse to leave her practice.

I spent a lot of time driving across the water to Christian Psychotherapy that year, grateful to have found a team of doctors who prioritized the integration of faith in mental health treatment. I did solo counseling every week, premarital counseling when Charming was in town, and psychiatrist medication check-ins every month.

Looking back, I'm struck by how often the bridge tunnel became a metaphor for my journey—crossing back and forth through that water, literally traveling between my broken reality and the hope of healing. There was something sacred about that repetitive pilgrimage, as if each crossing was a small act of faith that wholeness was possible on the other side.

My new psychiatrist started me immediately on anti-anxiety medications. One after another. From August to December, we experimented with six different medications. And I dropped two dress sizes. My hypomania was activated. I slept inconsistently. I felt, at times, overmedicated, and would opt to work through the sleeplessness rather than take the prescribed benzo pill. I recall planning a *Wizard of Oz* spin-off skit for the homecoming pep rally in October and things going sideways, my mood launching ahead of me, feeling like I was chasing achievements and falling short. I made it bigger than it should have been. Kids didn't have the attention span for a skit like that at a pep rally.

Meanwhile, Charming and I were planning the wedding of the century come weekends. My parents hosted us in Syracuse for an open house at Thanksgiving for friends and family to meet my fiancé. The weekend was hazy. In fact, the next few months were hazy. I'd take an Adderall in the morning, work, hit the gym, play Pokémon Go at increasing intervals of time, then take my prescribed benzodiazepine, clonazepam, with a swig of rum and sleep. Repeat until Christmas vacation when Charming took me home to Syracuse again. I had a meltdown, but I don't remember why. I can remember fighting with my mother, growing hot all over, still taste the salt in my angry tears, feel the tightening of my chest. It was my first panic attack.

It was just a month later that I'd be back at my parents' house because my grandmother passed away. The only lucid thought I can anchor to is I didn't want Charming to drive me home for the funeral. In five days, I compiled a montage tribute to Grams, weaving together video clips and still images to bring her to life again at the service. It was an entirely manic endeavor. I was to marry Charming in five months, but it seemed like less anxiety and stress for me to make this trip without him. He insisted. I picked up Charming in DC. He drove us the rest of the way. My extended family loved and accepted him. I was a wreck the whole weekend.

Charming talked with my family about my moods. They were worried. We left Syracuse with a plan for Charming to attend my next doctor's appointment with me. I remember none of this clearly or chronologically. Days bleed into one another. I use my blogs and date info from phone photos to recreate the timeline for much of this chapter. I don't remember snooping on my fiancé's phone to discover the email he wrote to my therapist after the funeral. I took pictures, though. Researching today for my timeline, I found those photos. It was as if I was reading it all for the first time.

My heart breaks for the man who wrote that email. He was desperate for my doctor to get me some help. Reading his words now, I see love in action: someone refusing to let me disappear into the darkness alone. Perhaps that kind of steadfast love is how grace shows up in human form, proof of providence when we least expect or deserve it.

I've been reminded of the preface to Terri Cheney's *Manic* as I compose this chapter. She explained her choice to write her memoir episodically instead of chronologically. "When I look back, I rarely remember events in terms of date or sequence," Cheney writes. "Rather, I remember what emotional state I was in…. Life for me is defined not by time, but by mood."[54] I took her advice, crafting the whole of part one episodically for this reason. It was easy to topically register qualifying details, tell you parts of my story that came up in context of a bigger picture context.

Attempting to tell this part of my story chronologically, however, is a perplexing challenge. When it comes to my acceptance timeline, I drafted it at my husband's prompting, only my memory mixed events up and left out things my blog and photos assure me happened. Charming's words give me an insight to myself I lacked at the time. I rely on these external tools to piece my tale together accurately. In some strange way, having to reconstruct my story from fragments felt like an act of faith— trusting that even the pieces I couldn't remember had meaning in God's larger design.

Perspectives Collide: Life in Hypomania from Inside vs. Outside

Charming's words, sent from a place of love and bewilderment, are now the best documentation about my mental state at this time. They accurately depict my decline. Better yet, they offer the opportunity for a comparative account.

At the time of his writing, I can affirm that I was taking the stimulant Adderall to treat ADHD as prescribed. While I occasionally took clonazepam to get a little sleep, I had stopped taking it daily for anxiety, explaining to my psychiatrist that I preferred the less sedative, shorter acting effects of marijuana. Being open with my doctors about my treatment protocol, including marijuana, didn't raise any red flags. Charming positioned himself as observer in the email, supplying evidence a doctor would need to provide a diagnosis of my mental state.

"She is not in a stable place. Her mental state is incredibly fragile and not resilient to even the slightest of life's frustrations," Charming began. "She seems incapable of delaying any emotion or compartmentalizing almost any concern." He described me perseverating, pervasively. He gave examples of my deteriorating state, like being driven to a fit of rage by something small like a check engine light or hole in my pants. In those tantrums, he quoted me saying I hated my life, questioned why I'd lost God's favor, and believed no one cared for me.

"She will sob by the second scene of a movie, or chapter of a book. She simply cannot be consoled after being frustrated. And when she gets frustrated, she often goes on angry tantrums, where she rages against the world," Charming explained to my doctor. I don't know about you, but I can conjure an image of Scarlet O'Hara in *Gone with the Wind* right now. Who knows? Maybe it was Vivien Leigh who taught me how to express my bipolar emotions all those decades ago.

After our trip to Syracuse last Christmas when he saw me fall apart and beat myself in the mudroom, my then-boyfriend Tony asked me when that behavior started. Charming's email confirmed my suspicions.

He describes that sometimes I'd repeat, "I hate me," like a mantra while hitting my thighs or forehead. "She bristles at any other sort of interpretation, assumes you are calling her stupid or questioning her character (even when your differing opinion is to value her character)," he wrote, "and then gets vindictive to turn the offensive on someone, something, anything else."

Charming describes our last Christmas together in 2017 much differently from how I perceived it. Mostly, I remember having a fight with my mom and escaping to drive around catching Pokémon for hours. In Charming's account, he uses Christmas day to show that, even with no planned events or deadlines, I constantly felt like I was being rushed, telling him I never had "enough time".

Before returning to this chapter today after unearthing the photos of Charming's email six years ago, my husband Tony had me read it aloud to him. It sounded familiar. Once I stopped sleeping consistently due to my back injury last fall, Tony had a front row seat to my hypomania. Tony could empathize with Charming. In the most ironic intersection of past and present, both men had witnessed how the slightest request might cause me to blow up in disgust or lash out.

"It almost seems like a sort of paranoia," Charming had written. "The highs are too high and the lows are deathly low."

Tony interrupted my reading at that line. "The difference between then and now is I could match those symptoms to BD," he told me. "I knew right away. I'd already seen it in my daughter's mother."

Charming was distraught by his inability to trust me and perplexed by my suicidal ideations. He describes well what loved ones experience on the other side of our intense moods, saying, "I do not know when she is merely crying wolf in bemoaning her life or if she truly wants to hurt herself." Five months from our wedding day, my fiancé was staring down the barrel at a marriage to a woman best described as "overtly mean, vindictive, selfish, and unloving". It is encouraging that, five months ago, Tony married a quite different, reformed version of me, and those adjectives no longer apply.

Perhaps the insight I most appreciated was Charming's take on happenings in my professional environment. In my opinion, until reading his account, I had faked my way through that last year at the high school in Hampton much better. Yes, I was on the "struggle bus" many days, missed a lot of work, dropped a few balls. But I managed to explain away each of these instances so well I don't remember them as he describes. That said, I trust Charming's account is the right one, not mine filtered through the rapid cycling haze of those days.

"Whereas in past years I believe they saw her as a model teacher, placing her in leadership positions, the administration at the school have conducted at least two 'interventions' with her this year," Charming explained to my doctor, citing alleged complaints from students. What interventions? How is it I can't remember?

It gets worse. "The principal sought to relieve her of some of her duties, recommended that she take days off for mental health, and had to cut her off during a speech at a student ceremony," he wrote. Relieved of duties? Take days off for mental health? Completely blank on those, too. The silver lining is I accurately recalled things went sideways at the National English Honor Society induction ceremony, just now I know what; nevertheless, I don't remember what I said in the speech or why I was cut off.

I can trust my memory of events no more than Charming could trust me at the time. It was humbling to realize how much I'd been living in my own reality, disconnected from the impact I was having on others. Maybe real healing starts when we're brave enough to see ourselves through eyes of love rather than through the distortions of our own shame. We still went to church together on Sundays, but I'd stopped having quiet times, journaling, and reading my Bible. I could not be slowed so, could not bear to face the disquiet within.

Despite my ability to explain away work snafus to my fiancé, he was not reassured. "I don't know how serious each of those items were individually," Charming wrote, "but collectively, they worry me and seem to suggest she is falling apart at work as well." I suppose I was. We saw each other in person only two days per week, but Charming was probably right to suggest to my therapist that things were much worse than I let on.

For the Love of Bipolar, Don't Label Me Depressed

Charming escorted me to my next doctor's appointment as planned, and I walked out with a diagnosis of depression and a prescription for sertraline, an antidepressant classified as an SSRI, or Selective Serotonin Reuptake Inhibitor. Now, if you've been paying attention, a red flag just went up. You're thinking of Suzy Favor Hamilton, perhaps. Good readers, this is why it is so necessary to accept a bipolar label if it fits. Depression is not a preferable diagnosis. Unknowingly prescribing antidepressants to a BD patient can go one of two ways: worsening depression symptoms by triggering suicidal ideations and behaviors or activating a manic episode.

Which way would it go for me?

A Fuzzy, Fuzzy February

I knew from experience it would take four to six weeks to see full effects of the antidepressant medication. I didn't spend the rest of the month waiting for the meds to kick in. Instead, I jumped the employment timeline and applied for English positions that were not yet vacant in some of the top-rated high schools in northern Virginia in preparation to join Charming in the DC area. I didn't stop at submitting applications through employment portals; it would likely be a couple of months before jobs for the coming year posted. I sent personalized cards with inspiring quotes to each principal along with letters of interest and copies of my resume.

It is difficult to recall this time in my life with clarity. Writing about it makes me sick to my stomach now. Applying for jobs in my mental state was excruciating. It would have typically been easy to brag about my educational prowess and pitch myself for teaching positions. This was different; I didn't have the energy or the optimism. Making it through the workday was a struggle. I had to find energy I didn't have in the evenings to knock out those job applications. Yet, in a way, my hypomania was looking for a way to be productive in the waiting room of balanced activity.

Leaving the job and life I loved in Hampton Roads to marry Charming was starting to become real. I retreated into my virtual reality game on my phone whenever the thought of moving away snuck back in. We got a snow day, and I wound up spending it with my neighbor. I'd met Van while playing Pokémon Go the previous summer. Van helped me shovel my car out of the driveway so we could go play our favorite game downtown. Planet Fitness opened midday, giving me access to my normal exercise routine. Van had a membership, too. During this storm, we started going to the gym together and playing Pokémon more often.

Mid-month, I had surgery on my right rotator cuff. Charming came to Hampton for the surgery itself, but as I recovered, I needed help nearby. Van was happy to oblige, driving me to the real gym and the Pokémon gym every day so I'd meet my most important daily goals, fitness and virtual. In retrospect, those are the only two things I seemed contented to do. Even the word "contented" feels wrong; it was more like going through the motions of living without actually feeling alive. The gym and the game had become my entire world, but it was a hollow world, stripped of meaning or real connection. I was functioning, but barely existing, clinging to routines that felt safe precisely because they demanded nothing of my heart.

Photos of me hooked up to a computer monitor registering my brain waves while I watched videos on a screen remind me that I started neurofeedback brain training at some point shortly after my grandmother's death. Charming funded the excursion at the recommendation of our Christian psychotherapist. It was another reason to brave unexpected tunnel traffic in the evenings twice a week, sometimes spending several hours traveling between Hampton and Virginia Beach.

In session, a woman hooked wired pads up to my brain like they do for heart monitoring. The goal was to rewire my brain by teaching it to regulate itself correctly. I could see my brain waves in real-time, but I didn't understand how it worked. I could watch anything so long as I remained looking at the computer monitor. It was torture sitting still and doing nothing for an hour. I'd console myself on the way home by playing Pokémon while I sat in traffic, even taking detours to chase rare spawns in the game.

All I've described was under the care of several mental health professionals. I sought help. I got some diagnoses. I got treatment. I took the medication they prescribed as directed.

But ultimately, it was the wrong diagnosis, the wrong treatment, and a lethal combination of medication assembling a nuclear bomb inside. Day by day, for half a year, they worked tirelessly, entering my blood stream, slowly building until the bomb went off. Out of the ashes, phoenix rose.

Chapter Seven: What Happens When Everything Falls Apart?

Let's recap the month prior to Fenix's arrival. I'd just lost my grandmother and was prescribed an antidepressant soon after. Meanwhile, I was planning a wedding and cross-state move, applying for jobs, recovering from shoulder surgery, preparing for my students' upcoming end of course test, producing the school yearbook, and somehow still acting as chair of my department. Outside of working and exercising, I was travelling to Virginia Beach two or three times a week for three types of doctor's appointments and playing Pokémon whenever possible.

By the end of the month, I started to feel an escape from the cycling depression and anxiety. Come March, I was feeling oddly happy, even.

Fenix Rising: Creating an Alternate Persona

Let me be clear. I don't have multiple personalities. I am not a schizophrenic. I am, however, creative and adept at compartmentalizing. During my state of growing elation in March, Fenix was born, and at my neighbor's prompting. I created a second Pokémon Go account in her name.

A phonetical spelling of the same, this character was a phoenix rising from the ashes.

It fit with how I felt inside, the darkness and irritability of the depression had been replaced by excitement over playing my virtual reality game with Van. I had sick days accumulated at work I needed to use or lose. I'd already interviewed and hired my replacement. A few times, I took a half a day off just to go to Fort Monroe beach and drive around hunting for Pokémon.

It was euphoric. My therapist says brain fog is common for a manic episode; with rapid firing neurons from imbalanced neurotransmitters, my brain overloads, affecting my memory. While I am spared vivid memories of these days, those who loved me were not. They likely remember watching in shocked horror as I systematically imploded my charmed life.

Van liked to encourage Fenix to come out and play. She was the sexy, carefree version of me. I'd never had much of a libido which made it easy to wait for marriage with my fiancé. Whatever Charming was, Van was not. Where Charming was financially stable, godly, generous, kind, and good, Van was not. I quite rarely went out on a school night, but Van started bringing me to the bar with him. I took Tramadol for the pain after my shoulder surgery for a while. The bottle said not to mix it with alcohol. My antidepressant had a similar warning. I ignored them.

I'd never lost time before. I lost it with Van. I'd always said I wanted to marry a Christian man, and here I was choosing the opposite of everything I'd claimed to value.

I was taking Adderall plus the antidepressants and the pain killer, all as prescribed, but mixing that with two drinks was enough to make me black out. These blackouts went beyond brain fog. I had conversations. I was awake and interacted. For months to come, I would introduce myself to an acquaintance of Van's only to discover we were already familiar, friendly even. We'd met in that bar on one of these nights. I could conjure no memory of having met these people before (though I quickly learned to just pretend I remembered them as fondly as they did me).

One of Van's friends was someone I already knew. He was the son of our school librarian. She was a colleague I considered a friend. I don't remember drinking with him, but Van was quick to tell me the next morning that the librarian's son had asked him what drugs I was on. A legal, lethal combination? Another time, I woke up in the passenger seat of Van's car with the windshield cracked. He told me I'd kicked it so hard it shattered. I was apologetic and paid for it, but I had no memory of the event.

I was also suddenly increasingly aware of my sex drive. It seemed like the antidepressants were starting to kick in. I felt happy if I was with Van. Waiting for marriage with Charming hadn't been an issue, but my typically low libido was in overdrive. My neighbor was prepped to fan that flame. It did not matter then that Van was *not* my type. A short, slender Asian who himself claims to be incapable of loving another human, I find nothing attractive about him in my right state of mind. One day he encouraged Fenix to come out and play, just not with Pokémon. I slept with Van.

The memory is fuzzy, though in my mind, Fenix was with Van, not me. The next day, I awoke to a double life. Yes, and. *Yes,* I was going to be Charming's wife in July, *and* I was going to play Pokémon with Van until I had to move to DC. I still wanted the good life we had planned months down the road. I would enjoy this alternative, good life while I could. Manic reasoning doesn't pass logic checks. It made sense at the time.

A Manic March in Two Worlds

Van hated the smell of smoke. It wasn't a suggestion; it was an order. I quit smoking clove cigarettes overnight in March, replacing them with vaping. A friend hooked me up with a mod and a juice flavor I liked. I recall how puzzled Charming was the first time he saw me make a cloud of vapor. I'd forgotten to tell him I'd quit smoking and switched to vaping. I guess it slipped my mind.

I know my bridal shower was that month, too, in Charming's parents' hometown up north. Without the pictures and invitation, my account of that day would be inaccurate. I was present in body, but I wanted to be playing Pokémon instead of getting expensive gifts. I was a terror to my mother and sister-in-law, who were only trying to give me a beautiful party. Several photographs capture me scowling in disgust at one of them.

Fenix's role in my life increased. The game required us to be physically present at real locations to play—churches, parks, museums. Some battles needed multiple players working together, so Van and I created extra accounts and used multiple phones. We became obsessed with reaching the highest levels possible, which meant we could spend hours together every day, just the two of us, winning battles that felt more real than anything else in my life.

On the weekends, I wedding planned with Charming. During the workweek, I got to focus on leveling my second account up as high as my main account. I began treating Fenix like her own person. I was with Charming. Fenix was with Van. Since Van preferred blondes, I bought a wig. He took me shopping at Forever 21 when I dropped another size or two. Fenix was blonde and wore crop tops and miniskirts. Van liked to take her on fake dates to Virginia Beach or Norfolk on the other side of the bridge tunnel where no one would recognize us. I was reserved and repressed. Fenix was the life of the party.

I wish there were another email from Charming so I could write about this month with as much clarity as the preceding one. Alas, we're reduced to my ill-attempts to recall a month that is to me a single, endless day of blissful ignorance. I had been medicated right into my first, truly obvious, unconcealable manic episode. The signs were textbook. My doctor missed them. Fenix was the product of putting a bipolar patient on an antidepressant medication.

April Fool's: We're Going to Germany

I had interviews scheduled with two schools in northern Virginia when Charming complicated the plan. I knew he was trying to decide where to take his career next after his DC job ended in June. The first of April, he broke the news. He had been offered a three-year post in Germany. Government job. Highest pay. No brainer. There would be no interviews in northern Virginia. In four months, Charming would move to Germany. He'd return to marry me in July, and then I'd return to Germany with him for the next three years.

I've had many years to consider our ill-fated love story. I believe this was the beginning of the end for Charming and me. Germany. I did not know I had BD, could not have consciously protected myself from upending my life in this way. In the DC area, we had three years building relationships at church and with our small group. Charming's friends and family were there. I had a job lined up there. It was only a few hours from my brother's family. I could still be there for my nieces' and nephew's big events.

Three years in Germany? I know I did not want to go, but I also thought it didn't matter. A good wife would set her reservations aside in support of an incredible opportunity her husband would be a fool to turn down. My best explanation is that my mind fractured, but it had help. April Fool's Day was also Easter that year. It was my third and final Easter Sunday at our church in Alexandria where we were no longer going to live.

Merely days later, I was in Tampa Bay unplanned. It was spring break. I told Charming I had to get away by myself and reset in good weather. Really, there was regional Pokémon that only spawned in Florida, and Van and I were driving our many accounts down there to catch it. I remember feeling joy basking in the Florida sun. I don't, however, remember the name of the rare Pokémon worth all that driving. Van posted a photo of us on one of his social media accounts at a bar in Jacksonville on our drive back home, or I wouldn't be able to tell you we stopped there, too.

One moment stands out, though, amongst all the others. One singular moment of clarity. Driving on I-75 with Van sleeping in the passenger's seat, I called my psychologist. I left him a voicemail so calm it feels scripted, like I was neutrally observing somebody else. "Hey, doc. I'm making decisions out of character for me, not acting like myself. I'm really happy, but I don't need sleep," I'd told him. "Something's off. I think I should go off the antidepressant." He called me back immediately, agreed with my side-effect evaluation, and approved my plan to taper off sertraline.

After studying my illness, I don't need a degree to recognize a manic episode. I understand the red flags and warning signs. When I meet people on the bipolar spectrum now, I recognize them. Absent shame, I'm excited to find another unquiet mind navigating normalcy like I do.

My doctor, however, had a PhD after his name. This doctor built a practice that treated mental health issues through a Christian framework. Looking back, I can see the signs were all there—Charming's detailed email in February, my own phone call in April describing textbook manic symptoms. If I can recognize a manic episode now without a degree, how did a trained professional miss it?

When I searched for him years later to understand what happened, I discovered he had died in 2020 and his practice had closed suddenly due to financial problems. I felt a strange mix of sadness and frustration— sadness for his passing, but frustration that this missed diagnosis changed the entire trajectory of my life. The wrong help had sent me spiraling into the most destructive episode I'd ever experienced.

An Overseas Move, Doubts, and a Trip to the Courthouse

The rest of April is a surreal blur. I didn't understand exactly how it worked, but Charming's new job affected our marriage timeline. For my "household" in Hampton to be included in his move to Germany, we had to be legally married within three weeks' time. Van joined me and a couple of my closest friends for an early bachelorette party despite the fact our real wedding wasn't set for another three months.

I'd never been to one before, and Van easily convinced me a bachelorette party was a girl's once in a lifetime excuse to go to a strip club. The night itself is a string of still images, no real memories, other than the impression this strip club was underwhelming, far less glamourous than in TV shows, and even Fenix couldn't bolster enough courage to feel comfortable in a place that reeked of desperation. I don't know whether my fiancé knew about the bachelorette party or not.

In the end, Charming and I waited until the last possible day to tie the knot. Even then, the night before, we argued about whether we should still get married. By two o'clock in the morning, we agreed to move forward in the darkness with the decision we had made in the light. We went to the courthouse and made it official for the move, parting ways from there. I drove back to Hampton to teach a half a day. We were only ever husband and wife on that piece of paper. We planned to wait until we were married in the eyes of God to consummate our union.

What Happens on Prom Night

I do not remember much of May. The month is fragmented like a highlight reel: playing Pokémon, grading books of poetry projects, choosing bridesmaid dresses, going to the bar and gym with Van. If I did not have the photographs to jog my memory, I'm not sure I could piece these events together properly. I slept little, ate less. I was increasingly unable to be at work for an entire school day. My blog reads like I have it all together, reflecting a perception on that time I can't trust was entirely accurate. Again, I'd love another of Charming's emails to show me what I really looked like during this time.

One day stands out from the monotony. I caught a man taking photos with a digital camera in my yard. When I confronted him, he said he was taking photos of my neighbor's house. Paranoia or intuition, I guessed Charming had hired a private investigator. My best friend came to a bridal shower held in the library at my work. I was suspicious of her conversations with my coworkers, later surprised she was texting with my librarian friend, mother to the young man concerned about what drugs I was on that time I blacked out.

The nineteenth of Saturday was my high school's prom at the Virginia Air and Space Museum in downtown Hampton. Charming was coming to chaperone with me while I took pictures for this fourth and final yearbook edition. My best friend was involved somehow, maybe also chaperoning, a detail that never registered as odd until now. At some point, I caught her texting Charming. She had told him about my affair with Van. The gig was up. I ran away from prom. I don't remember whether I drove home or had Van pick me up. I know I played Pokémon for a while. There are no surviving messages, photos, or emails to fill in the gaps for me.

Whenever I did get home, I remember walking into what was left of an intervention attempt. I don't remember who was there. Charming, at one point. My best friend? I know my neighbor came outside when my parents showed up. Why weren't they in Syracuse? Charming had hired a private investigator, and together with accounts from my best friend and the librarian at school, my family had concluded I had a drug problem. They had planned to talk to me together after prom and send me to rehab to ride horses and heal.

This is among the most painful nights to be someone who loved me well, I imagine. I wish I could remember more of it, for their sakes. I'm not certain, but I think I climbed out my bedroom window to escape and played Pokémon with Van all night, leaving my family bewildered and reeling in my rented bungalow.

That was the end of Charming and me, and it was the end of my career at the high school near my older brother's house. I was not getting married. I was not moving to Germany. In a month, I would have no job. I could not face this reality. The following week at school, I got stuck with an unexpected task during my planning block. A student came to my room to remind me I was scheduled to proctor an exam. I ranted the whole way down the hall about how I had too much to do for the yearbook to watch kids test, and apparently said, "Just shoot me in the head."

The student, concerned, reported this to admin. They came looking for me during lunch, but I wasn't at school. This further concerned them. I had taken my students' poetry books to grade at Fort Monroe beach. When I returned for my last class, I was pulled into the conference room instead. My principal and assistant principal were there, I know, looking very confused. I assured them I was fine. No one could seem to be convinced.

I was put on immediate paid administrative leave and assigned mandatory therapy sessions. I did not finish the last two weeks of my four-year post there. It is among my greatest regrets. It is also the first time my BD could be documented by employers as a legitimate health problem, capable of damaging my career and reputation.

Would this be enough to make me realize the doctor was right ten years before when he suggested I had bipolar tendencies?

Accumulating Consequences, Physical and Legal

This chapter, I feel physically ill. Trying to access inconsistent memories nauseates me. At times the recollections are fuzzy, other times hazy, sometimes blurred together, but never clear. As a writer, I am ever in search of the truth. And I can't count on my mind to give me that for a period spanning a year and a half. Sending myself back in time to relive this was necessary. Facing the inconsistencies, trying to find the truth beneath my escape tactics—I am making peace with myself, then and now. I'm reconciling the memory books, balancing the scales.

In essence, I was not always actively participating in the present. Compare an exegetical sermon to a topical one. The former unpacks a passage of scripture, verse by verse, to arrive at varied conclusions. The later begins with a premise, then crosses between old and new testaments to find scriptures for support. The exegetical sermon is typically chronological, points made as the verses unfold within the greater context of the chapter, or book, examining the voice of the author. The topical uses disparate voices in disparate moments to illustrate, offering a surface level analysis of the context or greater framework. Writing this chapter requires both an exegetical and topical approach, simultaneously. My perspective, when I was not actively participating in the present, must be supplemented by other narratives.

Perhaps most relevant here is I can best recall events I was promptly forced to talk about and process, even if my conclusions at that time were inaccurate. Whether in conversations with friends or authorities, the months to come would elicit opportunities to face the possibility an undiagnosed mental illness was at the heart of my soul's unrest.

I think it's hardest to remember the months I was mostly escaping reality in passive avoidance of the destruction I'd left in my wake. I thought I should be job hunting, but Van pointed out I had a paid two-week vacation. It was just me and Van against the world. At the start of June, I was a lifetime brunette. At Van's urging, I began to look more like Fenix's avatar. I got blonde highlights at first, then went platinum blonde a week later. I played hard without sleep for a few days, playing the game all night, then crashed quickly and repeated.

While my students were finishing out the schoolyear, Van and I played Pokémon. We had about eight accounts between us by then, and we played them all at the same time. I crafted a special gaming tray that could hold four phones. I joined online communities to be notified of rare spawns so I could drop what I was doing and get out to catch them all. In the wake of the Charming debacle, I'd been uninvited to my cousin's wedding. I pretty much cut my family off.

There was a waiting period before I could file for divorce, which I promised Charming I would do the day I returned my engagement ring. Ironically, we would have qualified for an annulment had I been able to acknowledge I was mentally ill then. I tried returning wedding gifts and canceling related items, but my brain was becoming increasingly disorganized. I made mistakes and couldn't focus to finish a task.

By the end of June, I still didn't have a job lined up for August. Van took me on a trip to the mountains a few hours away. A bunch of his friends had rented a place. Everyone brought something for the weekend; my contribution was marijuana. Van drove us there in my car on a Friday evening. The first night around the campfire was fine. When everyone else went to bed in the cabin, sleep was elusive. In a house full of people, I was alone. There was also no cell service, which meant no Pokémon Go escape.

Even worse, Van was asleep with my car keys in his pocket. I felt trapped. I didn't have a book to read. I journaled. Turning my gaze inward somehow made me more anxious. I walked outside, lush mountain canopy filtering the moonlight. I jogged. Sprinted. Tried to tire myself out. It was dawn when I returned to the cabin. I simultaneously woke and started a fight with Van, who at first refused to give me my car keys. When pushed to anger, he agreed to let me leave, but he would drive us back home in my car. I resisted at first, but I had embarrassed us both in front of his friends. Distraught, I complied. We packed up the car and started down that narrow, winding mountain road.

I tried to calm myself. Van was seething. He'd calmed me down more than once by punching me in the face. I hoped to avoid that. Heck, I didn't blame him. I deserved it. His rage and my shame stole the oxygen from the car. I didn't know what I was experiencing was a panic attack, that the train of thought about Van hitting me only heightened my fight or flight response. My blood was hot in my veins, my chest tightened, and I couldn't get enough air. I begged Van to pull over the car and let me out. In his defense, there was no place to do this safely. We were driving down and around a mountain at twenty miles per hour with barely enough room for two cars to pass each other.

"Stop right now and let me out, or I'll jump out the window," I demanded with Scarlet O'Hara-like dramatic flair.

"Okay," he laughed. "I dare you."

I did it. This scene I can picture clearly, lucidly, like my mind took command to record this epic scene from outside the vehicle. I dive out, headfirst. I am momentarily airborne. I hear a sickening thud. I do not instantly register the sound as the back of my head connecting with the gravel road. I try to stand. A wave of dizziness smacks me back down. I put a hand up to the back of my head. I connect with something sticky. I draw it back. Blood.

Van came back and collected me. He thought I'd be fine without medical care. I called my nurse friend for a second opinion. Her description of all the things that might be wrong caused another physical response. Again, I didn't understand the way a panic attack worked. The increase in cortisol and adrenaline masterfully mimicked the adverse symptoms my friend narrated. I wound up calling 9-1-1. We were in the middle of nowhere. Van was directed to a gas station where the ambulance would meet us.

Twenty minutes later, I was lying in the ambulance being assessed when I heard a deep, male voice say, "Do I smell marijuana in the vehicle?" The question was directed at Van. From my vantage point, I couldn't see either man. I asked the EMT who was talking out there. He explained it was a small town. The sheriff liked to drop in on calls like this. We had a short conversation while the sheriff poked around my car.

"Have you been in trouble before?" the EMT asked.

"No, never."

"He'll let you off with a warning, then. Just be honest."

When the sheriff confronted me, I told the truth, assured him this was my first time.

Just my luck, a new first time offender's program was in place in Virginia, and the sheriff was excited to dispense this tidbit. I'd go to court twice, first for sentencing. Then I'd return in January after six months of probation, seventy-four hours of community service punctuated by meetings with my probation officer, random drug tests, and drug education classes. If completed successfully, my misdemeanor marijuana possession charge would be dismissed.

Picking Up the Pieces, Poorly

My next clear memory is interviewing with a school district on the other side of the James River a week after I jumped out of the car window. My toes, cut up from their meeting with the gravel road, would not fit nicely into any of my dress shoes. Road rash covered a third of my back and shoulders, hidden well by a nice dress. I presented well. I was offered the job. I accepted, hoping to be hired before a background check could flag the drug charge. It was a forty-minute commute without traffic, but the unpredictable Monitor Merrimack Bridge Tunnel can double that easily.

Gaining employment was the first step to picking up the pieces of my life. I finished the last administratively appointed session of talk therapy in July, proud to tell the counselor I was now settled. I don't remember our meetings in any detail, but I presented well there, too. I didn't think I needed her help and resented being forced into what felt like therapy jail. I also didn't mention the drug charge to her—another secret I was keeping. I was eager to be done with mandatory counseling, especially since I'd be starting probation. I thought once school was in full swing, I'd find a rhythm, and life would be normal again.

I had three different courses to prep for, more than anyone else in the department, added to the learning curve of being new to the school and district: AP Language and Composition, English 11, and Yearbook. I'd balanced teaching three courses before and thought I'd be fine, accustomed to having a planning block every day. At this school, we had duties every other day, cutting planning time in half. A first-year teacher next door was my one spot of joy that year. She used my curriculum with her juniors; our partnership motivated me to stick with that job as long as I did. She reminded me of myself in my early years in the classroom.

I continued blogging every Tuesday night. It became increasingly difficult to focus that long. Plus, my life was full of things I couldn't write about. I honored Charming's wishes by not mentioning our legal union in my blog posts. Filing for divorce without a lawyer, *pro sé* they call it, with a man living in another country—this adventure was not fit for print.

Likewise, I had to serve out my new prison sentence. I tried to quit smoking marijuana. The longest I made it was three days. Smoking pot was the singular thing that made me feel sane. I could find sleep for about four hours if I smoked a bowl and downed one of my benzos with a shot of spiced rum.

I don't remember the name of my probation officer or what she looked like, though I met with her several times. I was more focused on the detox drinks I'd buy at the tobacco shop before each appointment— expensive solutions that let me keep smoking pot rather than actually quit. Even facing legal consequences, I couldn't imagine getting through a day without the one thing that helped me sleep.

I failed my first drug test.

My probation officer seemed to have been counting on this. That's what the coming drug education classes were for, after all, and I would be expected to pass the remaining drug tests to get this charge dismissed.

I used this as leverage. It would be easier to quit smoking pot if there were lower stress environments for serving my community service hours, like the local library. There was a branch two blocks from me, I reasoned. The evening and weekend operating hours worked well with school and commuting. The library was not an approved location. In the end, I convinced my probation officer to let me ask.

Seeking Solace for My Unquiet Mind

I walked into the library branch by my house and explained my situation to whomever was manning the front desk. I waited to speak with the head librarian. We met in her office. She told me that the library used to let probates work of their community service hours at the library, but not anymore; there were too many problems. I imagine she tolerated this line of questioning because I was a career English teacher holding down a day job presenting professionally.

The interview was on track until the librarian asked me what charge I was facing. When I explained this was my first time in trouble, she practically kicked me out of her office. "They don't mandate seventy-four hours of community service for a first-time offense," she spat and began handing me back the form for my probation officer. I told the librarian I'd thought the same thing, but this was a new program, and my presence in her office started to make sense. I leaned into credibility and respectfully begged. As an English teacher and lover of the written word, would she let me serve out my time in a safe, calm environment where I could be useful?

She agreed to give me a try. I started in October after my next scheduled meeting with my probation officer. I used Van's urine to pass my remaining drug tests. Life was too busy and hectic to quit. Without marijuana, I'd never have slept. I can only imagine how much more damaging that would have been to my career.

The unpredictable commutes across the James River were bookends to a stressful school day with too many expectations for teachers and not enough time to realistically meet them. This issue was systemic in the district, or at least in my school. Commands passed down from higher-ups lacked buy-in from building-level administrators. Teachers were spread thin. Burn out was high. Principals were instructed to enforce protocols that weakened school morale.

My workday was a tedium of writing daily lesson plans for three preps. I'd set a standard of excellence in a time of mental wellness that I could not maintain, particularly when my planning time had been cut in half. I longed for my classroom with the stage back in Hampton with my yearbook crew and my blogging club. Perhaps I lacked investment over there because I quickly decided this was a post for just one year. I was determined to make it out of this occupational jail cell and back to Hampton where I belonged.

Yet, I wasn't sure if I would be welcomed. There were question marks around my departure, and I sensed I deserved this suffering as karma for what I did to Charming. Fitting in seventy-four hours of community service between work and all the other drug charge related appointments spread me thinner still. I played Pokémon Go whenever I was driving, my consolation prize for this awful existence. My closest friends were animations. I was happiest inside my phones. My hair began cutting itself from repeated bleach treatments. I remained cut off from my family. Van controlled our free time, practically lived at my house. I cooked for him obsessively.

I've never been so isolated. I pray I am never so again.

It was inside the public library that life slowed down. Seventy-four hours of quiet. No Pokémon. No Van. No students. It could be sunny or rainy, day or night, but inside the library, it was the same still, silent wonder. In the beginning, it was torture to unplug, but the more hours I accumulated for my probation officer, the more I began to look forward to serving my time.

Oh, this is the first time in this chapter that the heaviness lifted. The library was my sanctuary for healing. Something about the stillness reminded me of sitting in church as a child—that same sense of peace settling over chaos.

Forced to set aside my escape tactics, I became increasingly aware of the disorder in my brain. My thoughts were disorganized. Tasks that used to come naturally were overwhelming. Not at the library, though. My jobs were simple, at least in the beginning. I reshelved books. I pulled reserved titles. I re-alphabetized the DVD section a couple of times a week, something the staff came to count on.

Often, I worked too quickly through the amount of work assigned and would have to fill the extra time on my scheduled shift. One method was to choose a section of the library and tidy up the shelves. I could reshelve misplaced titles, shift books, and pull duplicate items for the librarian to review. There were nights I had the time to peruse the labels, flip through some pages. When I had to reshelve or pull books with call number 616.8, I took my sweet time.

In the Dewey Decimal System, the nonfiction psychology books about mental disorders and mental health live in this spot, starting with 616.8. I'd always believed God could work through doctors and medicine, but I was still surprised to find hope hiding in a psychology section.

In my branch, these titles were nestled into the farthermost corner of the library. It was eerily quiet and unpopulated in that section. I picked up books about things that fascinated me like narcissism, borderline personality disorder, depression, anxiety, and bipolar. Hidden between stacks, I'd read a few pages, then get back to work. It was about this time that I quit blogging, when I began checking out the 616.8 books.

My medication protocol hadn't changed. I took Adderall in the morning, clonazepam at bedtime, and marijuana as needed for anxiety and sleep. But by January when I completed my community service and fulfilled all the criteria to have my charge excused, I was thinking more clearly. I remember the library vividly even when the rest is blurry.

I saw the head librarian a few times to get her signature on my community service log before monthly check-ins at the corrections center. In the end, I think she genuinely liked me. Before I left, she gave me a final project of retiring a collection of titles as part of an expansion plan, resulting in shifting a dozen full rows of shelves and creating new labels for the stacks. I couldn't have done that when I started. The library slowed me from my busyness to face the confusion inside.

Sufficient Shame, Sufficient Consequence, Sufficient Stillness

Two significant events define January 2019. First, I got my drug charge dropped and my life back. That's an obvious landmark. Second, I stood up to Van. We had been out late dancing one night and were driving home, playing Pokémon in our neighborhood. We got in an argument. It turned physical, as it often did when alcohol was involved. I got out of the car intending to walk home. Cops showed up. A neighbor had called it in. The armed pair took a visual inventory and tried to coax a statement.

"Come on, you've got marks on you. This is the time to report it."

I lifted my hand to my cheek. Swollen. I brought it back down, a flashlight beam resting on a bruise on my bicep. Report him? Van had a record. This would not be a small thing. I refused, telling the officers I still wanted him to be there when I got home.

In my next conversation with Van, I told him he'd put his hands on me for the last time. Another strike, and he'd be out of my life. That was, in fact, the last time Van ever hit me. Maybe he was just waiting for me to take a stand. For the first time in over a year, I felt like I'd listened to the voice inside that had been trying to protect me all along.

Two significant events define February, as well. The first is simple. The judge finalized my divorce to Charming. The second would be the proverbial straw that broke the camel's back of my acceptance timeline. Even with my drug charge behind me, Van's hands off me, and the divorce final, I was still depressed. Then came my thirty-sixth birthday. I remember thinking this wasn't the life I'd prayed for as a little girl, but maybe it was the one that would teach me what I needed to learn.

It was a Wednesday. While I was working with a student, a boy secretly put his phone on the classroom floor and recorded a video up my skirt. On Thursday, my classes drove me crazy with their distractions; senior boys whistled at me in the hallway. The day unsettled me enough to put in a sub request for Friday. I was at home when my assistant principal called to tell me what happened. She had to explain what it meant that my student airdropped this video of my thong to the school on Wednesday, that students and teachers with iPhones received it. The previous day made sense, the distractions and whistles.

My response was I felt violated and asked what I could do. My assistant principal replied, "Wear longer dresses." It matters not that my dress was knee-length; this student was intent on exploiting me, and he'd been creative about it. She apologized for being so insensitive in our next conversation, but the damage was done. She'd sown doubt I was to blame.

The next week, circumstances grew worse still. This boy was captain of a team, a ruffian well-liked by his peers, his girlfriend in another of my classes with all his teammates. The school was required by law to press charges. He was expelled. The authorities found videos on the boy's phone of him engaged in sex with minors. Though a junior in my class, he was legally an adult. I had to go to the police station and watch these videos, identify my underage female students filmed without their consent.

It was the very next Wednesday after my birthday at a faculty professional development training after school entitled More than Sad that it finally clicked. The American Foundation for Suicide Prevention (AFSP) created this program session to teach educators how to recognize signs of mental health distress in our students. I, however, was seeing it in myself.

I was more than sad. This training wasn't restricted to depression. BD was on the menu as well. My moods had been up and down, controlling my life. This was a bipolar low. I knew it. I'd found myself in the 616.8 section of the local library. Medical professionals had suggested it not once but twice. It happened first at age twenty-four in the emergency room after my first week of sleeplessness when my ex cheated on me. It was again suggested in the fall of 2018 immediately following my diagnosis of ADHD combined type with anxiety. My nurse practitioner, Leslie, said it then, and I fired her, moving all my appointments to Christian Psychotherapy.

I guess for me, I had to experience sufficient shame, sufficient consequence, and sufficient stillness to face, process, and accept that BD had run my life since I'd been taken off quetiapine in August 2018. I had to feel exposed, see my masks weren't working to hide the chaos within anymore. I had to break, break, break again.

And if I'm really seeing things clearly, I also had to stop avoiding reality. Seventy-four hours of community service at the local library forced me to do that. Serving my sentence literally put the books in my hands that led me to qualify my disordered thinking, define the uncertainties, and get help.

When did I get diagnosed? When I could be honest about what life since February 2018 had been like for me, it was easy. Setting my faith aside, I could finally see the signs and admit, "I have bipolar disorder."

Now what? What comes next?

Chapter Eight: How Did I Find Real Help?

When I was finally diagnosed, my psychiatrist didn't hand me a book recommendation or a roadmap for what came next. I was left to figure out treatment on my own, piecing together guidance from memoirs and my support group. That's part of why I'm writing the book I needed back then.

What I wish someone had told me was this: expect that what comes next will be difficult and uncertain. If it's not, consider yourself blessed. But for most of us, finding the right treatment is like house hunting—you might get lucky on the first try, but more likely, you'll need to keep looking until you find the right fit.

From my weekly support group, I've learned that finding a treatment protocol that works for your specific brain and body takes purposeful experimentation. Every story I heard had the same theme: the first medication rarely works perfectly. Sometimes it makes things worse before they get better.

I learned this the hard way. Several times in my life, I saw psychiatrists who diagnosed me with depression and prescribed antidepressants—the very medications that would later trigger my most destructive manic episode. But I was only telling them half the story. I omitted past manic behaviors because I couldn't identify the symptoms myself until after diagnosis. I was too embarrassed to mention the times I'd felt "too good," thinking that happiness couldn't possibly be a problem.

Looking back, being open and honest about those embarrassing moments might have led to an accurate diagnosis in my late teens or early twenties. I don't regret the life I've lived, but I do wonder what might have filled the past twenty years if I'd taken control of managing my BD back then.

So, here's what I learned about treatment—with a little help from textbooks and memoirs, but mostly just from living it.

Doctor Shopping for My Mind

When I accepted I had BD, I knew I needed to make two appointments. I called my psychiatrist across the water and at Christian Psychotherapy and filled in the missing details I'd been hiding for years, and medication experimentation began. I also made an appointment with that mandated therapist from the previous summer. I was finally ready to talk about the things I'd never mentioned—like my drug charge and what had happened with the student in my English class on my birthday.

I was fortunate to have existing professional relationships and wasn't in crisis when I sought treatment. I wasn't manically destroying a marriage or contemplating suicide. I was stable enough to make rational decisions about my care, which I now realize was a privilege not everyone has when they reach their breaking point.

I think about Kay Redfield Jamison, who had a colleague brave enough to confront her with a manic-depressive diagnosis and then help her find treatment. "Together we tracked down everything we could find that had been written about the illness," she wrote. [55] Most of us don't have a psychiatrist colleague looking out for us.

When I was researching for this book, I noticed how the internet tries to help. On multiple platforms, searching for bipolar content redirects you to crisis support pages. You have to click a link confirming you're stable just to continue your search. It made me realize how many people must be looking for help in desperate moments. I remembered all the nights I'd prayed for God to make me normal, unaware His help might come through doctors and therapists instead of overnight miracles.

I've learned from support group that finding help can be complicated. Some people wait months for psychiatrist appointments. Others end up in emergency rooms during crisis, which I can tell you from experience as both patient and visitor isn't pleasant—but it does get you immediate access to medication and referrals.

I've also been in the position of trying to find a private mental health facility for someone I love. Even with money and insurance, finding an available bed was nearly impossible. I called seven facilities before finding one with an opening. The whole experience taught me that our mental health system, while better than it used to be, still leaves people scrambling for help when they need it most.

The goal of any hospitalization is to stabilize someone enough to transition to outpatient care. But for those of us able to seek help while stable, the path is different—and in many ways, we get to be more intentional about building our treatment team.

The Search for the Right Therapist

The second piece of my treatment puzzle was finding a therapist, and honestly, this felt more urgent than the psychiatrist appointment. I could get a therapy appointment within days, while psychiatrists were booking months out.

I've seen seven different psychologists or therapists over the years, and here's what I learned: chemistry matters more than credentials. Four of them made little impact, likely because I was "voluntold" to be in their offices. The woman I met with after my manic episode was competent, but we lacked that spark that makes you want to come back.

That might seem silly—shopping for a therapist based on chemistry—but if you're committing to spend hours talking with someone about your most vulnerable moments, you need to feel safe with them. In Syracuse, I had that magical relationship with Dr. Dennis Bogin. We worked through my divorce and starting over, long before I'd come to accept the mood disorder he already knew I had. Therapy with Dr. Bogin felt like intellectual exchanges between colleagues. After he died in 2017, I thought I'd never find that connection again.

After my student air-dropped my thong to the entire student body in February 2019, I returned to that female therapist a few more times. We still didn't click. So, I did what I now know was a terrible mistake: I quit therapy entirely. I didn't return until March 2024—five long years later.

I convinced myself that staying on medication and reading books about BD would be enough to understand myself. I was wrong. For five years, I carried confusion and shame that bubbled and boiled inside me. I thought I was managing my illness, but I wasn't truly living with it.

When I finally found my current therapist Renee in 2024, everything changed. For the first time since Dr. Bogin, I had someone who understood my faith and my mental health could coexist; I didn't have to choose between trusting God and taking care of my brain. After about eight months of talking specifically about BD, I wasn't afraid, ashamed, or angry anymore. I began to embrace the bipolar parts of me. That's when I realized something crucial: medication will help stabilize your moods, but it won't help you accept or live well with BD. That deeper work happens in talk therapy.

Many people in my DBSA support group prefer telehealth appointments, especially those who struggle with agoraphobia or find leaving the house triggering. However you connect with a therapist—in person or online—the important thing is finding someone who specializes in mood disorders and makes you feel heard.

Permission to Fall Apart Properly

I get it. Taking time off from work isn't an option for everyone. But if I could go back and do one thing differently, it would be giving myself permission to fall apart properly while figuring out the right medication. I was so used to white knuckling through everything, thinking that's what faith looked like, when maybe the faithful thing was to admit I needed help.

For years, I'd been trying to escape the classroom. I got my graduate degree to teach teachers how to integrate technology, applying year after year for instructional coaching positions that would give me regular hours in an office with grown-ups instead of teenagers. I was rejected every time, often passed over for internal candidates. My priority was always financial stability over mental health—a choice that would cost me dearly.

When I was finally diagnosed in February 2019, I was working full-time and didn't want to immediately go back on quetiapine. I hoped to find something pregnancy-safe instead. Part of me still wondered if taking medication meant I wasn't trusting God enough, but life was forcing me to believe God works through medicine, too. What followed was a nightmare of medication roulette while trying to hold it together in the classroom.

My doctor started me on something that made me restless and agitated at school—a place already stressful enough after the student incident. The court case was dragging on, his parents had money and a good lawyer, and I was barely holding it together. In March, my doctor and therapist encouraged me to transfer to another building, citing a hostile work environment. I took over a sixth-grade classroom at the elementary school down the street.

Next came Latuda, which was pregnancy approved. By April, my thinking was organized enough to lesson plan and make presentations, but I felt completely disconnected from my students and colleagues. In May, my doctor switched me to lithium, which requires regular blood work monitoring.

Lithium was supposed to be the gold standard—it's been around since Kay Redfield Jamison's time and remains one of the most prescribed drugs for BD. For me, it killed everything. All emotions, good and bad. I didn't want to sing along to worship songs on the radio that used to move me to tears. It felt like losing a part of how I connected with God. I became a loner, severely depressed and isolated. Every day

I'd leave school, drive across the Monitor Merrimack bridge to the gym, get nowhere on an elliptical machine, then go home and eat half a family-sized bag of tortilla chips with an entire tub of white queso dip. I ate too much, slept too much, felt nothing.

I don't know how I made it from February to June, switching medications every month, without completely tanking my career. The medication rollercoaster had taken its toll. Once school was out and I had space to think, I realized I hadn't received appropriate care.

I called Leslie, the nurse practitioner who'd managed my mental health previously. I left a message that she'd been right about the bipolar diagnosis, I was sorry I'd fired her, and I was ready to come back if she'd have me. Desperate for stability, I let her put me back on quetiapine. Within weeks, my thinking was organized again. I could feel emotions. I felt balanced for the first time in nearly two years.

Looking back, I should have taken medical leave during those months of medication experimentation. Jamison describes her early treatment as "endless and terrifying days of endlessly terrifying drugs—Thorazine, lithium, valium, and barbiturates." At least she had time off to experience those highs and lows without jeopardizing her career. I was trying to fake my way through a forty-hour work week while my brain chemistry was in chaos.

The cumulative damage of prioritizing work over mental health makes me feel traumatized at the thought of returning to a classroom. My husband Tony provides me the space and time now to write this book, despite our lack of financial security. He reminds me every day that this book is my job. It doesn't generate income yet, but writing it improves our family's quality of life daily.

Trial and Error (Mostly Error)

Every drug comes with trade-offs, and quetiapine taught me that lesson harshly. It's a second-generation antipsychotic that soothes my brain, but I hate what it does to my body. Within three years of taking it, despite exercising seven days a week, I gained twenty-five pounds and went up three dress sizes, developing high cholesterol, high blood sugar, and high blood pressure along the way.

When I was later diagnosed with ADHD and switched to Adderall, I returned to my high school track days' size within months. All my metabolic problems disappeared, proving quetiapine had been the culprit. That means when I returned to Leslie and my quetiapine routine in July 2019, I was knowingly agreeing to gain the weight back.

It wasn't until a doctor prescribed Metformin—a diabetes drug that helps counteract weight gain from antipsychotics—that I found some relief. For the past couple of years, I've maintained my weight at 125 through a combination of quetiapine, Metformin, daily exercise, and strict intermittent fasting. I restrict my calories to 1200 a day unless it's a special occasion. It works, but it's exhausting to maintain this level of control, and I suspect it makes me more irritable and anxious.

I know someone else who faced the same quetiapine dilemma. Every time he got frustrated with weight gain, he'd stop taking it. The pounds would come off quickly, but his wife learned to watch for the warning signs: he'd grow more animated, agitated, paranoid that she was cheating with a neighbor. She became expert at coaxing him back to his medication before things got worse.

This cycle illustrates why people with BD go off their medications—we want to escape the side effects of the very drugs that stabilize our moods.

I dream of finding another solution, but every medication comes with its own issues. Some people in my support group have paid hundreds of dollars for genetic testing through companies like GeneSight to avoid the trial-and-error process. Others swear by Francis Mark Mondimore's guide *Bipolar Disorder: A Guide for You & Your Loved Ones*, which breaks down medication options in clear, understandable terms. His chapter on creativity helped me start to like myself again after diagnosis.

But ultimately, medication management becomes a deeply personal negotiation between what your brain needs and what your body can tolerate.

My Amateur Brain Chemistry Education

When I was first diagnosed, I became obsessed with understanding how my brain worked differently. I did what any former teacher would do—I made a spreadsheet. An epic one. I listed every medication I tried, its effect on me, and how it worked at the cellular level. This helped me identify patterns—like how antidepressants consistently triggered my manic episodes.

Francis Mark Mondimore's guide helped me understand the basics without getting lost in advanced biology. He compares the brain to a computer that receives information, processes it, and delivers output in the form of behavior. But unlike a computer with simple on-off switches, the brain operates more like the internet—billions of neurons that are each little processors themselves, constantly adapting and reprogramming based on their environment. [56]

This concept of the brain's ability to rewire itself—called neuroplasticity—became crucial to my understanding. As Mondimore explains, "Areas of the brain are constantly remodeling themselves in response to changes in the environment; the brain's capacity to do this is called *neuroplasticity*." [57] This gave me hope. My brain wasn't permanently broken; it could adapt and heal via medication protocols to enhance neuroplasticity.

Neuroplasticity fascinated me. Science was confirming what I'd always believed about God's design: our bodies have an incredible capacity for healing and renewal.

The key insight was that medications enhance neuroplasticity by protecting existing neurons or triggering new ones to develop. My brain has "programming issues at the design level"—problems regulating chemicals like serotonin, dopamine, and norepinephrine that work together to stabilize moods. [58] I started to think of it less like a manufacturing defect and more like needing different software to run the same beautiful hardware. With the right medication, my brain could literally reprogram itself to better manage these chemical imbalances.

I started listening to health and wellness podcasts, picking up fragments of brain science that felt relevant to my experience. When I heard about "Brain-Derived Neurotrophic Factor" (BDNF), I researched its connection to BD and discovered that decreased levels show up in both depressed and manic states. Suddenly, my exercise routine wasn't just about managing weight—it was about supporting my brain's neuroplasticity, its ability to adapt and heal.

My spreadsheet became my security blanket. When my neurologist recently prescribed nortriptyline for nerve pain that was keeping me awake, I objected because it's also used for depression. He assured me that at the lowest dose, this tricyclic antidepressant wouldn't trigger mania. I consulted my spreadsheet—I'd never tried this class of medication before. After clearing it with my psychiatrist, I decided to try it.

I took the medication for two months, asking Tony to watch for signs of mood instability. The result? I slept through the night for the first time in years, which meant better mood management during the day. Now I play this careful game with every drug I take, even cold medications, always asking: How does this interact with my other medications?

The right medication will improve neuroplasticity, your brain's ability to adapt. That should encourage you to continue fighting until you discover together the correct means for maintaining that delicate balance of neurochemicals for maintained mood stability. Your medication needs won't necessarily stay the same because of the cyclical nature of this disorder, underscoring the need for a supervising physician and close mood monitoring and record-keeping.

There are limits to what I can research on my own. My psychiatrist already knows the mechanisms of action I've been charting in my epic spreadsheet. But my research helps me be an informed partner in my treatment instead of a passive recipient. That's why ongoing monitoring and record-keeping matter so much, and why I need a doctor I trust to help navigate these decisions.

Understanding neuroplasticity changed everything for me. It means that with the right treatment, my brain can continue to improve its ability to regulate serotonin, dopamine, and the other chemicals that keep my moods stable. My spreadsheet might make me feel more in control, but ultimately, managing BD is a collaboration between my amateur curiosity and a belief in God's sovereignty; He built healing and renewal into my brain's design.

Finding My Treatment Team

Getting the right help for BD isn't a destination—it's an ongoing journey of building relationships with the right professionals, understanding your own patterns, and learning to advocate for yourself.

My treatment team now includes my psychiatrist, who manages my medications with patience and expertise; my therapist, Renee, who helped me embrace rather than just manage my BD; and Tony, who watches for warning signs and reminds me that my mental health is worth prioritizing over everything else.

It took years of wrong turns, failed medications, and mismatched therapists to find this combination. Still, understanding that my brain can heal and adapt through neuroplasticity gave me the hope to keep trying. The spreadsheet might make me feel more in control, but ultimately, recovery is a collaboration between my curiosity, professional expertise, and my brain's remarkable ability to rewire itself.

Treatment isn't just about finding the right medication—it's about building a life that supports your mental health. That was the lesson I learned the hard way, and the foundation I needed before I could truly thrive with BD.

Chapter Nine: What Else Do I Need Besides Pills?

Stabilizing with medication is just one aspect of living well with BD. In this chapter, I suggest a host of other management strategies. While these recommendations represent current best practice, I've also had personal experience testing them out. Managing my mental illness by taking quetiapine for a decade helped me sleep; it didn't help me navigate triggers for mania or depression. It served as a mask of mental health during times of peace. Events could still tip me sideways emotionally. It was not enough just to take a pill. I needed to understand who I was.

How My Bipolar Library Became My Lifeline

After my diagnosis, I felt a strange mix of vindication and overwhelm; I had, after all, figured it out for myself before my doctor did. She rattled on about options for dual treatment of BD and ADHD—antipsychotics, mood stabilizers, benzodiazepines, stimulants—and I found myself nodding with recognition. Those late nights in the 616.8 section had prepared me for this turning point: acceptance.

Still, there's a difference between reading about bipolar disorder in the shadowy corner of a library and having it officially stamped on your medical chart. The textbook knowledge I'd quietly absorbed suddenly became personal, urgent, real. Psychiatrists and psychologists aren't the only ones who can "get" how we tick. I wasn't just curious about mood states anymore; I wanted to understand them, maybe learn to master them so they could not derail my life again.

That's when I made a decision that changed everything: I was going to become the expert on my own brain. My first stop was Amazon. I preferred online shopping to standing exposed in the psychology section of a local bookstore with "newly diagnosed bipolar" written across my forehead. Reviews analyzed, I dropped ten titles in my cart and waited expectedly for that blue truck with the smiley face to deliver my lifeline.

The first book that saved me was Dr. Francis Mark Mondimore's *Bipolar Disorder: A Guide for You & Your Loved Ones*. Finally, someone was speaking my language—or rather, translating the medical jargon into something I could understand. When he explained brain chemistry using technological analogies I could grasp, scary words like "psychosis" and "mania" started feeling less like death sentences and more like... well, data points I could work with.

For the first time since my diagnosis, I didn't feel broken. I felt informed.

Then came *Bipolar Disorder for Dummies* by Candida Fink and Joe Kraynak. Yes, the title stung a little—nobody wants to feel like a dummy about her own mental health. But this book walked me through practical stuff: how to pick a doctor (wish I'd had this earlier), medication options, and most importantly, survival skills for the day-to-day reality of living with bipolar.

Julie Fast's *Take Charge of Bipolar Disorder* hit differently. Here was someone who got it—diagnosed in her thirties, just like me discovering this wasn't something I could just medicate away. Her 4-step plan, the Take Charge Program hinges on the fact that medication alone doesn't promote long-term stability. This was a read I shared with my husband as we were both the target audiences, and it gave Tony a road map for life management strategies to use in our home.

My psychiatrist underestimated the value of having a few book recommendations for me. Reading about my illness was therapy. Every page I turned was psychoeducation, which research shows reduces relapses and hospitalizations. [59] More than that, it gave me back my power.

Now my curiosity is insatiable. I subscribe to psychiatric journals, follow bipolar researchers on social media, and yes, I still read everything I can get my hands on about this disorder. Because here's what I believe, truly: when people with BD become experts on our own condition, we improve our quality of life and simultaneously chip away at the stigma that says we're too unstable to understand our own minds.

When I was teaching at alternative school, our principal had the students and staff recite a daily motto: "This is my life. This is my story. I will love it or regret it based on my daily choices." Reciting it every day for nine months impacted me, too. Choosing to study the dark passenger within was the first daily choice that led me toward living my life with BD instead of battling against it in private.

Finding My People in Print

After devouring those guidebooks, I still felt like I was looking at bipolar from the outside—clinical, sterile, academic. I needed to hear from people who had lived this, who could tell me what it felt like from the inside.

That's when I discovered bipolar memoirs, and everything changed. I figured, if I wanted to know the truth about the seriousness of our mental health conditions, I'd spend a little time with someone like me who cared enough to write it down.

Carrie Fisher's *Wishful Drinking* was my gateway drug. Here was Princess Leia, for crying out loud, talking about electroshock therapy and medication cocktails with the same wit she brought to a galaxy far, far away. I read it in one sitting during what I now recognize as a hypomanic episode—perfect timing, really. Fisher made me laugh about BD for the first time ever. Given my conservative upbringing, some of her language made me blush, but I desperately needed someone to show me this disorder didn't have to steal my sense of humor.

Kay Redfield Jamison's *An Unquiet Mind* destroyed me in the best possible way. Here was someone who made BD her life's work because she had it, not despite it. Reading her memoir felt like watching my own mind unfold on the page. I started scribbling notes in the margins— angry notes, grateful notes, "Yes, exactly!" notes. Those margin scribbles eventually became the idea for this book. The last day we recited our daily motto at alternative school, I committed to take a year off to write this manuscript.

Then came Andy Behrman's *Electroboy*, and I had to put limits on myself. One chapter at a time, max. Behrman somehow managed to capture the detailed chaos of mania in a way that made me feel like I was right there in his spinning brain. It was terrifying and fascinating and completely necessary reading. His story showed me the absolute worst-case scenario of untreated bipolar and made me grateful for how far treatment had come since his early experiences.

Terri Cheney's *Manic* gave me permission to blow up my career. Here was this successful Beverly Hills lawyer whose bipolar brought her entire professional life crashing down. Reading about her journey made me realize that sometimes protecting your mental health means making choices that look crazy to everyone else, like taking a sabbatical from the classroom to write a bipolar memoir. Her story bridged the gap between Behrman's chaos and the possibility of rebuilding.

Suzy Favor Hamilton's *Fast Girl* hit closest to home. Olympic athlete, overachiever, someone who ran from her madness—literally and figuratively—until she couldn't run anymore. Her breakup stories had me back in my boyfriend's driveway the night my pastor, his dad, called the cops. It was nice to know I'm not the only one who turns breakups into crises. Her story of facing the illness and finding peace gave me a snapshot of what healing might look like.

Each memoir showed me a different facet of this disorder. In their stories, I found pieces of my own: the medication trials, the questionable decisions, the relationship wreckage, the moments of brilliance, the crushing lows. Words like "bipolar" and "episode" stopped feeling like slurs and started feeling like… just words, important words that described real experiences. The fuzzy haze over the last year I spent with Charming made sense using the right words.

Before I found these authors, I thought I was the only one who made spectacularly bad decisions during mood episodes. I thought I was the only one who couldn't remember chunks of time when my brain was spinning too fast. These memoirs didn't just validate my experience, they normalized it.

Reading about bipolar became my form of therapy, my way of taking control when everything else felt chaotic. Because here's what I learned: when you have a disorder without a cure, when you can't control the triggers or fast-track a psychiatrist appointment, there's still one thing you can always do.

You can educate yourself. It's not just helpful. It's your responsibility. Fast and Preston put it perfectly: "Early recognition and appropriate treatment are important in trying to stop BD before it ruins a person's life." [60] The key word there is *before*. Education is prevention—preventing years of misdiagnosis, preventing ineffective treatment, preventing the kind of life destruction I saw in some of these memoirs and, admittedly, my own life.

Our minds are fascinating, complex, and worth understanding. These authors became my teachers, companions, and proof that people with BD don't just survive the illness. No, we tell stories, win Olympic medals, create art, and sometimes even help others find their way through the darkness.

I'm still reading every bipolar memoir I can find. Each one adds another piece to the puzzle of understanding not just BD, but myself.

Training My Support Squad

I made a huge mistake early on: I thought bipolar was my problem to solve alone.

After my diagnosis, I dove headfirst into research, reading everything I could get my hands on. But I kept it all to myself, like I was protecting everyone else from the messy reality of my brain. What I didn't realize was that I was also protecting myself from the one thing that could make the biggest difference: informed people who loved me.

The wake-up call came during a family conflict last year. I'd had a heated conversation with a loved one—defensive jabs, high emotions, the whole nine yards. They hung up and immediately called another family member, declaring I was "clearly manic." That family member, who has their own mental health challenges triggered by my episodes, panicked and canceled an upcoming family gathering.

Meanwhile, I was at home doing my own emotional temperature check: Had I slept? Yes. Taken my meds? Yes. Eaten properly? Yes. I wasn't manic—I was just having a difficult conversation like any human being might.

But here's the problem: they'd skipped the most important step. They talked about me instead of with me. In trying to protect everyone, they'd created exactly the kind of crisis they were trying to prevent. As one expert puts it, "Don't create a secret society with the goal of protecting your loved one. Doing so can make her feel as though everyone wants to gang up on her—as if she's the family problem."[61] That's exactly how I felt in that moment.

That's when I realized I'd failed to train my support squad.

My husband and stepdaughter have learned tools to help navigate my moods. On good days, they ask direct questions: "How are you feeling? Did you sleep okay? Do you need to take a step back?" When these check-ins happen, I've learned not to be defensive—they're data collection, not attacks. However, I'd be lying if I said this happens consistently. Tony has his own battle with depression, and when he's struggling, he doesn't always have capacity to check in on me. Some days he forgets the tools entirely. Some days his mental health collides with mine, and we both spiral. Training a support squad is ongoing work, not a one-time achievement.

Moreover, they've also learned an equally important lesson through those check-ins: not to interpret every strong emotion as a symptom. [62] My husband doesn't assume I'm manic just because I lose my temper. Instead, losing my temper becomes an emotional temperature check—a chance to assess sleep, medication, diet, and stress levels before jumping to conclusions.

I'd never thought to extend that education to my wider circle.

My sister-in-law Gabrielle became my gold standard for how this should work. During my manic episode before my wedding to Charming, she didn't abandon me, but she was careful to avoid conflict that might escalate things. Since my diagnosis, she's spent hours talking with me, asking questions about what I've learned, what helps, what doesn't.

The last time we had a family conflict, it started with a late-night text exchange. I felt myself spiraling—waking up at 2 AM, ruminating, having imaginary arguments in my head where she said things that sounded nothing like my sweet sister-in-law. Instead of letting it fester, I texted her asking for a call the next day. I woke up my husband, told him I was ruminating, and he rubbed my back while I gave my worries to God in prayer.

When Gabrielle called the next day, we had a wonderful conversation. But the best part? She told me she wasn't afraid to make that call anymore. She trusts the changes she's seen since I've been in therapy.

Here's what I learned: love without education is just good intentions waiting to backfire.

The research backs this up: people with bipolar are much more likely to relapse in family settings with high levels of conflict and criticism. [63] Learning about the disorder increases empathy and reduces blame, but more importantly, it teaches people how to focus their anger and frustration on the illness, not the person with the illness.

The people closest to me needed to understand that I can't just "snap out of" a mood episode, no matter how much I want to.[64] They needed to know that positive events—weddings, promotions, vacations—can trigger episodes just as much as negative ones. [65] They needed to recognize that paranoia, anxiety, or restlessness might signal trouble just as much as classic mania or depression.

Most importantly, they needed to know how to talk with me, not about me.

I still haven't had the conversation with my nieces and nephews about my BD. I've rehearsed it in my head: "Your auntie has something called bipolar disorder, which means my moods can get really big sometimes. If I seem mad or sad, it's never your fault. If something I say or do upsets you, please tell me or talk to your parents." I keep putting it off, telling myself they're too young or it's not the right time. The truth is, I'm still working up the courage.

Because here's the truth: my moods affect everyone around me. The least I can do is give them the tools to navigate loving someone with bipolar. When my family understands what they're dealing with, they can support me better—and protect themselves too. My faith community's response to my diagnosis would also become part of my healing journey—some embracing, others uncertain about how mental health and spirituality intersect.

Building a support squad isn't about finding people to take care of you. It's about creating a team that knows how to spot trouble brewing and isn't afraid to say, "Hey, let's talk about what's really going on here."

In theory, Tony and Calista understand our home needs to support my stability. We've talked about protecting routines, limiting last-minute disruptions, and keeping conflicts from escalating. [66] Sometimes this works beautifully. Other times, Calista wants a last-minute sleepover, Tony prioritizes her happiness over our agreements, and I'm left managing the stress alone. I've learned I can't make my home my sanctuary—not when it's shared with two other humans who have their own needs, moods, and limitations. The only sanctuary I can count on is the one I find in God, who never forgets our agreements and never prioritizes something else over my wellbeing.

The Holy Trinity of Stability

I learned the hard way that medication alone wasn't going to save me. Even with my quetiapine keeping me stable for a decade, life could still knock me sideways emotionally. I needed something more foundational, something I could control when everything else felt chaotic.

That's when I discovered what I call the Holy Trinity of bipolar stability: sleep, diet, and exercise. [67] The spiritual language felt right— there was something sacred about learning to care for the body I'd been given, treating it like the temple I'd learned about in Sunday school. Everything in moderation, everything on schedule, everything intentional.

Sleep became my religion. I didn't need a book to tell me I go sideways emotionally when I don't get my eight hours, but the research confirmed what my body already knew: when your sleep-wake cycle gets out of sync, your mood pays the price. [68] I've had friends call me selfish for declining late-night events or backing out when I realize something will mess with my bedtime. But here's what I've come to acknowledge: protecting my sleep isn't selfish—it's survival.

As I learned to manage my symptoms, I began to wonder how God fit into this new understanding of myself. Was taking care of my mental health actually a form of stewardship?

I monitor my substance intake like a hawk now. That daily energy drink I consumed for over a decade? Gone. I was less anxious within weeks of quitting. Even something as innocent as DayQuil can spike my anxiety, so I keep a running list of medications and their effects on my mood. Sometimes I'd rather suffer through cold symptoms than deal with the emotional fallout. Marijuana is a similar threat; while it might mellow me out, most experts agree it's ineffective as long-term treatment and might even worsen symptoms. [69]

Exercise was where I made my most spectacular mistakes. Senior year of high school, I got obsessed with track and field and started what I thought was a "disciplined regimen." I ordered supplements online: Xenadrine for weight loss, creatine for muscle building, St. John's Wort for anxiety. I exercised three times a day—lunch break, after school practice, then the gym.

I was in the best physical shape of my life, and my moods were absolutely wild.

My best friend and I skipped school to get our nails done. I used a teacher's access code to sneak back into the building and got caught by another teacher, ruining that relationship forever. Just before graduation, my boyfriend proposed, I accepted, and I slept with him despite my lifelong plan to wait for marriage. He was an abusive alcoholic, but I'd made my choice and felt I deserved whatever came next.

Looking back, I now know people with bipolar should avoid all three of those supplements I was taking. I was basically mainlining mania-inducing stimulants while wondering why I was making such poor choices.

Now I approach exercise completely differently. I schedule a little movement every day—nothing crazy, just consistent. Physical activity helps with depression without triggering mania, but timing matters. [70] I learned the hard way that working out too close to bedtime creates energy when I need to wind down. My daily exercise routine is scheduled earlier in the day, and it's become as non-negotiable as taking my medication.

Diet became my most fascinating discovery. I understood sleep and exercise before my diagnosis, but I was completely oblivious to how food affected my moods. For two years, I followed a ketogenic diet with a boyfriend—this was during my "remission" period with Dr. Bogin. Cutting out comfort foods was challenging, but my mood stability was superior to anything I'd experienced. The science makes sense: blood sugar swings create mood swings. When I was eating carbs all day, my insulin was constantly spiking and crashing, taking my emotions along for the ride. [71] The ketogenic approach gave my brain a steady, slow-burning energy source instead of the rollercoaster.

I've also battled metabolic syndrome using intermittent fasting, targeting a caloric deficit, and taking Metformin. But honestly, the ketogenic approach seems like a better solution than the mood instability my current eating plan sometimes promotes. A strictly keto diet reduced my hunger, and my brain felt more balanced—like I was giving it the right kind of fuel. "Don't eat your feelings," isn't just a cute saying—it's practical advice. [72] Many bipolar medications cause weight gain, so being proactive about food choices becomes even more critical. I've learned to treat food like medicine, asking myself: Will this fuel stability or chaos?

The seasonal piece was my final puzzle piece. I cycle down every winter like clockwork. After reading about bright light therapy for bipolar depression, I bought a device and sat in front of a light box every morning from October through March; it genuinely lifted my spirits when the winter blues hit. Now that I live five minutes from a beach, however, I prefer twenty minutes of actual sunlight at sunrise every day.

Creating this lifestyle—prioritizing sleep, exercising smartly, eating strategically—became my prescription for mood stability. It's not glamorous, and it requires saying no to things other people take for granted. But it's the difference between surviving with bipolar and actually thriving with it.

The holy trinity isn't a cure, but it's the foundation that makes everything else possible.

Let's Talk about It… in Therapy

Reading about BD gave me knowledge, but it couldn't give me what I really needed: a safe place to fall apart.

My bipolar diagnosis was traumatic. [73] Not just the label itself, but everything that came with it—the fear about how it would affect my life, my relationships, my future. I was emotionally reeling, and all the books in the world couldn't talk me through that turmoil. I needed a real person, sitting across from me, helping me make sense of the chaos.

I should have started therapy immediately after my diagnosis. Instead, I waited five years—five years of struggling alone with thoughts and feelings I was too ashamed to share with anyone. Research shows psychological treatment is most helpful in that first year after diagnosis. I could have saved myself half a decade of spinning my wheels if I'd been brave enough to find help sooner.

When I finally found Dr. Bogin in Syracuse, everything changed. Every Tuesday night at 7 PM, I'd walk into his office knowing I had an hour to be completely honest about whatever was rattling around in my head. The fact that I looked forward to those sessions told me I'd found the right match.

Our progression was telling. In the beginning, we unpacked my pending divorce and the wreckage of leaving behind a decade of life in Nashville. I was drowning in disappointment—my life at thirty looked nothing like what I'd imagined. I was depressed, pessimistic, convinced I was fundamentally broken.

Slowly, our conversations shifted to present choices and stalled career plans. Then to my new dating relationship and what I actually wanted my life to look like. By the time I moved to Hampton Roads sixteen months later, we were talking about possibilities instead of problems.

The transformation was subtle but profound. I entered therapy seeing myself as a failure. Dr. Bogin helped me reframe my perception of who I was becoming. Somewhere along the way, I started liking the woman I saw in his eyes—someone resilient, someone capable of growth, someone with a future worth building.

That future perspective became genuinely optimistic for the first time in years.

Here's what therapy gave me that books couldn't: objective feedback when my thoughts were spiraling, solid encouragement when I couldn't see past my current crisis, and most importantly, a confidential space to be honest about the unsettling thoughts and feelings that come with BD. [74]

Because here's the reality: relapse is always a possibility with bipolar. Mood episodes are traumatic, and we need a safe place to navigate them as they're happening, not just analyze them afterward. [75] Therapy became my early warning system, my processing center, and my reminder that even on my worst days, I was still worth investing in.

The books taught me about BD. Therapy taught me how to live with it.

Beyond Talk Therapy

If sitting in a room just talking sounds like torture, there are more structured approaches that can be incredibly effective for BD.

Cognitive Behavioral Therapy (CBT) saved me during my darkest period. After the birthday "thong airdrop" incident and getting transferred to sixth grade, I was spiraling into depression. I gave myself a crash course in CBT and completed enough exercises to see its power, though I was often lost without professional guidance.

The theory behind CBT makes perfect sense: Dr. Aaron Beck discovered in the 1960s that depressed people develop distorted views of themselves and the world, creating thinking patterns that actually perpetuate their problems. We think negatively, interpret experiences negatively, and expect the worst from the future. Beck called these "automatic negative thoughts"—things like mind-reading, all-or-nothing thinking, and fortune-telling that happen without us even realizing it. [76]

CBT taught me that my thoughts were literally making my problems worse. I'm a catastrophizer by nature—traffic on the way to the airport sends my heart racing because my automatic thoughts jump to: "I'm going to miss my flight. I'll be trapped here. It will cost a fortune." CBT gave me tools to replace those thoughts with realistic ones: "If I miss my flight, work will cover it. There's a hotel at the airport. I can write from anywhere."

My nephew Joseph is a highly sensitive, deep thinker—the kind of kid who processes everything intensely. During the pandemic quarantine, all that extra time at home gave his mind too much space to spiral. When he was struggling with negative thinking, my sister-in-law had to get creative. She found a book called *Captain Snout and the Super Power Questions* by Daniel G. Amen, a board-certified child psychiatrist. The book teaches kids how to question the negative thoughts that bring them down, calling these troublesome thoughts "ANTs"—automatic negative thoughts. I chuckled to learn, while writing this book, that we both discovered the same strategy during the same season, a whole generation apart.

Dialectical Behavioral Therapy (DBT) takes this further, focusing specifically on emotional regulation—perfect for people with bipolar who struggle with intense feelings. It's about defusing emotional situations before they explode and being prepared for crises. [77] I wish I'd discovered this earlier. It wouldn't come into play until I started biblical counseling.

Family therapy, however, taught me what NOT to look for in a therapist.

Tony's newly licensed therapist offered to see all three of us on short notice. Red flag number one: she was clearly Tony's advocate, not a neutral party. Red flag number two: after I told her my name multiple times, she asked if she could just call me Laura instead. When I declined, I could see I'd already lost her respect.

The session went downhill fast. When I got emotional discussing my relationship with Calista, the therapist asked why I was crying.

"I have bipolar disorder," I explained. "My emotions are big sometimes. Do you know much about bipolar disorder?"

"Yes, I know bipolar people. They are…"

I stopped listening. Bipolar people. Not "people with bipolar disorder"—bipolar people, like that's all we are. I expect ignorance in the real world, but not in a therapist's office.

When she asked if I felt safe, I was honest: "No." I was sitting next to the door, considering bolting while her unsilenced phone notifications punctured every tense moment.

The worst part came when I started crying again. She leaned in and asked, "Are you on medication?"

"Yes," I replied.

Her eyes widened in genuine surprise. "Really?"

"Yes, really. Did your eyes just widen?"

"Yes and…" I couldn't hear the rest. The damage was done.

This disaster taught me what to look for: therapists who understand BD, respect your identity beyond your diagnosis, maintain professional boundaries, and don't express shock that you're managing your condition responsibly.

My current support group has been transformative. After completing training through the Depression and Bipolar Support Alliance, I'm now hosting a local in-person group. There's something powerful about sharing experiences with people who truly get it—no explanations needed, no shocked expressions, just understanding and practical wisdom.

Peer support isn't a replacement for professional therapy, but it's an incredible supplement. [78] Sometimes you need someone who's lived it to tell you that yes, medication can take months to find the right combination, and no, you're not crazy for grieving the person you were before diagnosis.

The goal isn't to find the perfect therapy approach—it's to find what works for YOU. Whether that's traditional talk therapy, structured CBT exercises, family sessions with the right therapist, or peer support groups, the key is finding professionals who see you as a whole person, not just a collection of symptoms.

The Critical Role of Stillness in the BD Brain

Here's my bipolar early warning system: missing journal entries.

Show me a time in my life when I was severely manic or severely depressed, and I'll show you gaps in my writing. When I'm least emotionally stable, I discontinue my normal practice of daily self-reflection. Because I could never hold a train of thought long enough to pray in my head during mood episodes, I've written my prayers in journals every morning for most of my life. When I can't bear to sit still for fifteen minutes to look inward, that's a red flag.

My mother modeled this practice without realizing she was teaching bipolar management. She started every morning with prayer and Bible study—what the world now calls "mindfulness." As a Christian, I was initially cautious about meditation trends, but I've come to realize that mindfulness is simply becoming aware of something. That's exactly what we do when we pray or have devotional time.

When my emotions spiral out of control, I surrender them daily to a Creator who is in control. There's a spiritually-adjacent CBT at work here: I bring my negative thoughts captive before God in prayer (the mindfulness aspect), then examine them in relation to a Savior, which creates a new narrative of grace, peace, and freedom.

My fifteen-minute rule became non-negotiable: every person with bipolar needs at least fifteen minutes daily to intentionally inventory thoughts, moods, and behaviors. For me, this looks like journaling prayers when I can't focus mentally. It creates a log of mood symptoms that signal when I need intervention—the whole goal of mindfulness for bipolar patients.

I also use a smartphone app to track activities, emotions, energy levels, menstrual cycle, and family dynamics. Seeing the trends helps me course-correct before I crash.

Guided meditations became my secret weapon. My husband insists every bipolar patient should have a breathing control meditation downloaded for when emotions grow too big. He tells me to take a timeout when I need one—it puts physical and emotional distance between feelings and thoughts. After fifteen minutes of focusing on my breath, I'm in a better position to process through prayer or journaling.

Initially, I worried about meditation contradicting my faith. But when a voice told me to "feel the source of love and light within," I automatically qualified that as the Holy Spirit living in me. I was learning to see my bipolar disorder as part of how God made me, not as a punishment or spiritual failing. Most scripts never challenged my beliefs.

Writing is where I make sense of life, but others will need their own forms of stillness. In different seasons, I've kept three separate journals: prayer, diary, and poetry. I've cycled through scrapbooking, crocheting, and photo montages. The bipolar brain needs an outlet for all that interconnected thinking—some productive hobby to expend extra energy without the stimulation of exercise.

The key is having your stillness practice ready before you need it. Because when your brain is spinning too fast or sinking too low, you won't have the capacity to figure out what might help. You need something familiar, something that's already proven to ground you.

Stillness isn't about emptying your mind—it's about becoming aware of what's actually happening in there so you can respond instead of just react.

Insanity is Doing the Same Thing and Expecting Different Results

The definition of insanity, they say, is doing the same thing over and over while expecting different results. For the first five years after my diagnosis, I was clinically insane.

I kept thinking medication alone would fix everything. I kept making the same choices—ignoring my sleep schedule, loading up on caffeine, skipping therapy, isolating myself from the people who loved me. Then I'd wonder why I kept cycling through the same emotional chaos.

Everything changed when I stopped expecting medication to be my magic bullet and started building a life that actually supported my brain.

Reading became my foundation—understanding that I wasn't broken, just different. Training my support squad gave me allies instead of critics. The Holy Trinity of sleep, diet, and exercise became my daily scaffolding. Therapy taught me how to live with bipolar instead of just survive it. And stillness—through prayer, journaling, and meditation—became my early warning system and my reset button. Prayer didn't cure my BD, but it did give me strength to pursue treatment and hope healing was possible, as are all things with God[79].

None of these strategies are glamorous. None of them are quick fixes. But together, they've transformed my life from surviving with bipolar to actually thriving with it.

Some people with mood disorders seem to function with minimal disruption—they probably already have effective coping strategies in place, whether they realize it or not. The rest of us have to build them intentionally, one daily choice at a time.

Here's what I've learned: you can't just treat the symptoms. You have to build a life that makes stability possible. For me, that life had to include space for both medicine and prayer, therapy and faith, acknowledging that God might work through doctors just as much as through miracles. That means saying no to things that seem harmless to other people. It means protecting your schedule like your life depends on it—because it does. It means surrounding yourself with people who understand that your "big emotions" aren't character flaws, they're data points.

The goal isn't perfection. It's progress. It's building a toolkit so comprehensive that when life inevitably knocks you sideways, you have multiple ways to find your footing again.

Because here's the truth: we can't control having BD; however, we can absolutely control how we live with it.

Chapter Ten: Who Am I Now?

The question that haunts every newly diagnosed person: Am I still me?

For months after my diagnosis, I felt like I was living in a strange dual reality. There was the "before Laura Joy"—the woman who thought her dramatic mood swings were just personality quirks, who blamed her impulsive decisions on being "passionate," who had no idea why relationships felt so complicated, who thought staying up all night writing a song to God was spiritual devotion. And then there was the "after Laura Joy"—armed with a diagnosis, medication, and suddenly seeing patterns everywhere I looked.

But here's what I've discovered: I'm not two different people. I'm one person who finally understands how her brain works.

My mood state is in constant flux—that's literally the definition of BD. Euthymia, that neutral state, sits at the center like home base. I'm not always in crisis mode, not always manic or depressed. As one researcher puts it, people with bipolar "aren't always insane; in fact, they're usually sane. Their illness is the susceptibility to mania or depression," not the constant reality of it.[80]

I could be manic, depressed, neutral, or somewhere in between— headed toward one state or recovering from another.

The old psychiatric term "manic-depressive" actually captures this fluidity better than our modern compartmentalized labels. There's continuity between all these mood states, a spectrum I navigate rather than distinct boxes I get trapped in. I find it easiest to understand who I am now as someone on this mood disorder spectrum, more like Kraepelin's all-inclusive title.

We get around, emotionally speaking. And that's not necessarily a bad thing.

This chapter isn't about managing symptoms or following treatment protocols. We covered that. This is about identity—understanding who we are now that we have language for our inner weather patterns, and how that knowledge changes everything about the choices we make moving forward.

Because the goal isn't to become someone else. It's to become the fullest, most intentional version of who we already are. The more sense I made of my diagnosis, I found myself praying differently. I stopped asking God to fix what was "broken" in me and, instead, give me wisdom to navigate this new understanding of how He made me.

My Personal Mood Disorder Hopscotch Board

And to become that best version, I needed a map for my brain.

All the clinical descriptions and diagnostic criteria felt abstract, disconnected from my actual experience of waking up each morning and wondering, "What version of me am I today?" So, I created something you won't find in any textbook: my personal mood disorder hopscotch board.

Picture a hopscotch court, but instead of numbers, each square represents a different mood state. Euthymia—that balanced, neutral state—sits right in the center. It's home base. The goal. The place I'm always trying to get back to.

From the center, I can move in three directions:

Down: One step to mild depression (the world feels gray, motivation disappears). Two steps to severe depression (I can barely get out of bed, everything feels hopeless).

Up: One step to hypomania (I'm energetic, confident, maybe a little too chatty). Two steps to mania (sleep becomes optional, my judgment gets questionable, consequences pile up).

Out: This is where things get scary. One step out to dysphoric mania—those terrible mixed states where I'm simultaneously wired and miserable. Two steps out to psychosis, which thankfully I haven't experienced yet.

Here's the game-changing insight: euthymia is never more than one or two steps away.

Even when I'm in severe depression or full mania, I'm not lost forever. I'm just a few intentional moves away from center. The hopscotch board makes concrete what used to feel impossibly abstract—the idea that I can navigate these states purposefully instead of just being a victim of them.

The visual gives me power. When I notice myself stepping toward hypomania, I can course-correct before I reach full mania. When I feel mild depression settling in, I can implement strategies before I sink to the bottom.

Progress isn't about traveling some linear path toward "cured." It's about how close I can stay to that center tile. Some days I'm right there in euthymia. Some days I'm one step away and managing well. Some days I'm further out, but I know exactly where I am and what direction leads home.

The board also reminds me that some paths back are longer than others. Cycling "out" toward mixed states means I might trample on loved ones in the process, making the return journey more complicated. It's not just about regulating my brain chemistry—it's about repairing relationships and rebuilding trust.

This isn't a tool for self-diagnosis or treatment—it's a way of understanding my own patterns and having honest conversations with my doctors and family about where I am and where I'm headed.

What does your hopscotch board look like? What are your steps back to center?

The Family Connection I Can't Ignore

When you get a bipolar diagnosis, you can't help but start seeing patterns everywhere.

I know my questions make my family uncomfortable. When I ask about relatives across generations—whether they showed signs of mania, depression, anxiety, or hospitalization—I can feel the tension. The unspoken objections: "Isn't it enough that you're writing this book and exposing yourself? Can't you just leave the rest of the family alone?"

But here's what anyone with a bipolar diagnosis needs to understand: this isn't about casting judgment. It's about understanding why you're not alone in this.

Without a genetic predisposition, your odds of developing BD would be incredibly low—less than one percent. But if one identical twin has bipolar, the other has an 85% chance of developing it. For siblings, it's 5-10%. Depression is about half genetic, half environmental. [81]

Here's what makes family history so crucial: many people fall on the bipolar spectrum without meeting full diagnostic criteria. Remember, the DSM recognizes bipolar I, bipolar II, cyclothymia, and "soft" disorders—bipolar NOS (not otherwise specified). [82] This is where some family members might land.

People with bipolar NOS might be "dominated by depressive symptoms and show only the slightest coloring of mania." They might have brief periods of elevated mood they don't consider abnormal, but when examined closely, show hallmarks of hypomania: decreased need for sleep, increased energy, uncharacteristic overconfidence, loss of inhibitions. They might have periods of agitation lasting only hours— mild mixed states that get dismissed as "bad moods." [83]

Sometimes a family history is the only hint that what looks like depression is actually part of the bipolar spectrum.

This isn't about blame. It's about making sense of your story.

I spent years wondering why my brain felt different, why relationships were so hard, why I made choices that seemed inexplicable later. Getting my diagnosis finally gave me answers, but it also made me realize I wasn't the first person in my family to navigate these waters—I was just the first to have language for it.

Some family members have their own hopscotch boards of mood states they've learned to navigate. When I recognize patterns in relatives, living or dead, I'm not diagnosing anyone. I'm learning from their coping strategies, their lifestyle choices, how they managed without ever having a name for what they were experiencing.

Here's why this matters for anyone reading: If bipolar tendencies run in families (and they do), we can watch for early signs in the next generation. We can recognize that some people might be prone to obsessive thinking, might struggle with major life transitions, might need extra support during stressful times.

A family history of mental illness must start somewhere. For many of us, we're just the first ones brave enough—or desperate enough—to seek professional help and get an official diagnosis.

For the children and grandchildren in families affected by bipolar, this knowledge is a game-changer. Instead of wondering why someone seems "moody" or "dramatic," families can recognize potential symptoms early. They can teach kids that seeking help is strength, not weakness. They can normalize therapy and medication instead of treating mental health like a shameful secret.

Here's what I'm *not* saying: that everyone in families with bipolar has the disorder.

Here's what I *am* saying: that genetic predisposition exists, and environmental factors can trigger it. Stress isn't just a six-letter word for families like mine—it's something we need to take seriously and help each other manage.

The good news? Our brains are more adaptable than we once thought. Researchers believe bipolar results from problems with neuroplasticity—the brain's ability to remodel itself. While medication helps alter brain chemistry, we can also improve neuroplasticity through lifestyle choices: sleep, diet, and exercise. [84] Genetics might load the gun, but environment pulls the trigger—and environment is something we can influence.

Both genetics and environment matter. Those with genetic predisposition might never develop symptoms if not triggered by environmental factors. [85] But if you're raised by a parent with bipolar, the odds increase significantly—both because of shared genes and shared environment. The family influences bipolar expression in multiple ways.

The goal isn't to pathologize family trees. It's to understand why some people might need extra support, why certain lifestyle choices matter more for some than others, and why early intervention can prevent years of unnecessary suffering.

I'm not asking families to change how they see themselves. I'm sharing why I had to change how I see myself—and why that understanding might someday help someone else find their way to stability sooner than I did.

This knowledge isn't a burden. It's a gift we can give to future generations. I find peace knowing if any child in our family inherits this genetic predisposition and experiences the environmental factors to activate it, at least they won't have to spend decades wondering what's wrong with them like I did.

Under the Influence of Stress

Stress isn't just uncomfortable for people with bipolar—it's quite literally toxic to our brains, no hyperbole.

While the general population needs to manage stress for overall wellness, for us it's a requirement for survival. Chronic stress disrupts neuroplasticity, making our already-struggling brains even less able to regulate moods. When we're stressed, our bodies produce cortisol, which suppresses the cellular growth our brains desperately need to create new neurons. [86] Our hippocampus—the learning and memory center—can't do its job of sprouting new connections and maintaining the ones we have. [87] Translation? Stress makes it harder for our brains to stabilize our moods.

I learned this the hard way when I had to evaluate a ten-year friendship.

Bob and I had never had a conflict until this summer. When we finally did, his response was to ghost me—no communication for five days while I spiraled with anxiety, waking up all night ruminating about our friendship. During those sleepless nights, I found myself returning to old patterns of frantic prayer, begging God to fix the situation instead of asking for wisdom to handle it well. When he finally reached out, he claimed he was waiting for an apology I'd sent two hours after our fight.

I recognized Bob's conflict avoidance as a trigger for my hypomania and communicated this to him, asking him to talk through problems instead of disappearing. A month later, when he was upset about something else, he went silent again. This time, his only communication was a series of texts reaching back six years to my antidepressant-induced manic episode as "evidence" of my poor character.

That's when I knew: some relationships undermine mood stability, and I had to choose my mental health. I had to choose to trust God had given me both wisdom and medication for a reason; promoting my mental wellness wasn't selfish, it was stewardship.

Ten years of friendship, and I had to let it go. I couldn't expect Bob to change his conflict style for me, but I also couldn't subject myself to the stress of his disappearing acts.

The hardest part about managing stress with bipolar is that our capacity changes with our mood states. What I could handle before my diagnosis—like hosting two parties and driving to a football game in one weekend—became impossible. The first time Tony and Calista saw symptoms of my hypomania was during exactly that kind of overscheduled weekend. By the second party, I was showing enough concerning behavior that Tony's mother questioned him about it.

That's why I got married with five days' notice. I wanted to be stable on my wedding day—to feel joy, remember what the pastor said, notice the sunset fading as we made our vows. I skipped the stress of wedding planning to prioritize my mental health, and it was the right choice.

Here's the tricky part: cortisol doesn't discriminate between good and bad stress. Bad stress (distress) makes me anxious. Good stress (eustress) energizes me. Both can trigger episodes. Teaching is a perfect example—it provides financial stability and health insurance (reducing distress), but the emotionally demanding nature of the job creates eustress that can still be overwhelming.

The key insight: I can't navigate this alone anymore. My husband and stepdaughter don't just need to help me choose less stressful paths—they also need to protect me from unnecessary stressors. Making our home a sanctuary isn't just nice to have; it's essential for my brain's ability to function. Though creating this physical sanctuary with Tony and Calista was crucial, it would only take me so far. There was another kind of refuge that made all the difference—but that's a story for part four.

Living with bipolar means accepting that stress management isn't optional—it's a medical necessity. Some people can power through exhaustion, relationship drama, and overpacked schedules. We can't. And that's not weakness; it's just biology.

Experts agree stress reduction requires intentional life restructuring. This might mean navigating decisions about returning to work, whether to disclose your diagnosis, requesting workplace accommodations, or finding more suitable employment. As one guide puts it, "Stabilizing your moods requires extra work on your part. You need to manage your medications, make lifestyle adjustments, and possibly face periods of unemployment and diminished cash flow." [88]

The goal isn't to live a stress-free life (impossible) but to structure our lives around what our brains actually need to stay stable.

Episodes Don't Define You, They Transform You

I tell my students: "Our mistakes don't define us. They teach us." Mood episodes, however, aren't mistakes. They're something else entirely.

When I ask people without bipolar to think of their most joyful moment, they smile. They remember celebrations, loved ones, accomplishments. Those memories make them want to experience more days like that.

When I think of my most joyful moment, I grimace. The most euphoric I've ever felt was during my antidepressant-induced manic episode when I destroyed my life and Charming's. I was on top of the world, completely absent of worry or fear, thinking I was living my best life. Nevertheless, the memories that accompany those feelings of elation are a terrible string of ill-informed choices I can only hazily recall. The cruel irony of bipolar is that our highest highs come with our lowest consequences.

For a while after my diagnosis, I lived terrified of happiness. My medication kept me stabilized just south of a good mood because I was terrified of getting "too happy" and triggering another episode. When my husband and stepdaughter made me genuinely happy, I'd instantly start evaluating my mental stability instead of just enjoying the moment.

Tony and Calista convinced me that avoiding good moods was a lousy compromise. They're right. I've been happy most of my life—childhood, adolescence, adulthood were all colored brightly by mostly good times, punctuated by brief depressions. The longest, deepest depression only followed the most epic, euphoric high.

Here's what I'm really afraid of: I'm not afraid of being happy. I'm afraid of who I became during that manic episode.

Van gave her a name—Fenix—and it fits. I'm afraid she'll return like a raid boss, rising from ashes she created, to manically, joyfully, forcefully torch my sanity again. I resent the depression that follows, the personality my ex-husband likened to Eeyore from Winnie the Pooh.

Our episodes don't define us; they transform us. Our brain chemistry literally changes when we move from tile to tile on our mood disorder hopscotch boards. Unlike mistakes we can learn from and avoid, we can't promise not to have another episode. We're always just a step or two away from becoming someone different.

Episodes change us because we have to live with the consequences of choices we wouldn't have made in our right state of mind. We lose friends, lovers, jobs. We rebuild trust. We make amends. We learn to recognize early warning signs. But we also know our moods are prone to cycle again.

Maybe that's why I've always been obsessed with butterflies—their ability to metamorphose from something so completely different. People with bipolar have a similar quality. We transform, adapt, emerge changed but not broken. The goal isn't to avoid transformation. It's to navigate it purposefully as a part of our story, designed by God, even when the process feels destructive.

In the next sections, we'll explore practical ways of dealing with changing mood states—naming them, making amends for them, and learning to live with a brain that's capable of remarkable highs and devastating lows, sometimes within the same week.

Calling My Moods by Name

Carrie Fisher named her moods, and it changed everything for me.

"Roy is Rollicking Roy, the wild ride of a mood, and Pam is Sediment Pam, who stands on the shore and sobs," she explained. "One mood is the meal, and the next mood is the check."[89] That last line hit hard—it's easy to feel like depression is payback for mania, a deserved punishment for feeling too good.

Tony and I decided to name all my moods too.

Laura Joy is my euthymia—that calm, neutral center state we target during instability. When I'm stable, when I'm myself, when I'm most me. This is who I was when I left Dr. Bogin's care in remission.

Eeyore is my depression. My ex-husband gave her this name years ago, and Tony likes the label. Tony hasn't met her yet, and honestly, I hope he never does.

Fenix is my mania—the personality that rises from ashes she creates to manically, joyfully torch everything in sight. Tony hasn't met her either, and I pray he never will.

But we needed one more name. What about that ever-changing mass of contradictions? Winston Churchill was open about his periods of depression, naming this mood "The Black Dog".[90] However, Churchill's military chief described him as "either on the crest of the wave or in the trough, either highly laudatory or bitterly condemnatory, either in an angelic temper or a hell of rage." [91] That sounds more like hypomania to me.

During a fight early in our relationship, Tony made a joke that stuck: "Right now? You're just Laura. I want Laura Joy back."

Laura became the name for my hypomania. When I'm engrossed in a task, annoyed by distractions, irritated by interruptions, hypermotivated until I finish—I'm just Laura. It's me without the joy, me running a little too hot, me one step away from the center tile.

When people ask if I go by both names, I tell them it's a mouthful, but I try to live up to the second part. I want to take joy with me wherever I go, like my mother and namesake always seems to do. There's something in her steady faith that anchors her joy—a quality I'm still learning to cultivate.

These aren't separate personalities living inside me. By naming my mood states, I can characterize the thoughts, behaviors, and tendencies of each state like characters in a story. These character sketches give me and my loved ones essential observation criteria.

When we see signs of "just Laura," we make immediate lifestyle or medication adjustments to bring Laura Joy back.

Could naming moods be an effective strategy for others with bipolar? Maybe it sounds silly, but I agree with Carrie Fisher—we need to not take ourselves so seriously all the time. This is a serious illness, but that doesn't mean we can't find ways to make it more manageable. Moreover, it's a practical approach that feels like stewarding the mind God gave me, even when it doesn't work the way I wish it would.

Whether I'm acting like Laura, Eeyore, or Fenix, I'm still responsible for my actions and decisions when I've stepped off the center tile of mood stability. That's why learning to apologize well is particularly important in the bipolar patient's toolkit—something we'll explore next.

Making Amends for Bipolar Misbehaviors

If you've been diagnosed with bipolar later in life and haven't left a wake of broken relationships behind you, you have my utmost respect.

I know it's possible, but that's not the story I see in most memoirs or hear in support groups. Most of us have damage to repair.

Tony knowingly married a person with mental illness. When he said "in sickness and health," he committed to love me through all my mood states. However, he didn't agree to be on the receiving end of emotionally abusive temper tantrums without apologies.

During premarital counseling, our pastor suggested Gary Chapman's *The Five Apology Languages*. This book changed everything for us. It explores five different ways of expressing and receiving apologies: expressing regret, accepting responsibility, making restitution, genuinely repenting, and requesting forgiveness.

Here's what we discovered: Tony receives forgiveness when I repent—when I commit to changing the behavior to avoid repeating it. I know he's sorry when he expresses regret, showing genuine remorse for the pain he caused. We were speaking different apology languages, which meant my attempts at making amends weren't landing.

Learning to apologize well became essential for our relationship. Tony's expectation for a real apology is that I commit not to make the same mistake again, then actually follow through. He gives me grace, understanding that my commitment and follow-through don't always match up perfectly. His forgiveness isn't all-or-nothing, and this compromise leaves room for me to develop new habits rather than expecting me to be different overnight. In any event, Tony's willingness to continue extending this grace is a daily mirror of the unmerited favor I've received from God, challenging me to offer the same patience to myself and others.

Before my diagnosis, I was terrible at apologies. I withheld them because I was aware I'd done things I couldn't expect to be forgiven for. I thought I was good at starting over, but really I was just good at burning bridges. I'd make new friends to replace the ones I'd wronged, move cities, get new jobs, keep trying to reinvent myself as Laura Joy again.

Getting my diagnosis was like someone teaching me names for primary colors. Things I'd seen and processed now had names, belonged to categories, had origin points. I could map my mood states over the decades, making it easy to determine which decisions were made during stable versus unstable times.

I genuinely wanted to go back to everyone I'd hurt and apologize.

It was a great thought in theory, but I was in a dark depression and taking Lithium at the time. In the end, I prioritized one apology: Charming.

About a year after that fated prom night where Fenix destroyed everything, he met me at a restaurant in Richmond. I don't think my apology made much sense—I hadn't read Chapman's book yet. It was my first time saying, "I have bipolar disorder. I was in a manic episode. I wasn't acting like myself."

I'm not sure I even asked for his forgiveness. I didn't think I deserved it.

Charming was bewildered. It wasn't the closure either of us expected, but it was my first attempt at coming back from a mood episode instead of just running away from the wreckage. Looking back, I think God was teaching me that healing starts with taking responsibility, even when the outcome is uncertain.

Learning to apologize well isn't just about repairing relationships—it's about taking responsibility for our actions regardless of our mood state. Whether we're "just Laura," Eeyore, or Fenix, we're still accountable for the choices we make when we step off that center tile of stability.

The goal isn't perfection. It's genuine accountability paired with the commitment to do better next time that's like a form of worship, an attempt to honor God by stewarding my relationships well even when my brain doesn't cooperate.

Mood States Impact Choices, For Better and Worse

There is one apology I can never make.

Between Charming and Tony, a childhood sweetheart snuck back into my life. Joshua and I had dated in college before parting ways—him for Los Angeles, me for Nashville. We kept in touch over the years, and shortly after my bipolar diagnosis, we rekindled our romance.

Following the total decimation of my life during the Charming episode, a long-distance relationship with Joshua gave me hope. He was running a comedy club in Nashville while I was teaching in Virginia. We fell back in love through video calls in the fall of 2019. My visits to see him at Thanksgiving and Christmas are sepia-colored memories I'll cherish forever.

He loved me when we were kids, and he loved me as an adult with a bipolar diagnosis.

But I was still largely unaware of how my moods dictated the trajectory of my life. As things got serious between us, I tried switching medications—going off quetiapine and starting lurasidone, the one mood stabilizer I knew was approved for pregnancy. When Joshua came to visit me in February, I was depressed.

Looking back, it's easy to see how my low mood miscolored our entire time together.

A month later, the pandemic shut down the world. His comedy club closed, school went virtual, and we were both isolated. In my estimation, we were both depressed when we decided to break up. It wasn't Joshua's fault that his visit didn't lift my spirits like my trips to Nashville had.

I'm sorry that, in my depressed state, I pushed away a good man who loved me exactly as I was.

Joshua died of a heart attack in his sleep three years later.

I attended his memorial service at the chapel where we'd talked about getting married. We scattered his ashes at the farm where we would have had our reception. I hugged his mother Marci, and we wept together for what might have been. Standing in that chapel, I felt both the weight of my regret and the strange comfort that comes from believing Joshua was finally at peace.

Had I kept a mood log like I do now, would I have recognized that depression and avoided making such a big decision? I don't know, but that's my regret about Joshua.

If he were here, I would tell him I'm sorry I let him go, that he was enough, that it was my illness tricking me otherwise. He's not the first relationship I sacrificed during a depression, but I pray he's the last. Joshua was a casualty of my sickness—which is exactly why doctors recommend not making major life decisions during mood episodes.

The silver lining is his mother Marci. Since Joshua passed, we've enjoyed a sweet friendship. Having both known depression, we slipped easily into kinship and mutual encouragement. Marci has been my top supporter throughout writing this book. I've read her whole sections over the phone and hang up inspired to continue.

Because I suspect my bipolar got in the way of my relationship with her son, it's cathartic talking with her about everything I'm learning to make better choices now. Like Joshua, Marci knew me when I was young, happy, and carefree. Like Joshua, she loves me as I am—BD and all. In our conversations, I often sense God's grace working through her, transforming what might have been unbearable guilt into something redemptive.

When you're trying to live well with this illness, recognize the impact of decisions made during mood episodes. Give yourself grace. Make amends where you can, and make changes where you can't.

Some losses teach us lessons we wish we'd never had to learn. From my experience, though, in my gravest regrets, God doesn't waste our pain. He uses it to teach us to love better, choose wiser, and hold tighter still to what matters most.

Who I Am in the Light

Who am I now?

I am Laura Joy who happens to have BD, not a bipolar person who happens to be named Laura Joy. The difference matters because identity comes from whose I am, not what I have, and I belong to a God who calls me His beloved daughter, bipolar brain and all.

I am someone who has learned to map her emotional landscape. My hopscotch board of mood states gives me a visual for where I am and how to get home to center. I understand that my family's genetic patterns aren't a curse—they're information that helps me make better choices. What used to feel like a generational burden now seems surely part of God's intricate design, whether I understand the purpose or not.

I am someone who has learned to call her moods by name. Laura Joy, Laura, Eeyore, and Fenix aren't separate people living inside me— they're different versions of me that emerge under different brain chemistry. Naming them gives me and my loved ones the language to navigate them purposefully.

I am someone who has learned the cost of unmanaged episodes. I carry the weight of choices I made when my brain was lying to me about reality. I live with the grief of a relationship I sabotaged during depression, a man I can never apologize to because he's gone. These aren't punishments—they're the teachers that forced me to take this illness seriously.

I am someone who has learned to make amends rather than burn bridges. Instead of running to new cities and new lives every time I mess up, I've learned to stay and do the hard work of accountability. I've learned that Tony's forgiveness isn't about perfection—it's about genuine effort to do better.

Most importantly, I am someone who has learned that having BD doesn't make me broken. It makes me someone who experiences life at extremes, someone whose brain is capable of remarkable highs and devastating lows, someone who has to work harder than most people to stay balanced. This extra work isn't punishment; it's spiritual discipline that keeps me dependent on God's grace and strength.

When well-managed, our manic energy can accomplish extraordinary things. When properly supported, our empathy can help others feel less alone. When we share our stories honestly, we can light the way for someone else still stumbling in the dark.

I am not defined by this illness, but I am refined by it. Every episode taught me something. Every breakdown led to a breakthrough. Every loss showed me what was worth fighting for. Besides, through it all, I've been held by something bigger than my diagnosis, something that doesn't diminish when my brain chemistry shifts, something that whispers "Beloved" in the darkest depressions. The goal was never to become someone different. It was to become the most intentional, self-aware, purposeful version of who I already was.

In the light, I can see clearly: I am fearfully, wonderfully, and yes—bipolar-ly made. And that's not something to hide from anymore. David's psalm was never meant only for people with "normal" brains—it was written for all of us, including those of us whose minds work in ways that seem chaotic but might just be part of a larger design we can't yet see.

Part Three: Ending the Stigma—Spotlight on Bipolar

Chapter Eleven: How Did I Step Out of the Shadows?

Nathaniel Hawthorne's *A Scarlet Letter* inspired my perception of the way I interacted with life after diagnosis. As a punishment for infidelity, Hawthorne's leading lady Hester Prynne is forced to wear a patch with the letter "A," printed in red, to publicly shame Hester for her sin of adultery.

Being diagnosed can feel like being similarly branded. The stigma surrounding BD positions me as a disgraced member of society. Unlike Hester's scarlet letter, imposed as a punishment for sin, this diagnosis doesn't equate to shame or judgment, but it took a while to come to terms with how God made my particular mind.

I'm not literally walking around with a flashing sign reading "insane" or "unstable," but put in a position to disclose my diagnosis, am I afraid of being misunderstood? Deep down, beneath all the strategies for bipolar mood management, fear of prejudice lurks, waiting to disrupt our best attempts at stabilizing moods. No, the weather is not bipolar today, it just changed since this morning.

I'm convinced that this fear undermined my progress. My husband supports this by offering observations from family gatherings over the past year. Hiding my disorder took effort, negative effort at that. Fear of showing signs of BD and being rejected wound me up, an anxious pull cord easily triggered to unravel. I was, in essence, less stable emotionally out of fear of being exposed, with my BD brand flashing in neon red. When a trigger did happen, I was primed to pop.

Since coming out about my illness to Tony's family, he's observed a significant improvement in my mood stability in those large gathering settings. Freed from fear and the effort of hiding my BD, the result was that I began acting more normally, more like the "Laura Joy" Tony fell in love with, and it makes sense, really. We can continue to interact with the world around us ashamed of our illness, but I'm afraid we're setting ourselves up for failure. Living in shame about something God allowed in my life feels like rejecting part of His design simply because I don't get His purpose.

Not Ashamed of Bipolar Disorder

I am not ashamed of BD. If you're reading this book, I challenge you to join me. Say it out loud, "I am not ashamed of bipolar disorder." If you can't believe it yet, that's okay. Sometimes faith comes before feelings, declaring what we know to be true even when our hearts haven't caught up yet. Saying it will help you know where you're starting from on this journey of acceptance. Whether you or your loved one is living with BD, success in managing this illness is largely determined by getting rid of that scarlet letter to be defined by truer qualities.

In her memoir, Terri Cheney captures something I understand completely. She writes about how the object of her shame shifted—not the condition itself, but its consequences. "I believe in this diagnosis. It's as true to me as being a redhead," she says. "Despite the constant shifting of the earth beneath my feet, I feel grounded at last." [92]

That's exactly how I feel now. Our label isn't a punishment—it's a lens. Through it, I finally see myself clearly. The diagnosis that once felt like a brand of shame became the key to understanding my whole life. Why I felt so much, so intensely. Why I could accomplish amazing things and then crash spectacularly. Why relationships felt like such high stakes.

Our label is a gift, not a curse. With the right diagnosis, I can now take responsibility for living well—not despite BD, not because of it, but with it as part of who I am. I imagine God sees my diagnosis similarly, not as a mistake to be ashamed of, but as part of the fearfully and wonderfully made design He had in mind.

Living Responsibly with Bipolar Disorder

A few years ago, I stumbled on an article that changed everything for me: "Learning to Live Responsibly with Bipolar Illness" by C.S. Herrman, a man who shares my diagnosis. His central idea hit me like lightning—that BD traits aren't inherently good or bad, but become problematic only when they cluster together in certain ways. With the right medication and self-management, he argued, we can harness our positive traits while managing the challenging ones.[93]

This wasn't just theory to me—it was hope. For the first time since diagnosis, someone was telling me that quality of life wasn't entirely beyond my control. I couldn't change my genetics or rewrite my past, but I could take responsibility for how I managed my future. It reminded me of the Serenity Prayer—accepting what I cannot change while taking action on what I can.

Reading Herrman's work, I realized I'd been carrying around a dangerous narrative. I'd been seeing myself as a victim of my brain chemistry, powerless against mood swings, destined to hurt the people I loved. But Herrman challenged me to flip that script. Even medicated, yes, I'm "compromised in accessing, appreciating and properly acting upon otherwise normal cues."[94] However, I also have the capacity for self-reflection and authentic conversation with the people who love me. I can be made aware of my mood state.

I've known people with BD who use our diagnosis as a free pass for bad behavior. They're often the loudest voices representing us, and unfortunately, they fuel the very stigma we're trying to overcome. That's not the person I want to be. I want to honor both my diagnosis and my faith by taking full responsibility for my choices, regardless of my mood state.

I made a commitment to myself and my loved ones: I will live responsibly with this diagnosis. That means learning everything I can about BD, staying compliant with my medication, and building the support systems I need. It means acknowledging that while I can't control my symptoms entirely, I can control how I respond to them.

This isn't about perfection—it's about intention. If we want to change how the world sees BD, we have to start by taking ownership of our own lives.

Fighting the Stigma with a Voluntary Chosen Dependence

For years after my diagnosis, I felt like I was failing at being an independent adult. I needed Tony to help me recognize mood shifts. I couldn't miss therapy appointments. I had to limit social commitments to protect my energy. I felt ashamed of all the supports I required, like I was broken, needy, less than.

Then I stumbled across a Swedish study with a title that stopped me cold: "A Dependence that Empowers." The researchers had interviewed adults with BD who were living well, and they'd discovered something revolutionary: the people thriving with this illness had learned to embrace strategic dependence rather than fight it. [95]

This went against everything I'd been taught. American culture screams independence. Pull yourself up by your bootstraps. Stand on your own two feet. Nevertheless, what if that's exactly the wrong approach for people like us? Even in my faith, I'd been taught that dependence on anything other than God was weakness. Maybe I'd misunderstood what healthy dependence looks like.

The study called it 'voluntary chosen dependence'—deliberately choosing supports that actually give you more freedom and control, not less. [96] The researchers captured something I'd felt but couldn't articulate: "Life with BD is characterized by a strong, restless desire to be able to conduct one's life, and thus having a greater possibility of living a good life, which means a life corresponding to how one perceives oneself to be." [97]

That hit me like lightning. I had that exact restless desire—I wanted my reality to match who I knew I could be, and I need to stop apologizing for needing what I need to make that happen. It struck me God might have designed us to need each other, that my dependence on Tony, my therapist, my medication wasn't failure, but part of how He intended life to work.

I turned the course of my life by accepting that I would always need supports—and that this wasn't a character flaw. I started protecting my energy by saying no to commitments that would drain me. I embraced being needed by Tony, by my students, because that responsibility actually helps stabilize my moods. I built trusting relationships where people can tell me honestly when they see warning signs. And I learned to use my past episodes as landmarks to navigate future challenges. [98]

Most importantly, I changed the story I told myself. The old narrative was all shame:

"Laura Joy, something's wrong with you. We're going to hide it the best we can. You can't trust yourself. You can't be alone. You're controlling, obstinate, and powerless."

But that victim story was keeping me stuck. Now I tell myself the truth:

"Laura Joy, you never miss a medication dose or therapy session. You're responsible. You rely on the stability and perspective your husband provides. You know your triggers and have strategies. You prioritize sleep, eat well, exercise. You protect yourself with boundaries. You talk openly about BD to help others."

This voluntary chosen dependence transformed how I see myself. I don't struggle with BD anymore—I live with it, I manage it. By embracing the supports I need instead of fighting them, I gained the very independence I thought I was losing. There's a difference between codependence and God-honoring interdependence. The Swedish study helped me recognize my need for support as part of how God designed His people to care for one another rather than a spiritual shortcoming.

If we want to shatter misconceptions about BD, we have to stop acting like victims of our diagnosis. We can arrange our lives intentionally, build the support systems we need, and yes—have hope for a good life.

Bipolar Disorder as Depicted in Entertainment

Before my diagnosis, what I knew about BD came mostly from TV and movies. When I thought "bipolar," I pictured Jack Nicholson's character in *One Flew Over the Cuckoo's Nest*—basically, the psychiatric ward. [99]

Then I discovered *Homeland* during my engagement with Tony. We binged the series together, watching CIA agent Carrie Mathison navigate her career while managing BD. Carrie was brilliant, driven, successful—but always thirty minutes away from going off her meds to "think clearly" and either saving the day or destroying everything. [100]

I could relate to Carrie sometimes, but her episodes were more extreme than mine. She had BDI; I have BDII. When I was first diagnosed, part of why I resisted the label was because I didn't see myself in Carrie's chaos. Her manic episodes required hospitalization—mine flew under the radar as hypomania.

Later, I watched Andrew Deluca's storyline unfold on *Grey's Anatomy*. In one devastating episode, he correctly suspects a patient is being trafficked, but his growing mania makes everyone doubt him. His sister tries to help him see his symptoms, but he can't see himself clearly. Even though he was right about the trafficking, his manic behavior destroyed his credibility. [101] Terri Cheney's words echoed in my mind: "Manic intentions are always good; manic consequences, almost never."[102]

Watching Andrew speed away on his motorcycle after losing everything, I wept. I knew that urge to race away from the mess you've left behind. But I also saw something hopeful—Andrew wasn't just a "crazy person." He was lovable, charming, someone viewers had invested in. When he fell apart, I wondered if other people watching felt empathy for him.

That's what's missing from most portrayals—we're shown at our extremes because conflict drives plot. But what about stories where we're successfully managing our illness? Where we're taking our meds, going to therapy, living well between the poles?

I want to see characters with BD who aren't just heroes and villains of their own stories. I want representation that shows us as teachers, doctors, parents—real people managing a real condition, not walking disasters waiting to explode.

If we want better representation, we have to share our real stories. We're not fictional characters—we're your neighbors, your coworkers, your family members. When we stay silent, the only narrative people know is the dramatic one from entertainment. We're also the people sitting in your church pews, leading youth groups, singing in the choir— faithful people who happen to need medication and therapy to be our best selves.

That's why I'm telling my story, to show what living well with BD actually looks like. If we know BD is not a death sentence or a scarlet letter, our silence only contributes to the stigma.

My Dream Life as the Next Carrie Fisher

Recently, I was listening to one of my favorite podcasts, *The School of Greatness with Lewis Howse.* The episode featured an interview with entrepreneur Rory Vaden. At one point, I stopped and went back because I had to write down what I'd heard. Vaden said, "You are most powerfully positioned to serve the person you once were. Find your weakness and exploit it in serving others." Naturally, I connected the dots: I want to help people like me with BD live better. The context of this episode prompted me to envision a career doing just that.

I let myself dream big here. Since dreams don't have consequences, it's safe to lean into the grandiosity my illness affords me. I have a dream that this book sparks conversations that spark conversations that exponentially positively impact the lives of people with mood disorders and those living with people with mood disorders.

Then, I become the poster child for BD like Carrie Fisher, devoting my life to informing others about the illness and crushing the stigma, leading to an increase in accurate diagnoses and better self-management strategies and supports. Fisher blazed the trail as a secular advocate—I dream of following her path while adding something of spiritual value: showing how faith and mental health treatment can work together, not against each other.

My book is an open invitation for honest conversations. People accept my challenge and reach out wanting to share their stories on my podcast, and I host a range of successful individuals on the BD spectrum that inspire a contagion of better living. My podcast, *Manic Superpowers*, fueled by a pilfered motto that with our great bipolar power comes great responsibility, gets attention. I'm invited to speak at a TED Talk, where I share my vision for an annual bipolar convention.

People catch my vision. While we're in the planning stages, I keep busy by travelling a high school circuit as a motivational speaker for faculties and student bodies, inspiring a message of hope about mental illness that empowers. Churches will invite me to speak there, too—

places where Fisher's message might not have reached, but where people desperately need to hear about God's heart for the mentally ill.

The convention is a hit. Kay Redfield Jamison is our keynote speaker. Selena Gomez follows with a touching performance of her song about living like us, "My Mind & Me".

The weekend features topics targeted at supporting the range of mood states and diagnoses within the BD spectrum and supporting the people who love us, with a range of sessions for every relevant topic. Experts and people with positive lived experience share best practices and current research, just like at education or English conventions I've attended in the past. Only, for this convention, tickets are refundable and can be purchased at the last minute. That accommodation just makes sense for us.

The convocation's culminating event features an interview panel with several celebrities living with BD who advocate for mental health, including Mariah Carey, who gives the final performance of the evening with a new song she wrote reflecting her personal story of walking in our shoes and relying on God's daily renewing grace, a reformed message on a secular platform about whole healing. Of course, that song goes viral, and it inspires Bradley Cooper to rally TV execs behind production of a new series featuring a faith-based, multigenerational mentally ill-family powered by bipolar management.

I'm naturally a part of this conversation, so Bradley (we're on a first name basis by now) connects me with a screenwriter, and we can afford to contract Catherine Zeta-Jones to play the moody matriarch since, positioned as her daughter, would be moody me at a fraction of the cost. Also, my book is influential in leading a young adult female celebrity to an accurate diagnosis of BD, and this girl rounds out the cast family as my daughter. When this third-generation representative had shown symptoms in early adolescence, her mother intervened giving her access to services, and though moody and temperamental at times, she has yet to develop BD.

The show's vibe is that of ABC's *Cougartown*, a series which features an apparently undiagnosed female lead with ADHD played by Courtney Cox. Ours is similarly funny punctuated by serious, demonstrating the everyday challenges someone with this disorder overcomes. The multigenerational framework facilitates relevant conflict and theme development, providing opportunities to see different strategies for self-management and demystify life on the mood disorder spectrum within the plot of a single episode. Bipolar pride suffocates the life out of stigma, and it's okay to own who we are without fear of rejection outside our home sanctuaries.

And if you pick up the original face of BD's memoir *Wishful Drinking*, you'll find my grandiose posturing emulates Carrie Fisher in this dream sequence of becoming the next "her," letting the humorous string of ideas make me a frontrunner in the early mental health industry, in a way that pays respect to Fisher's masterful, integrative complexity.

It's a beautiful dream, but that's not how most of us are realistically going to affect change. How do we inform, educate, advocate, scaffold, and combat stigma in our everyday lives? How can the teacher or realtor, the doctor or cashier, carry a torch for BD without launching a new career? I declined a sixth-grade teaching contract last summer to prioritize writing this book. My book is nearly finished. My stepdaughter's school offered me the job again, and I signed that contract while developing this chapter. I'll start after winter break, and Lord willing, have finished my book by then.

Soon, I'll be an English teacher again. It's not the vision Rory Vaden inspired, but his words still apply: "You are most powerfully positioned to serve the person you once were. Find your weakness and exploit it in serving others." I was once an adolescent with undiagnosed issues trying to accommodate my way through a cloud of high expectations, questioning purpose and meaning in life, seeking to connect with the God who designed me this way.

I'm powerfully positioned to serve these kids. It is not separate from my vision; rather, it's a part of it. I'll make an impact where I am and pray that circle of influence grows.

Becoming Bipolar Ambassadors

After everything I'd learned about living well with BD, Tony and I realized we wanted to do more than just manage our own lives—we wanted to help change how the world sees people like us. "We should become bipolar ambassadors," he said one evening. Representatives for BD to the community at large. I felt a stirring in my spirit, like God was calling us to use our experience for something bigger than ourselves.

The idea excited me, but I'm a teacher—I need structure. So, we sat down to figure out what that actually meant. What's our mission? What are we working toward? What values should guide us?

It took a few hours, but we crafted our mission, our response to being called to love our struggling neighbors: to foster understanding, compassion, and support for those affected by BD by sharing personal experiences and insights. We want to break down stigma, promote open conversations, and create a community where people can share their stories, find hope, and inspire resilience.

Our vision is simple: a world that embraces individuals living with BD with understanding and compassion, free from stigma and discrimination.

We needed more than lofty statements, though—we needed principles to guide our daily choices. We identified seven core values that would shape how we interact with the world:

- **Empathy** - Understanding and accepting people affected by BD
- **Awareness** - Educating others to combat stigma
- **Compassion** - Creating safe spaces for people to seek help
- **Resilience** - Celebrating the strength of people with mood disorders
- **Authenticity** - Being honest about our experiences to encourage others
- **Hope** - Inspiring optimism for recovery and growth
- **Empowerment** - Providing tools for people to advocate for themselves

These aren't just words on paper. We're actively advocating, attending support groups, and training to facilitate our own in-person group. I'm pursuing a peer support specialist certification to help me be more effective serving others. I created social media accounts to share encouraging messages about living with BD. I blog about my experiences to model open dialogue. Our seven values mirror what I've learned about God's heart.

Most importantly, these values give me a framework for returning to the classroom. Empathy, awareness, compassion, resilience, authenticity, hope, and empowerment aren't just ideals for mental health advocacy—

they're perfect for education too. I can be a bipolar ambassador and a teacher simultaneously. In both roles, I get to show students and colleagues that God uses our struggles for good, ultimately, and there's hope when we intentionally mind the body and soul we've been given.

Writing and education are my wheelhouses for carrying this torch. What's yours? Do you want to rep for us out in the real world and help change the narrative?

A Challenge to Take Up the Torch

If my story resonates with you, maybe you want to become a bipolar ambassador too. Not in some formal, organized way—just in your own life, using whatever gifts and platforms you have. I believe God places us exactly where He needs us to make an impact, whether that's in a boardroom, a classroom, or a living room.

I think about Bebe Rexha's tweet from April 2019, just two months after I accepted my diagnosis: "I'm bipolar and I'm not ashamed anymore. That is all. (Crying my eyes out.)" [103] Over 26,000 people liked that tweet. I suspect many of them were trying to gather the same courage she had.

That's the power of one person's honesty. Selena Gomez sharing her journey through her documentary "My Mind & Me." Catherine Zeta-Jones, Russell Brand, Demi Lovato, and Mariah Carey each owning their diagnosis publicly. Faye Dunaway coming out in a 2024 documentary. Jane Pauley sharing her experience in her autobiography. Patty Duke not only writing about her illness but lobbying Congress for BD research funding. And of course, Carrie Fisher, who devoted her life to advocacy.

Each person used their unique platform to say, "This is who I am, and I'm not ashamed."

You don't need to be a celebrity or change careers to make a difference. You can be a bipolar ambassador right where you are. Maybe it's speaking up when someone makes a joke about mental illness. Maybe it's being the person a colleague feels safe confiding in. Maybe it's advocating for better mental health policies at your workplace. Maybe it's being the church member who helps your congregation understand that mental illness and faith can coexist.

For me, it's returning to the classroom with my seven core values—empathy, awareness, compassion, resilience, authenticity, hope, and empowerment. I'll be a teacher who happens to understand what it's like when your brain works differently.

Whatever your wheelhouse—whether you're an artist, healthcare provider, parent, or cashier—there's a way to carry this torch. The goal isn't to become a mental health expert. It's to be authentically yourself while helping create a world where people like us don't have to hide.

What would being a bipolar ambassador look like in your life?

How We Change the Perception of BD

I started this chapter zeroing in on Hester Prynne's scarlet letter, that symbol of shame she was forced to wear. But here's what I've learned: we get to choose whether we wear that letter or not.

When I stopped hiding my diagnosis, something remarkable happened. Tony noticed I was more stable at family gatherings. I stopped wasting energy on fear and started using it to actually live. The shame that once consumed me transformed into purpose. There was a point while writing this manuscript I could hear my mother reminding me as a young girl that what the enemy meant for harm, God used for good; my struggle is becoming my ministry.[104]

My diagnosis isn't a punishment—it's a lens that finally helps me see myself clearly. Yes, BD comes with challenges, but it also comes with gifts. The same intensity that can spiral into mania also fuels my creativity and passion. The depth that can sink into depression also allows me to connect with others in profound ways. The myriad facets of me are not flaws to hide, no. They're part of an intricate design that keep me ever in need of grace that's new daily.

I've learned to embrace what I call voluntary chosen dependence—accepting the supports I need instead of fighting them. I rely on Tony's perspective, prioritize my medication, protect my energy, and trust the people who love me to help me stay grounded. It isn't sinning, putting others before God; it's stewardship, utilizing supports that let me make much of God in stable mind. This isn't weakness; it's wisdom.

The old narrative I told myself was full of shame: "Something's wrong with you. Hide it. You can't be trusted." Now I tell myself the truth: "You're responsible, you know your triggers, you have strategies, and you help others by sharing your story." This new narrative aligns with what I believe God thinks about me. I'm fearfully and wonderfully made. I don't need to run from what's inside anymore.

This is how we change perceptions—not through campaigns or movements, but through living authentically. When I walk into my classroom next month, I'll carry my seven core values: empathy, awareness, compassion, resilience, authenticity, hope, and empowerment. I'll be a teacher who happens to understand what it's like when your brain works differently. I'll be living proof God can use people with mental illness to do meaningful work in His kingdom.

Every time we choose honesty over hiding, responsibility over victimhood, and hope over shame, we're changing how the world sees BD. We're proving that people like us don't just survive—we thrive.

That's how we step out of the shadows. Together, one story at a time. As we do, we're not only altering how the world sees BD—we're giving humanity a snapshot of how God sees each of us: beloved, valuable, and capable of extraordinary things.

Chapter Twelve: How Do I Help the Next Person?

Back in 2011, a grad school assignment challenged us to choose inspirational quotes fundamental to our teaching philosophies and post them on social media, a relatively new practice at the time. This was one of the few tasks comprising my 4.0 that I didn't overthink, easily selecting mine. Frederick Douglas was credited as saying, "It is easier to build strong children than to repair broken men." Even then, I had a fire in my soul to champion for mental wellness.

I might be focusing the spotlight on BD in this book, but I rarely meet anyone new to our support group who isn't juggling multiple diagnoses. I can't highlight BD without including a range of other illnesses and conditions that bridge adolescence to adulthood. Over the course of fifteen years, I was diagnosed with an eating disorder NOS, self-harming behaviors, depression, insomnia, anxiety, ADHD, PTSD, and BD.

I don't own all of labels because I find they situate themselves neatly within my BD—except for ADHD, and since I've been accommodating for that since childhood, I don't "struggle daily" so much as "overcome regularly". And for self-management purposes, I'm not sure it's necessary to differentiate between accommodations for ADHD or BD. My care of one encompasses the other, naturally.

Along the way, though, nonprofessionals hurled other labels offensively or embodied them subtly in an email: histrionic, borderline, or narcissistic personality disorder; premenstrual dysphoric disorder (PMDD), codependency or emotional abuse, substance abuse, and even demon possession. I don't identify with these labels, stones throne into tiny ponds, separate entities with characteristics overlapping with BD or with a person experiencing BD comorbidly with another disorder, like ADHD. They are unfortunate attempts to isolate features of episodic "craziness" in disparate ponds rather than assess the whole of them, their duration and intensity, their cyclical nature, and realize the stones all drop into one spiraling, bipolar river.

Tributaries branch out from it, deposit into it, the bipolar river. Other diagnoses and labels we picked up along the way, ones that permanently joined our streams or travelled with only until a better diagnosis came along. Still others join us for a time; my depression isn't a stagnant pond but a raging force that merges with my stream until spring forces it to branch off in its own way. Streams and waterways, similar and different, that can come together and separate, but all with the same origin: mental illness. We are, with our different labels, still running water, capable of shifting course.

What is in common with all my labels, true or false, is that I was not born with them. Nor would I be confronted with any diagnosis until onset of adulthood. Until age ten, I was a healthy, happy kid whose worst comment in school was socializing too much during class. In middle school, symptoms started. Kids hurled insults, labels I internalized, and by nature of my ruminating thoughts, I struggled to free myself from their entanglement. I can't help but wonder how life might have turned out differently if I'd been taught how to balance BD symptoms alongside algebraic equations.

The main premise of this chapter is that if we can teach our children how to think about thinking, they'll be better able to navigate internal and external conflicts, even if they never develop a clinical disorder or illness. I believe school-aged children need mental wellness scaffolds and supports in equal measure to other core initiatives as predictors for quality of life after graduation. Studies show such interventions in adolescence prevent some disorders from developing and improve success prospects if one does.

In middle school, we begin to develop our individual identity and perception of the world. We cement our ways of thinking about ourselves and the way we relate to that world. We are taught to multiply, memorize, and mimic.

We aren't taught to think, at least not with the same level of intentionality or support of latest research-based strategies as outlined for standards of learning with end of year tests attached. We can begin to reshape mental wellness in the next generation by looking backwards with purpose: What scaffolds or mindsets would have prepared us to endure our brands of future life turbulence? How might we have accommodated for impairments from a cognitive perspective? What strategies did we eventually find that would have alleviated childhood ailments?

Across this chapter, an adaptation of the bipolar ambassador's seven core values informs a set of six strategies for cultivating mental health. With a shift in descriptors to champion for the whole spectrum of mental wellness in children and young adults, these core values guided my selection criteria. We'll explore *modeling, reframing, informing, normalizing, counseling,* and *integrating* as six strategies for cultivating mental wellness.

Cultivating mental health in ourselves, our loved ones, and the next generation is as intentional as tending a garden, much like how my mother taught me to tend to my relationship with God through daily quiet times and prayer. It's a common analogy easily applied in a variety of frameworks and here helps us understand the importance of actively supporting mental health by fostering its growth from an early age. The dedicated gardener prepares the soil, creating a supportive environment conducive for development. She gives the plants what they need to survive. She exposes them to catalysts for growth. She patiently prunes and protects, giving each plant the unique care it needs.[105] It requires intention and daily maintenance. Planting seeds alone doesn't guarantee they'll thrive in this soil.

People utilizing these six strategies in daily life can cultivate habits of mental wellness in their own community gardens. It is easier, after all, to build strong children than fix broken men. The way we tend to our little seeds now helps define the harvest bounty, recognizing there might well be a child in you that needs this retraining to live well with BD inside your household.

The reality is this: by shifting the focus to improving the mental wellness spectrum for our youth, we gain a powerful motivator beyond ourselves to help us make the changes we need to make for our own peace and happiness. My desire to change for me is inherent, but it's boosted exponentially when factored with a desire to be better for my stepdaughter, nieces, and nephews and model the same kind of faithful perseverance my mother showed me through her own struggles.

Modeling: What They See is What They Learn

The first strategy I propose to help early mental health ambassadors in their efforts to promote mental well-being is modeling. Modeling, simply defined, means adults living out these core values in everyday interactions with those we value, including children and young adults—at home, at school, and within the community.

In grad school, study of emotional intelligence inspired me to integrate empathy in the curriculum in my tenth-grade autobiographical narrative unit in Nashville. I told my students the goal of this project was to "use their meaningful moments to evoke empathy in their peers."[106] To get kids comfortable with that idea, though, I had to put myself through the process as a model. Honestly, my lifelong battle with BD, in the undiagnosed and diagnosed stages, finds me in humble posture to relate to people, at all ages, who are struggling. I encouraged my students to take risks sharing about personal moments by teaching them first about what empathy is, how to evoke it, and how to respond with it.

Modeling empathy happens in daily interactions. I had one student in sixth grade at a school for the gifted and talented who was diagnosed with ADHD. Often, he forgot to take his medication. This explained certain behaviors I came to recognize. There was no stigma in our exchanges. He could vocalize, "I'm sorry. I forgot to take my meds." But there was a helplessness I could relate to as well, a frustration that we couldn't expect better from him today. He knew his teacher took medication, that she knew what it was like to feel like things were out of control, and that she had some strategies to cope on days like when he'd missed his medication. On such days, he'd adopt a spot on the floor near my desk and be quite literally underfoot, just to keep his attention on my ninety-minute block.

Other teachers complained about the same boy. He had an IEP in place with accommodations, but hyperactivity that interrupts the gifted teacher's lesson plan can frustrate us so that we miss recognizing that these behaviors frustrate the child, too. It's easy to target our frustration on the someone who is making things difficult instead of putting ourselves in his shoes to determine how to best hold him up. I laugh while remembering the way I tripped over him regularly; that was quality education, and we modeled empathy for that last block class all year.

What does it look like for a parent to model empathy for child? It happens in everyday conversations in our house. When I met my stepdaughter, she'd just started seventh grade. That was the worst year of my life, and I encouraged Calista by reminding her of that frequently along the way. Occasionally, I share age-appropriate stories from my own life that express feelings and emotions Cali can relate to. Replayed throughout the year with different antagonists, Cali navigated various ways to make peace with bullies by understanding them as similarly struggling with their own private issue. Some bullies even became friends.

I'm always tickled when grown-ups meet me and attribute certain positive character traits to say my daughter's just like me or that they can see my impact on raising her. Since Cali refers to me as mom outside the home, many people are unaware I'm not her birth mother. That position is reserved for a woman diagnosed with BDI who opts regularly not to take medication and has been in and out of drug rehab facilities, prisons, and psych wards; subsequently, she lost parental rights and is currently out of the picture. Should she stay clean and start responsibly managing her BD, Calista is open to pursuing a relationship with her again.

Calista is in the unique position of being raised by two women with BD. When I first met her, I recognized certain behaviors characteristics of mood disorders, but might she have just been mimicking learned behaviors from the years her mother was around? After nine months in therapy with our family having open conversations about mood states and collectively supporting one another in pursuit of stability, I see a difference. There are fewer concerning behaviors, and they're decreasing in frequency. She was also a part of a semester-long lunchtime support group for girls provided by her guidance counselor's latest intern. Calista can see the difference, in her and in me, through lived experience, of the improved outcomes when a person takes responsibility for self-managing mental health.

These are just a few examples of modeling empathy in exchanges with kids. When I walked into classroom as a substitute and a teacher left me names of students to expel from class in case of misbehavior, I mentally renamed that list: Kids I Need to Make a Relationship with When They Walk in the Door. What guides my interactions with those "problem students" are empathy and compassion, and as result, they're not so problematic. I greet every misbehavior as an invitation to a conversation about what's going on in there. I assume each kid, including my own, has a worry or problem, and this is a chance to intervene.

Despite my BD, or at times because of it, I model these core values for Calista. It doesn't matter whether I raise her from birth or from puberty, Calista will mimic what I model. I model awareness when I correct her with an unoffensive way, in the future, of describing unpredictable shifts in weather, not her original, "The weather is so bipolar today." I model compassion by comforting her after a setback and looking for ways to lift her spirits, and by doing the same thing for others, sometimes with her help. I model resilience and authenticity in the way I talk about my own setbacks. Living as someone managing BD, I model an empowered lifestyle. Modeling empathy was just the beginning of my advocacy journey. I realized I also needed to help people reframe how they think about their struggles.

Reframing: Flipping the Script

Modeling empathy was just the beginning of my advocacy journey. I realized I also needed to help people reframe how they think about their struggles. Our mindsets affect our motivation and achievement. During childhood development, we form mindsets that, for good or bad, determine how we interact with life. Do we believe we're stuck with what we have, or do we believe we can be more? How my stepdaughter responds to a setback or difficulty is, in part, determined by her belief in her own ability to overcome, learn, and be better in the future.

A growth mindset is at the core of everyday BD self-management. I read that self-managing would empower me, saw examples of others doing this, and believed God intended me to be an active participant in my healing, shifting my view of my limits and abilities. Choosing a voluntary dependence on medication and mood monitoring, for example, improved my internal narrative about my independence. I perceive a better quality of life by believing I can better manage BD in the future. Similarly reframing a child's perception of himself contributes to three of our core values: empowerment, resilience, and hope.

The first time I was to present growth mindset was to a group of gifted sixth graders in September 2021. My older brother's son Joseph was on my roster. While on vacation in New York at my parent's house the month before, I contracted my oldest brother's kids to help me produce a public service announcement to show my students on the first day of school. The eldest, a passionate bookworm and gifted writer, played Jill, who was struggling to respond to our first writing assignment: a diagnostic essay about how to be successful in my class and give me an honest, initial writing sample for ELA (English Language Arts). Her younger brother played Jack, the growth mindset guru.

It was ironic recording Jill sitting at my parent's dining room table crossing out sentence after sentence in a notebook, saying, "How can I write an essay about being successful in ELA if I'm *not* successful in ELA?" Jill picks up her pen to try again, starts to write a word and scoffs, "It's too hard. I don't know how." She throws up her hands in frustration before tossing the pen down. "I give up," Jill says, crossing her arms over her chest. Suspenseful music builds to a fairy dust sound effect, and my nephew as Jack pops up from under the table all in black with sunglasses and a backwards hat, growth mindset's fairy cool-father.

Jack breaks the fourth wall as he encircles his sister. "Could it be? Do we have yet another case of the fixed mindset? I think so." The footage then shifts to a visual diagram depicting growth and fixed mindsets, with subsequent images scattered throughout the PSA. Someone with a fixed mindset would respond to this writing challenge the way Jill has. Jack models how to use a growth mindset instead.

Jill looks up at him incredulously. "I just can't do it," she says.

"You're still learning," Jack replies. "You just have to try."

"I'm not good at this," Jill objects, shaking her head.

"What can you learn to be better at it?"

Jill's unconvinced. "It's too hard."

"With more practice, it'll be much easier," Jack reassures her.

And then it pours out, what's often at the heart of the matter with gifted education students. "I'm afraid of making a mistake," she admits.

"Mistakes are how you learn."

Jill is considering it now, and her next sentence is more of a question. "I don't know how."

Jack was waiting for this cue. "You can learn how," he tells Jill. "You can learn to develop a growth mindset." From there, he shows how Jill's statements evidence a fixed mindset, while his retorts evidence a growth mindset. He suggests a shift from thinking she can't do something to thinking she can learn to do something.

When she finally gets it, a smile spreads across her face, and she reframes the prompt using a growth mindset. "So, I can learn how to be successful in ELA?" Jill asks. When Jack pops back out of the picture, Jill confidently returns to that same assignment—with a different attitude, different mindset. One that empowers, encourages resilience, and inspires hope that we can be yet better.

Educators, parents, and mentors are all in positions to encourage growth mindsets in our children and youth by playing out Jack's half of that conversation. On the first day of school, my nephew Joseph watched his cousins perform in our PSA back in Virginia. It was a hit. I onboarded a hundred plus new recruits to growth mindset in one day. Kids held one another accountable to the themes and statements upholding a growth mindset all year long. Though I've consulted research, none evokes such an emotional response as remembering the way my students learned to thrive together again post COVID-19 with a simple mindset change.

Moreover, a growth mindset encourages self-efficacy. If I can develop through hard work and effort, I have agency to influence my own outcomes. It's been a central theme of my book. I don't believe it's ever too late to develop a growth mindset; however, I'll admit it gets harder to change programmed thinking reinforced over time, which is why I emphasize the importance of early childhood intervention in thinking about thinking.

A growth mindset encourages us to set personal goals and take ownership of our learning to achieve them. For example, recognizing sleep deprivation is a trigger for mood instability, I'll never volunteer to serve at an overnight lock-in at school. Is that a limitation of my BD? Or an expression of my voluntary, chosen dependence to live well? Learning about my illness has made me better able to manage it.

While teaching in alternative school, I met a sixth grader who was just beginning to learn to manage his dual diagnosis of ADHD and ODD (operational defiance disorder). Teachers described Allen as a problem child and behavior concern. Allen's mindset was, "I have this problem. I get mad when people tell me what to do." Administration trained us in de-escalation strategies for students with aggressive or violent tendencies, but what Allen really needed was a growth mindset to replace the internal narrative, "I can't control this. It's my ADHD's fault."

Presence of a disability doesn't abdicate us from responsibility. No, quite on the contrary, for a person with BD, ADHD, or another condition affecting everyday life, it demands we find strategies we haven't tried yet, day after day, lifelong—commiserate with our disorders and illnesses. Diagnoses give us access to resources we can use to set personal goals, and a growth mindset helps us achieve them. In part four, I'll consider this from a spiritual perspective.

A growth mindset reframes our response to bad behaviors, bipolar or otherwise. It says, "Ooops, I did that, but I have strategies to come back now," or, "I can learn to be more successful accommodating for my deficits." Reframing thinking in this way turns challenges into opportunities to change and setbacks become an expected part of the learning process. A growth mindset better positions us to recover from challenges and progress tenaciously toward goals.

A growth mindset is a friend to those on the mood disorder spectrum, assuredly. Let's be realistic. If we've been diagnosed with BD, we've probably already faced a lot of challenges. Given this is a lifelong relationship, we're going to face a lot more. Reframing the world from the starting point of a growth mindset empowers a move from victim to manager.

In *Growth Mindset, Resilience, and Grit: Harnessing Internal Superpowers for Student Success*, Dr. Raychelle Cassada Lohmann's emphasizes the importance of teaching children how to express their emotions through words. "As students grow up, not only will they have this language," Lohmann writes, "they will likely have healthier relationships because they can engage in emotional expression."[107] This emotional literacy serves us well on the mood disorder spectrum at any age.

Hope is paramount when possible diagnoses greet us. The average onset for major depressive disorder (MDD) is the mid-twenties; on the other hand, minor depressive disorder (a less severe depressive state) has an early onset, under age twenty-one. Is it possible intervention at the minor stage in adolescents prevents major depressive disorder from developing as adults? What about other disorders? Generalized anxiety disorder can start in childhood, and although BDI has a mean onset of age twenty, according to the APA, BDI and BDII occur in school-aged children, with cyclothymia typically starting in adolescence.[108]

Early intervention matters. How we think about ourselves and our labels informs our perceived quality of life. When that doctor back in Nashville said I had bipolar tendencies, I ran from the suggestion for a decade. Even when I eventually faced the truth, my response was largely to hide in shame, give up on my dream of a family, and accept BD would keep me from fulfilling my goals; I was hopeless. Reframing the way we see ourselves in relation to a potential diagnosis matters as much as any external trigger for stress or calamity—a growth mindset positions us to respond appropriately to new labels. Believing we have agency breeds hope.

How do we cultivate hope as extension of the growth mindset? My stepdaughter recently came home from school with a vision board she made during her girl's lunch group with the counseling office. Cali included words and pictures that encompassed her vision of what she wanted her life to embody. She glowed as she explained the significance of different choices. She was excited, optimistic, and hopeful in the present about the future self she is cultivating now. Goal-setting exercises, positive affirmations, and self-reflective journaling are some more easy ways to encourage the mindset necessary for gritty transitions.

And what's more effective than modeling the growth mindset? As we model these values in everyday reactions and reframe thinking through growth mindset, we can develop into confident, capable individuals who can better navigate adversity, with or without a diagnosis, no matter what age we begin. Winston Churchill likely struggled with BD, as explored in chapter ten. Without considering his family history of mental illness and his own experience losing two relatives to suicide, others suggest ADHD. Either way, Churchill knew the secret to struggle *and* thrive with a mental affliction is a growth mindset. To illustrate, I'll piece together several favorite quotes attributed to Churchill to create a motivational speech from beyond the grave.

"Attitude is a little thing that makes a big difference," he says. "If you're going through hell, keep going. Success consists of going from failure to failure without loss of enthusiasm," Churchill cautions. "The price of greatness is responsibility over each of your thoughts." Dramatic pause. "Success is not final, failure is not fatal: it is the courage to continue that counts." Winston Churchill models the core values of an early mental health ambassador and embodies the growth mindset I aim to make contagious.

Informing: Teaching What I Wish I'd Known

With modeling and reframing as my foundation, I discovered four more ways to put my advocacy into practice in everyday life. Stigma exists largely because we are misunderstood. I've seen from experience: awareness creates empathy and breaks down the barriers ignorance built. Whether I'm home or in the classroom, I see the power of informing to unite two core values where one fuels the other. It begins with a commitment to educate others about mental health issues, but combating stigma is just one face of a two-sided coin. We also need to recognize signs of emotional distress to promote understanding that leads to accessing resources.

One of my friends recently objected to a comment I made about writing this chapter. "Kids can't have bipolar," she'd interjected confidently. Practicing my BD self-management baseline of starting any argument with an assumption that the other person could be right, even if that likelihood is infinitesimal, I held my tongue and considered this carefully. My first student teaching placement was in fall of 2005. Nearly twenty years later, I can admit sometimes, though rarely, I've inherited a student with an accommodation for BD, specifically. Instead, school-aged children with a "diagnosable but unspecified emotional, behavioral, or mental disorder" severely impacting development ability are given the label emotional disturbance (ED).[109]

Children who live with conditions like anxiety, depression, BD, OCD, and PTSD all fit within an ED designation. Typically, I learned one of my students was struggling with symptoms of disorder by a combination of logging observed symptoms over time and personal conversations in context of established relationships where my student confides in me the diagnosis, a huge step in self-advocacy. Students with ED qualify for special education services, so if kids have been properly categorized, schools are required, by law, to help them be successful beyond disabilities.

In short, early diagnosis leads to government-sponsored supports I did not get access to as an adolescent. My stepdaughter just started an Individualized Education Plan (IEP) halfway through her eighth-grade year. Cali could identify that trying to reach her goals while fighting ADHD symptoms made her feel anxious and stressed. This IEP permits

Cali to take assessments in a small group setting with fewer distractions and use a number line on the end of course test for math. In place of one elective, Cali attends a skills class where she learns to accommodate for her ADHD in strategic ways. I'm proud of the strides Cali makes daily to champion her future.

Promoting awareness in the community is paramount. Those adults who associate regularly with children are the first line of intervention. Calista had a diagnosis of ADHD before we met; in fact, I attended her eligibility meeting for services on my fifth date with Tony. For seventh grade, we secured a 504 plan, which gave her access to supports to help her with adjustment issues in the short term. For example, Cali carried a check-out sheet to and from school each day. Her teachers ranked her behavior, attention, and assignment completion, noting upcoming assessments. She passed math for the first time since third grade. Establishing that link between school and home gave us the data we needed to implement an IEP this year, continuing supports provided from her 504 while giving her access to an additional forty-five minutes of math skills tutoring each week.

The transformation in Calista's character is well documented. In sixth grade, without accommodations, Calista missed thirty days of school and was tardy thirty days. She was best known for walking around school in her burrito blanket and sleeping or drawing during classes. She anxiously picked at her fingers, telling herself the same story every day, "I can't do math because of my ADHD." Her father manages life with ADHD; because he knew what signs to look for, Tony got Calista tested in sixth grade. The diagnosis explained the symptoms he'd observed. And when I came into the picture at the start of seventh grade, I knew what to do with that diagnosis.

Within the context of a family learning to support her development—imperfectly, with our own mental health challenges often complicating things—combined with 504 and IEP accommodations at school and a trusted therapist she loves seeing every other week, Calista has blossomed, as her guidance counselor put it. School is no longer a scary place she hates going to or something she must survive. Informing invested parties about Calista's ADHD and the way it impacts her learning created a safer environment in classrooms. She looks forward to school, made A/B honor roll last spring, and worries only that catching a cold might keep her from going. If Calista is drawing in class, it's a good sign she got lost, and her teachers can redirect her attention. That's a part of her IEP. The anxiety around school is gone. Cali's got a powerful team of adults encouraging her as she advocates for herself.

By the end of eighth grade, Calista would pass all her end of course tests on her first attempt, even math, but getting there took more than our combined willpower. Awareness about her disorder and its impact was the beginning of acquiring the services Calista would need to surprise herself at the successes she unlocked. God guided us to just the right professionals to intervene and change the story Calista told herself about her limits and abilities.

How do we raise awareness so other parents and teachers can help identify early warning signs and get support for navigating challenges before bigger issues develop? Untreated, Calista's ADHD significantly damaged the way she viewed herself. Her absences, tardies, and the burrito blanket evidenced a child who had shut down, withdrawn, and given up. These behaviors were symptoms of a bigger problem. We need to know what mental illness looks like to identify it.

We can collaborate with existing organizations to raise awareness in our communities. Many brochures, guides, and resources for families are available for free. The National Alliance on Mental Illness (NAMI), Depression and Bipolar Support Alliance (DBSA). Mental Health America (MHA), The Anxiety and Depression Association of America (ADAA), Child Mind Institute, and the National Institute of Mental Health (NIMH) offer comprehensive sets of awareness resources on their websites for free. I've connected with the local NAMI chapter president to partner with them as I consider starting a DBSA chapter in Virginia, making possible in-person support groups for individuals with mood disorders and their loved ones or caregivers in my state.

With little to no financial investment, we can educate and raise awareness by sharing information about mental health issues in schools, community centers, and online platforms. When we explain what mental health is, explore common issues faced during adolescence, highlight the warning signs of severe mood episodes, and connect our school-aged children with necessary support services, we grow mentally strong men and women. Equipping them with clinical knowledge is a step toward hope they'll realize they are fearfully and wonderfully made, too.

Normalizing: It's Okay to Not Be Okay

In addition to cultivating empathy, when we choose to share stories of other's personal mental health journeys, maybe even share our own, that begins the work of our next strategy: *normalizing*. We need to make conversations about mental health and well-being a standard part of daily living. In doing so, we create an environment where kids like my stepdaughter feel safe expressing their feelings and seeking help, understanding mental health is as important as physical health.

In parts one and two of this book, we emphasized the role that stigma plays in keeping us from getting help for symptoms of a mood disorder. I'm modeling this strategy by writing this book, owning my disorder and the life story it wanted to tell. Ultimately, normalizing mental health conversations dismantles barriers to care and promotes a culture where getting help is encouraged. This is how we change the cultural narrative surrounding BD and other disorders.

How do we apply the strategy of normalizing in everyday life, regardless of profession? It starts with open expression. Authenticity breeds trust and encourages a reciprocal response. When I spent one schoolyear in alternative school, I changed the way I saw labels. Kids came to me, age twelve to eighteen, with lots of different labels. Beneath them were children struggling massively with life's challenges, internal and external, with names and gifts and origin stories. Their labels opened the doors for conversation.

When we know we have a diagnosable condition that interferes with our daily functioning, we're not primed to stand on a stage and broadcast this news. On the contrary, we hope no one will notice we're struggling to perform or behave in a way appropriate to the situation. We pray our incessant foot tapping doesn't call unnecessary attention to our anxious undercurrent. We want control, want to be normal, want to pursue our dreams, and something inside is holding us back. Getting diagnosed, like Calista, also means getting access to tools that will help children take control, boost self-esteem, and pursue dreams unfettered. Knowing we have a condition means accepting we need help.

In alternative school, I used students labels to better understand their words and actions. I shared openly about my own mental health struggles when it was relevant to conversations with the kids. One of my students was diagnosed with BD; Addy was everyone's favorite student because she was in a very stable mood state during her time with us. When my old beaux Joshua died of a heart attack, I missed school to attend his memorial service. I blogged about this experience and chose to read this to my students when I came back. The kids were silent and well-behaved. I normalized grief and depression while showing them faith doesn't eliminate pain, but it is a companion to walk alongside us through it. Many could relate to losing someone they loved. Addy wrote me a note letting me know how I'd encouraged her. She started following my blog after that.

What if more people were willing to be so transparent and vulnerable? I imagine a future generation comfortable expressing emotions without fear of judgment, understanding vulnerability is not weakness, just a reflection of the courage God gives us to be authentic with one another. Instead of conforming to societal expectations, young people can choose the road not taken when it fits them best. Normalizing mental health discussions will, invariably, dismantle the stigma surrounding mental health topics today.

In short? People will be more likely to own and share their struggles and get access to the help they need, a natural byproduct of a vulnerably authentic culture.

What's more, we need redefine what's considered normal. Near daily, I'm confronted with the statistic that one in four people are affected by mental illness. I counted forty people at the gym this morning. Statistically speaking and using the terms that contribute to stigmatization, ten of us are mentally ill. "Normal" defines the characteristics which society deems ideal. Herein, normal encompasses a worldview that situates mental wellness as that ideal standard.

In 2023, Paige Lau published a manuscript entitled "Mental Illness, Normalization, and the Construction of the Abnormal Subject." Grounding her work heavily in contributions of French philosopher Michel Foucault, Lau examines the way we categorize subjects into healthy and unhealthy, thereby fundamentally shaping how they experience and express their mental illness. Lau observes that the "norm" describes an ideal type.[110] The normal subject, then, is only ideally and subjectively normal. Likewise, I am only anti-idyllically, subjectively abnormal.

Lau discusses normalization's dual nature—how it individuates while simultaneously imposing conformity. Consider the treatment of conditions like borderline personality disorder (BPD) and autism spectrum disorder (ASD), where therapeutic interventions focus on modifying behavior to align with societal expectations. [111] Mental illness is often treated with normalizing procedures aimed at transforming individuals to fit societal standards.

When I challenge the mental health ambassador to normalize mental illness, what I'm really asking for is a change in that ideal standard that constitutes normal. After all, for one out of four of us, it's normal to be abnormal, normal to be mentally ill. Moreover, the ideal of "normal" is subjective to each human experience, yet a pervading message about normalcy is an absence of mental illness. Like the visible, abnormal behavior patterns that can be modified to be made more ideal, the ideal of normalcy can be modified to more accurately reflect a reality that mental health is a continuum.

I will get a list of students with special education accommodations before I greet my next class. In a sea of a hundred sixth graders, there will be students, statistically speaking, struggling with mental health concerns without any supports. At home and at school, I commit to normalizing early mental health issues by providing the space to talk about it, modeling by example, and encouraging further dialogue. As an English teacher, it will be easy to incorporate topics that support mental health initiatives, to be further explored in a subsequent section. Choosing texts about coping and resilience-building strategies, providing tools for stress management and emotional regulation, and introducing mindfulness or journaling techniques all reinforce the message that it's normal to not be normal.

Ultimately, the goal is to destigmatize seeking help and teach children healthy coping mechanisms for managing their emotions. "Normal" becomes more accurately representative of people as on a spectrum of mental wellness—capable of being *more* or *less* "ill" through intentional management—and those mentally ill gain supports to stabilize them on intellectual and relational playing fields.

Counseling: Techniques from the Therapist's Toolkit

A person living with a mood disorder or loving a person with a mood disorder should learn some simple counseling strategies for several reasons. First, these techniques help us establish trust; when we feel heard and understood, we are more likely to open up about the internal struggles others can't see. Secondly, learning these techniques improves communication skills, guiding us to make meaningful conversations of routine interactions. Moreover, using basic counseling skills gives us opportunities to recognize signs of mental distress and respond with appropriate resources. Finally, these intentional strategies of thinking about thinking help us regulate and function better ourselves.

While these counseling techniques are powerful tools for managing our daily struggles, I've found they serve a deeper purpose in my life. When our minds are spinning in chaos—from mood episodes, ruminating thoughts, or overwhelming emotions—it's nearly impossible to engage meaningfully with anything beyond our immediate crisis, including our relationship with God. These practical strategies help stabilize our thinking and calm the unquiet mind, creating the mental and emotional space where authentic spiritual connection is possible. In part four, I'll explore how learning to manage my bipolar symptoms with counseling techniques ultimately opened the door to a faith relationship I never knew was waiting for me.

Using Scaling in Everyday Relationships

The first I'll explore here is called scaling, a solution-focused brief counseling approach. The idea here is that since our thoughts, feelings, and behaviors are abstract, it's hard to qualify their impact or severity. For a child who struggles with fractions, cutting a pie into four parts makes concrete this abstraction. In the same vein, we can use scaling questions to make our thoughts, feelings, and behaviors more concrete, and therefore, manipulable like fractions.

The heart of the scaling technique is empowerment via a sense of control where we can take ownership of our forward development. We ask a line of questions, starting with assigning an initial rating on a scale. Based on that ranking, we ask questions to determine what is necessary to move to a better number. Scaling techniques enable us to set goals for change and measure our progress toward accomplishing those goals.[112]

I recently had an opportunity to try this out with my stepdaughter. A friend gifted her chocolates on the last day of school before winter break. I might have warned her that bragging about those chocolates to my husband invited imposition of a "parental tax" where Tony is entitled to a piece of anything Calista brings into the house. It started off with cheerful giggles, but the tug of war in my kitchen escalated quickly when Tony raised a fist full of chocolates in the air, signaling victory.

Tony was still breathing hard and laughing; our thirteen-year-old was not amused. She screamed at her father and stormed out of the kitchen. I heard her stomp away. "What just happened?" I asked rhetorically before calling Calista back downstairs. I'd just read Erford's dialogues, one of which used scaling to reduce catastrophic thinking. I thought I'd try it out here.

"Calista, why are you so upset right now?"

"'Cause he shouldn't have done that to me. Those were my chocolates."

"They were your chocolates," I said. "Okay, on a scale of one to ten, with ten being the worst thing your father could do to you and a zero being he does you no harm, where does stealing your Christmas chocolates rank?"

Her emotions were still up at this point. "A seven," Cali retorted. I'm not a trained counselor in this technique, but I felt like her rating was a little high.

"Where would giving you a beating fall on that scale?"

"Oh, he did when I was little. A ten."

"Okay, how about forgetting to pick you up from color guard practice?"

"Like a seven?"

I reframe. "So, giving you a beating would be the worst thing he could do, a ten. Forgetting to pick you up from practice is a seven. You just said that Papi laughing with you in my kitchen pretending to steal your Christmas chocolates was a seven. Are you sure?"

Cali was good at this. Like, wow. "I guess it's not really a seven." By this point, all the processing had moved Calista to a calmer, more reflective state.

"Okay, so on a scale of one to ten, with ten being the worst thing your Papi could do, how bad was it when he tried to steal your chocolate?"

"Like a three."

"Wow, a three. So, he still messed up, but he can come back from a three, right? I mean he gave you back the chocolate. What would it take for him to get back to a one right now?"

Again, this wasn't a textbook execution, but as an experiment, it was effective. Calista was able to admit that her reaction was out of proportion to the catalyst, and when we further assessed that she was bloated and irritable beforehand, I got out a calendar. Calista's new to the PMS club, and this dialogue helped us make sense of the situation. Using the scaling technique saved family night. Instead of brooding in her room, we watched a Christmas movie together.

I started using the scaling technique with myself and wish I'd learned it sooner. I catch myself using it throughout the day to rank the severity of events or emotions so that I can figure out what needs to be done to move to a better number. Besides reducing catastrophic thinking to which I am most utterly prone, I can use scaling to assess my motivation for changing, getting on the same page in personal relationships, and even guiding suicidal assessments.[113]

Scaling isn't just restricted to numbers, either. I could use scaling pictorially, where I include emotions that fit on a continuum and visually represent them with cartoon faces or emojis ranging from frowning to smiling, for example. We start by identifying our starting emotion. Then, we identify our desired emotion. Finally, we determine the steps it will take to move to, or at least closer to, the desired emotion.

My husband and I developed a mood monitoring system for my BD I suppose would be considered a variant of the scaling technique using colors instead of pictures. On a scale of the rainbow, red is my worst mood state, purple is my occasional best, and I target the more neutral states of green and blue. Anger, shame, and grief fit in red. Fear, worry, and self-doubt in orange. Sadness, apathy, and jealousy in yellow. Neutrality, courage, and pride in green. Acceptance, willingness, and love in blue. Peace, joy, and enlightenment in purple.

It might sound silly if someone's walking by eavesdropping and my husband says, "Babe. You're in the red right now. Let's get you to green." He can also tell me, "I don't like your energy right now. Find a better color," and take his freedom to exit the room to keep me from crossing preset boundaries. Outside of the context of intentionally managing bipolar mood swings, one could mistake Tony's words as offensive. Not at all. Our scaling rainbow helps Tony make concrete that which is abstract so I can make the progress I committed to make. In moments like this, Tony's a coach, maybe even a counselor.

Still, I have to be honest: he's also human. He has his own battle with depression, and he doesn't always remember to use our tools. Some days he's my greatest support; other days his own struggles collide with mine in ways neither of us expected. We've had fights where his ring comes off and he says things that wound me deeply. We are two broken people trying to love each other, and some days we fail spectacularly. That's the reality of two people with mental health challenges trying to love each other well. It's why I can't make Tony my sanctuary—he was never designed to carry that weight. Only God can be my constant.

I wish I'd learned scaling twenty years ago. How many meltdowns could I have avoided? How many relationships might I have saved if I could have said, "Wait, is this really a ten, or am I just having a red day?" Still, I'm grateful Calista gets to learn this now, at thirteen, instead of figuring it out in her forties like her stepmom did.

Self-Disclosing to Disarm and Inspire

The scaling technique opened my eyes to how simple counseling tools could transform family dynamics. That's when I discovered another powerful technique. Fundamental to the effectiveness of my class management skills in middle or high school settings is knowing what's happening outside the four walls of my classroom that kids might bring inside with them.

For example, one day in the spring during our poetry unit, sixth graders entered my class buzzing about the latest news: the "couple" in our last block class had broken up earlier in the day. A few students wrote about it in their warm-up journals, including the girl who'd been "dumped"; one even shared aloud, without naming names, and the air was thick with the adolescent-sized white elephant in the room.

We'd been analyzing poetry. We were ready to start writing it. I pivoted. I jumped on the breakup story as inspiration for writing a poem. I told the kids about getting dumped when I was fifteen and how my boyfriend moved on to my best friend next. To an outsider, this might seem like an overshare; this self-disclosure had a purpose, though. I didn't know it was a counseling strategy, but what better way to normalize emotions than letting them know their rockstar teacher struggles, too? What better way to destigmatize being dumped? This was just the beginning of the self-disclosure lesson.

We brainstormed a chart on the whiteboard of possible thoughts and feelings during a breakup. Then, I wrote a quick poem about my breakup while students shot ideas at me for each stanza, modeling what they'd do next. Kids spent the next half hour writing poems, individually or in partners or in teams (based on level of comfort doing so), all about breakups. As it turns out, the recently single halves of a couple weren't the only ones familiar with heartbreak in that class; my share encouraged openness. In addition to normalizing emotions, self-disclosure lets us highlight coping strategies that work well in similar circumstances, practical tools others can use to work through a challenge—like writing a poem about it. Essentially, my transparency built a trust that put kids at ease sharing their own feelings and experiences.

There's two ways of implementing self-disclosure in a counseling setting. The first is in the way I just narrated with the sixth-grade breakup in poetry class. We share a personal experience to improve someone's perception of her current, similar situation; we normalize her struggle or validate her feelings. The second involves counselors sharing feelings they have during the session of those reveals will help counter negative self-concepts.[114] In other words, a counselor intentionally discloses specific thoughts, feelings, or experiences if he or she feels doing so will empower the client.

To begin, I've experienced firsthand the power of intentional self-disclosure in the counselor-patient relationship. Dr. Bogin and I met in his office in Syracuse for a year and a half. He had treated a sibling ten years prior and knew my family in a professional capacity. He did not regularly disclose personal details to me, such that when he did, it was significant. He was seeing me to work through what he called a situational depression caused by divorcing my husband and leaving a decade of adult life behind in Nashville. I was resetting in New York, but I didn't want to restart my life there.

Within the context I was frustrated my life didn't look like what I thought it would look, Dr. Bogin asked me if I knew he'd left Syracuse, had moved down south, and hadn't planned to come back? He proceeded, with only relevant details, to share about losing everything during Hurricane Katrina and returning to this position where I'd meet him in this office in New York every week—lightbulb—in a life that probably didn't look like he thought it would look. He'd struggled and lost, so he could relate. He was living a new normal like I would have to do now.

The above is an example of how Dr. Bogin used self-disclosure to normalize my struggle, validate my feelings, and give my perception a subtle but effective subjective redirect. There were also occasions where Dr. Bogin gave me some insight into his personal feelings. I can picture him peering out from behind his round wire rims inscrutably, eye gaze directed at me in active listening, a pen in one hand occasionally recording details in a notebook. Most often, Dr. Bogin's facial expressions and body language reflected a neutral posture during our hour together. And most often, when he spoke, it was to ask a question prompting me to talk more.

One day, I caught Dr. Bogin chuckling, briefly and uncharacteristically, at something I'd shared. I flipped the script and posed the question for a change. "Dr. Bogin, do you like working with me?" I asked. He put down his pen, and with it, temporarily lowered the veil. He told me that he did enjoy our sessions and noted a few specific things, like the depth of discourse and my progress, which made me believe he was genuine. In future sessions, Dr. Bogin's occasional, little laugh became synonymous with, "He likes working with you." I don't know if that was intentional.

It was not until after I interviewed at a Hampton-area high school in the summer of 2014 and told Dr. Bogin I was moving to Virginia come August that he disclosed more personal information. Dr. Bogin said he felt I was ready for this move and for this therapy to end. During our final session a couple weeks later, he gave me his email address with instructions to reach out and check in and a promise that he'd make time for a virtual session if I needed one. That's also when Dr. Bogin disclosed he'd been my neighbor for many years. We could see his house up the street from my parents' kitchen window.

I tried a few therapists over the years, but no one really measured up to the bar of excellence Dr. Bogin had set. When Tony challenged me to tame my temper and I had to accept my BD was winning, I made an appointment with a therapist online at Grow Therapy. In our first virtual session, I told Renee I all but believed that, with Dr. Bogin's passing, I'd lost my shot at quality therapy and would never find someone as good. "He made me feel the opposite of damaged," I informed her, "and I felt like he genuinely enjoyed our sessions."

Renee accepted the challenge. I respect the way she incorporated that success predictor into our professional relationship. She employs the self-disclosure technique occasionally with facial expressions or the insertion of a feeling. At the end of two particularly challenging sessions, Renee has closed with, "I'm proud of you for..." finishing the phrase with specifics related to progress marked during those sessions. She laughs at things Dr. Bogin would have laughed at, but she also mentions how things I say about myself make her feel, another feature of the self-disclosure technique. For example, if I string together a bunch of negative self-perception statements, Renee might interject, "I'm sad when I hear you say those things about yourself." I'm subtly redirected to replace that negative inner monologue with a better one.

On two occasions, Renee has used the self-disclosure technique sharing personal experiences related to navigating in-law family dynamics. Like Dr. Bogin, she never shares names, as her attempt is not to bond us in familiarity but to validate my feelings and normalize my struggle. I was concerned that going back to the classroom would prevent us from continuing our sessions, but Renee just posted new hours of availability that fit mine. At our last session, I bit my tongue when tempted to ask why her hours had changed, having studied the self-disclosure technique and now understand the effective boundaries therapists maintain.

I seek to model myself in relationship with others after Dr. Bogin and Renee. Given that I am prone to ramble, I think these stories provide a sensible framework of guidelines for how the everyday person can use self-disclosure as a counseling technique to help kids think critically about their problems and foster a growth mindset. Remember, our personal experiences and feelings are relevant to the extent they improve context for forward growth. We can disclose with facial expressions and body language, and feedback given as expressions of praise works best when tied to observable evidence, concrete rather than abstract, and is not overused.

Finally, self-disclosure is at the heart of the support group setting. Since none of us are qualified therapists, every meeting opens with an overview of the rules. We cannot make suggestions of what people should do, just describe our experience in a similar situation. I've landed in a small group with the same gentleman several times now. I'll call him Ernest because he is clearly earnest in his commitment to learning strategies for self-management in life with a mood disorder. In this group, participants ask for guidance about particular problems and other participants respond. Following suit, Ernest typically quickly sums up a relatable scenario, then offers practical suggestions that worked for him.

One week Ernest described his experience with CBT, and I could relate. Another week, he mentioned the acronym DIGFAST, a mnemonic device for recognizing the symptoms of mania. Nassir Ghaemi, author of *A First-Rate Madness*, explores this acronym in his book *Mood Disorders: A Practical Guide*. The letters stand for distractibility, impulsivity, grandiosity, flight of ideas, activity increase, sleep deficit, and talkativeness. We can use SIGECAPS for recognizing depressive symptoms: sleep, interest, guilt, energy, concentration, appetite, psychomotor, and suicide.[115] Doctors use these criteria to diagnose mood episodes, but people with BD and our loved ones can use the acronyms to help recognize warning signs and target early intervention.

It was also through one of Ernest's self-disclosures during DBSA support group that I discovered the 5-4-3-2-1 grounding method I'd adopted for panic attacks was working for other people, enough to include it as a part of the final counseling technique. I imagine it works similarly for Ernest when I share in group; I hope to inspire others it's possible to better manage our illnesses and live well. Ernest and others do the same in our mood management support group setting. Self-disclosure powers group therapy, encourages authenticity and vulnerability, and empowers through narrative reframing.

A little learning goes a long way, admittedly. Might also a little sharing go further than we realized? During support group, I hear God reminding me, "Comfort those in trouble with the comfort you've received from Me."[116] It's humbling, really. Whether I'm telling sixth graders about my teenage heartbreak or sharing my worst bipolar moments with strangers on a screen, the principle is the same: our pain becomes someone else's pathway to healing.

All those years I was just surviving my bipolar chaos, God was preparing me to sit in a classroom full of adolescents and a virtual room with strangers and say, "I've been where you are, and here's help with a side of hope."

A Synthesis of Thought Disruption Techniques to Quell Ruminations

Self-disclosure had been instinctive for me as a teacher. But I learned there was one more tool that could help when minds start spiraling. We've previously discussed how Cognitive Behavioral Therapy (CBT) is used to restructure our thinking and our behavioral responses. For example, I'm prone to catastrophizing, or making mountains of molehills. I'm also prone to jumping to conclusions, being a mind reader and fortune teller, and projecting my worries onto others and the future. Classified as a CBT strategy, the premise of the thought stopping technique is that we disrupt these automatic negative thoughts (ANTs). When we experience them, we say aloud, "Stop." This interrupts the unwanted thought sequence and gives us a chance to choose another, better response.[117]

For decades, psychologists have debated the effectiveness of the thought stopping technique, so I present it here as the first of a few steps to interrupt our negative thinking and replace it with a better narrative. In other words, I agree with researchers who believe stopping an anxious thought isn't enough to keep it from returning, just preventing a person from dealing with the thought.

I'd seen this before with young Allen in alternative school. One day he came to breakfast with a rubber band on his wrist. In traditional school, the elastic would be overlooked; here, however, a rubber band could be weaponized. When I asked him about it, Allen told me his therapist gave it to him. He was supposed to flick his wrist when he started getting anxious to make himself stop.

In theory, this was effective in helping Allen recognize when his anxious thoughts began. On the other hand, I'm not sure he knew what he was supposed to do next. That may have been discussed, but for a twelve-year-old with handicapping aggressive behaviors, identifying anxiety when it hit him was an empowering step, easy to use in public settings where audibly commanding yourself to stop might make you seem nutty. In my opinion, however, the rubber band sting can't be the end.

When you catch yourself thinking nasty thoughts, you say, "Stop it," while snapping your rubber band. Then, you take a deep breath and bring yourself to a calmer place in your mind, substituting positive self-talk. Slowing breathing alone makes me feel calmer and more able to make a good decision.[118] Stopping the thought is the first step. We interrupt the conversation in our brains so we can change it. We also need a new narrative to switch over to in these instances, and taking ourselves to a calming spot in the mind is a form of meditation.

In this section, I propose a synthesis of thought disruption techniques. We'll begin with this traditional concept of thought stopping. Now, let's layer it with the Mindful-S.T.O.P technique featured in Mindfulness-Based Stress Reduction (MBSR) courses. It's a well-known check-in technique for cultivating mindfulness throughout the day. Following the acronym's four steps inside of one minute, we can "log in" with our minds. For this reason, it serves well as a counseling technique anyone can use to deescalate a situation where anxious thoughts disrupt.[119]

Imagine I teach my stepdaughter about this technique, and we encounter a situation where it applies. I might walk her through it a few times before she feels comfortable doing it herself. She says, "Stop," out loud or in her head, and thereby takes the first step in the Mindful-S.T.O.P. technique. She interrupts the automatic thoughts. Then *T*, "Take a breath." A quick breathing exercise calms her body, and alters her physical experience, marking the change occurring. Now *O*, "Observe." She takes inventory of what's happening inside. Finally, *P*, "Proceed." Now that she's stopped, taken a breath, and gained awareness of herself and surroundings, she can reengage appropriately.

As an adult adopting CBT in daily life, I wrote a list of my most common automatic negative thoughts in one column of a chart. In the second column, I wrote positive replacement thoughts for each item in the first column. The concept was similar, only I memorized my flash cards, if you will. If I knew I was inclined to tell myself I was a failure, it helped to combat that negative thought with a pre-set, preferred response, "I've accomplished a lot learning from my failures."

In my experience, thought stopping techniques work best if you've prepared positive replacement affirmations. I didn't use the rubber band method, but I did carry a coin with the serenity prayer imprinted on one side and a butterfly on the other until I lost it. Turning the coin in my pocket turned my inner narrative, allowing me to respond to the ANTs. I think that coin was my first real attempt to blend clinical techniques with spiritual grounding—a combination that would become central to my lifestyle management. In fact, in part four, we'll revisit this strategy from a lens of gratitude in faith.

In the case of a panic attack, however, my prepared scripts hide in the abyss of logical thought, inaccessible to me. It feels like my heart is pounding fast and I can't get enough air. My chest goes tight. I'm lightheaded and start sweating. I feel like I'm losing my grip on reality, about to pass out. I've experienced these with the most common theme of facing a physical ailment that requires emergent care, when late for something important, or when faced with losing a loved one. Before writing my book, I didn't have genuine advice for managing an anxiety attack; I'd been largely unsuccessful.

In the act of writing my book, I learned not only to identify these physical symptoms but to credit them to cortisol production triggered by stress. The attacks don't happen to me: my thoughts cause them. My obsessive, automatic negative thoughts are so profound and all-encompassing that I can activate a fight or flight response in my body akin to a soldier in combat. During a panic attack, I've learned that I can't depend on positive affirmations. This is where I find the meditation alluded to by the counselor in Erford's example most beneficial.

I first learned about the 5-4-3-2-1 grounding technique at a Florida airport by searching for a good meditation for ending a panic attack. I had just recovered from one while driving through traffic that delayed my arrival at the car rental return. I'd been able to stop the thinking, interrupting the train of thought causing the physical symptoms. I took deep breaths, steadying my heartrate. I observed what was happening inside, rejected the train of thought, and focused instead on the cars and exit signs between me and the airport. Now that I was waiting to board a plane, I found it prudent to search for a new tool try out in case I had a panic attack while trapped in a seat in the sky.

Negative thoughts spark an anxiety attack. Begin "Mindful-S.T.O.P.5," my synthesis technique: stop, take a deep breath, observe what's happening inside, and proceed to a five senses check-in. I start by naming five things I can see, then four things I can touch, three I can hear, two I can smell, and one I can taste. This method is easy enough to remember, though I'll add a few tips. If it's dark, it's okay to name physical objects present without turning on a light. If I'm having trouble finding enough objects to name, this prompts me to go outside, the act of which is calming. And in case moving locations isn't an option, I like to keep gum or mints and scented lotions or sanitizers on me just in case I need one thing to taste or smell to finish my mini meditation.

From traditional thought stopping to the Mindful-S.T.O.P. and my addition of the 5-4-3-2-1 grounding technique, we have tools available to make us mindful and self-aware enough to stop negative thinking patterns and replace them with constructive, problem-solving based skills.

These Counseling Tricks Aren't Just for Kids

Though I've been pitching these as tools for helping kids, let's be honest—I needed every single one of these techniques myself. At forty-two. Because apparently nobody taught me how to scale my emotional reactions or stop my brain from catastrophizing every minor inconvenience into a full-blown crisis.

The beautiful thing is, it's never too late to learn. Whether you're teaching a thirteen-year-old how to rate her chocolate-stealing trauma or using the techniques on yourself when you're spiraling about work emails, the principles are the same. And if bipolar disorder lives in your house like it does mine, these aren't just nice-to-have skills—they're survival tools that can mean the difference between a family movie night and everyone retreating to their separate corners.

Integrating: Making it All Click

The final strategy for early mental health ambassadors to affect change is *integrating*. By this, I mean embedding core values like empathy, awareness, compassion, resilience, authenticity, hope, and empowerment into core curriculum areas in the classroom. The method described herein is best enacted by educators or parents wishing to extend learning beyond the classroom, but anyone can advocate for such curricular framework to be implemented in his or her community schools.

My suggestions, therefore, should spark further conversation about what's possible for early intervention and prevention if we support mental health initiatives alongside reading, writing, and arithmetic. Those in a position to teach can teach. Others among us can find and distribute resources to our schoolteachers, asking for representation. I aim to do both, having shaved six thousand words off this chapter by reserving specific curricular integration suggestions for my next book, focusing here instead about ways I've integrated successfully.

Recall the vision boards we can create to promote hope. I incorporated them into an eleventh grade English unit on The American Dream, calling it the "Future Fit Fix" project. We used dozens of old magazines and cut out images the old-fashioned way, but technology could take this project to another level. I modeled the project. I made a vision board full of my hopes and dreams, like getting married and having a child, things I projected into the future I would soon realize.

Really, it was a visual of everything I'd been asking God for in prayer. It's easy to integrate mental wellness into other discipline areas using vision boards.

As a child, I never dreamed I'd be good at math. I much preferred English. That was until eighth grade when I met Ms. Casey. Oh, how patiently she tolerated my ADHD. I had a hairbrush I pulled out in class so frequently Ms. Casey named it Ditzy. It was more like comic relief than admonishment, then, when she told me to put Ditzy away and work out math problems. Her attention didn't stop there, though. She pushed me to join the mathletes competition team and changed the way I saw myself and math. Ditzy was, in a sense, a coping strategy. Ditzy disappeared after our first mathletes competition.

Ms. Casey was a rockstar ambassador who taught me making math work wasn't about being naturally gifted—it was about having someone believe in you. She saw past my fidgeting to the potential underneath. That's the kind of teacher I wanted to become. Moreover, now it's the kind of advocacy I want to spread. Every child deserves his or her own Ms. Casey.

As a career English teacher, I've used my district's curricular framework to guide my course development, and I use what leeway I have to choose literature featuring mental health themes for students to analyze deepens understanding and empathy. Reading an article about the six domains of resilience, for example, is the perfect gateway to begin a unit designed to teach kids they can cultivate resilience in a variety of ways. I would come to use this strategy with my sixth graders at Calista's school while editing these chapters.

The International Center for Functional Resilience (ICFR)
developed a framework for understanding and building resilience called
the PR6 model, which presents six factors that serve as predictors or
contributors to resilience. These include vision, composure, tenacity,
collaboration, health, and reasoning. For someone who lives with a mood
disorder, the composure domain might be problematic, like me.
However, I have a clear sense of purpose and prioritize my physical and
mental well-being, which means I've got the vision and health domains
working for me. My students and I rated our levels of tenacity,
collaboration, reasoning, and the previously listed domains, then
generated ideas for improving strength in weak-area domains. I
convinced three classes of twelve-year-olds, and myself, that resilience
isn't a trait you're either born with or without.

Freewriting is an easy skill anyone use to help process thoughts and
emotions. It's a lot like writing in a journal and can be modified to fit
within time constraints. The restrictions are that it's quiet, no one moves
around, and the subjects keep their pencils moving. They don't have to
worry about spelling, grammar, punctuation, using shorthand, fixing
mistakes, or anything that interferes with their ability to follow their next
thought to the next thought to the next one. In this way, it works a bit
like free association. Freewrites can be focused or unfocused, and it's
easiest to teach this by starting with a focused freewrite where you pick a
starting word like the color blue or memories. I teach my students to use
freewrites like I did, as material for writing poems or songs.

From vision boards to Ms. Casey and Ditzy, from cultivating
resilience with the PR6 model to freewriting for emotional expression,
the integration technique's become the heartbeat of my home and

classroom. God was weaving these tools into my story long before I recognized His hand in it all. When we look backwards with purpose to what we lacked as adolescents or what empowered us, to the contents of our prayers, we see what's needed to reshape mental wellness in the next generation.

How this Spotlight Ends Bipolar Disorder Spectrum Stigma

When all is said and done, our labels remain. From our perspectives, they are firmly in the spotlight. As we conclude part three, does the BD brand flash in neon red, causing fear of exposure and stunting progress?

Or have we subtly moved beyond that, challenged to take up a torch as advocates who can say with some confidence now, "I'm not ashamed of BD. This label isn't a punishment; It's a lens through which those diagnosed can see themselves clearly." Armed with self-education and management techniques, there's no reason why a person on the mood disorder spectrum can't expect to live better tomorrow than in the past. I hope to change the way people like us are perceived and received.

It begins, as explored in chapter eleven, with turning the course and seeing ourselves and our illness from a new paradigm. We weaken the negative ties to BD by making a choice to live intentionally and responsibly with the brain-body chemistry we have and encouraging those we love to do the same. Collectively, such choices will rebrand our disorder and dismantle competing misconceptions, but those diagnosed with BD must accept a voluntary chosen dependence and commit to rely on necessary supports such as medication, routine and steady balance in the sleep-diet-exercise trifecta, and trusted others' perspectives to evaluate stability.

Ultimately, chapter eleven surveys the impact of accepting a personal responsibility to manage our mental wellness culminating in a challenge to take up the torch to end stigma as bipolar ambassadors. I present a mission to support those affected by fostering understanding, breaking down stigma, promoting open conversations, and cultivating a climate of acceptance. I outline seven core values requisite to such a mission: empathy, awareness, compassion, resilience, authenticity, hope, and empowerment.

In the next chapter, I both broadened and narrowed my scope, focusing my efforts on ways to change the face of mental health and wellness for the next generation. As early mental health ambassadors armed with the same seven core values, we can opt to harness the power of six techniques to champion the whole spectrum of mental wellness in ourselves and our loved ones: modeling, reframing, informing, normalizing, counseling, and integrating. If we can teach kids how to think about thinking, they'll better navigate inevitable conflicts.

I believe it's necessary to teach mental wellness alongside academic subjects; until that's the standard, we must fill the void ourselves. The most actionable strategy to prevent broken men and women is to teach ourselves and our loved ones how to think critically about thoughts and emotions now. These six strategies transformed me from someone hiding my bipolar diagnosis to someone proudly carrying the torch for others. Each technique I learned for helping kids also helped me manage my own mental health better. That's the beautiful thing about advocacy: when we lift others up, we lift ourselves, too.

These strategies—from scaling techniques to growth mindsets, from self-disclosure to advocacy—have transformed not just how I manage my bipolar disorder, but how I see my place in the world. Yet, while I've been learning to carry this torch somehow proudly and humbly, I know the light I'm holding isn't entirely my own. There's been a source of light and life—steady as a sunrise, faithful as dawn. In part four, I'll share how my journey from the shadows of stigma led me to a call to advocacy and respite in a sanctuary for the bipolar brain.

Part Four: Finding Hope—The Source of Light

Chapter Thirteen: How Did I Find My Sanctuary?

As I stepped into my role as a mental health advocate—carrying that torch somehow proudly and humbly—I quickly discovered secular strategies and professional techniques, while essential, didn't answer my soul's deepest question: What do I do with all this shame? That source of light and life I'd glimpsed was drawing me toward something I'd been avoiding for too long.

Over the course of the preceding twelve chapters, I prioritized characterizing bipolar accurately and evaluated it through myriad lived experience, contextualized it historically and clinically, and supported it largely with conventional, secular insights. Simultaneously, I've defined myself by this condition. I am a person with BD. Each chapter thus far has developed themes related to living with BD, Christian walk minimized, saving the best part of my story for last, in my opinion. If anything, I suppressed the spiritual lens until now to make possible diagnosis and treatment courses and establish a baseline for everyday living.

In part one, I surveyed life in the darkness, before a diagnosis switched on the bulb that made everything make sense, illuminating progressive symptoms of mood states of BD to make diagnosis possible. In part two, I unpacked what it's like to be diagnosed and explore treatment options. I outlined necessary supports of medications, doctors, therapists, and self-management strategies. In part three, I examined how we can change the way our illness is perceived and experienced moving forward, again in a secular context. I began by detailing a commitment to live well as positive, contributing members of society and called others to advocate similarly.

In essence, to change the way BD is perceived and experience, we begin by accepting the personal responsibility to manage our illness that our diagnosis demands. We change the stigma at an individual level. Each of us with this condition lives better, lives differently, starting with accepting a diagnosis and beginning a treatment protocol of self-management. We change the stigma by talking about the experience of having a mood disorder or loving someone with a mood disorder. We change the stigma by normalizing mental illness at an early age, intervening with scaffolds of support while kids are still developing their ways of thinking. But there's more we can do to proffer hope to people on the mood disorder spectrum.

My early exposure to God, church, faith, scripture, and worship shaped my worldview and self-concept. I have a profound reverence for God and His creation. For most of my life, I have, in fact, felt tethered inextricably to Him despite a mounting closet of secret shames. We all make mistakes, fail, and fall short of true love and respect. I understood biblical principles and had memorized songs and verses as a child the Lord would whisper into unfilled adult silences. After my diagnosis, I would question how to reconcile my disorder with faith in loving God and find the answer in Jesus Christ, my redeemer and advocate before Him. This tether, this connection, is why I never took my life in the lowest of lows. He never failed to uplift me, and that story's played out in various settings with different supporting characters always to reveal the same theme.

This chapter aims to bridge the often-divided worlds of faith and mental health, inviting readers to reconsider perceptions of BD within the Christian context that they too might find sanctuary for the BD storm in the arms of a loving Savior, the true source of light that illuminates the path toward complete healing. In this world we will have troubles, but I take heart in the One who has overcome the world. The challenges of mental illness beg for unwavering, unconditional love. I call for a faith community who knows how to embrace people like me compassionately and provide genuine sanctuary and support, and I speak vulnerably from personal experience to give Christians the proper foundation to accomplish this goal.

My identity as a Christian is not diminished by BD; rather, my illness powers a divine tether to the God who made me exactly as I am, capacity for alternating cycles of mania and depression included. With these two culminating chapters, I'll show you how I came to believe I was fearfully, wonderfully, and bipolar-ly made.

Breaking the Silence: Faith, Hope, and BD

While it was quite easy to access reputable and reliable sources for other chapters, what's readily available on the intersection of BD and Christianity is slender. There are few individuals with BD repping openly in Christian culture. The loudest stances are antiquated, remnants of earlier positions the church held before more was known about mental illness, echoes of an unproductive focus. Biblical scholars and theologians who wage war between God's word, the Holy Bible, and the APA's word, the DSM, are fighting the wrong battle.

When the church dismisses or minimizes biological causes of mental illnesses, it risks alienating those who struggle and perpetuates a harmful stigma. Moreover, all Christians are humans, but not all humans are Christians. People live with mental illness inside and outside of faith-based settings. The DSM functions to help doctors categorize sets of symptoms to connect people with appropriate supports, not fix their souls. Those categorized by the DSM are a mission field, primed by science for the gospel message. However, if I took the recommendations I've heard from most pulpits, I'd quit taking my medication, abide by a diet of prayer and scripture meditation, and if I wasn't cured of these symptoms, hide in shame and silence.

I've been there. It did not bring glory to God. No, we need to change the conversation around BD in Christian communities. The question should not be about whether a Christian can have BD, if it's real, if it's caused by sin, or if we should take pills. The question should be, "How does a person with BD find sanctuary in Christ?"

Ultimately, the ability to glorify God transcends mental health; the chief end of man is to glorify God, and I do that best on medication. To change the way BD is perceived and experienced, we begin by accepting the personal responsibility to manage the illness that our diagnosis demands. Any religious or cultural school of thought suppressing such a diagnosis handicaps its adherents. If you've had an encounter with a church in the past such as this, I'm sorry. I can relate. Living well with BD started with accepting the diagnosis. That became a label by which I identified myself starting at thirty-six. I am now a person with BD, and the themes thus far have characterized that identity.

I am also a Christian, and that's my primary identity. I've carried it since the age of five. It precedes and supersedes my bipolar label. I am a Christian saved by faith in Christ by His grace. I was a Christian before I was a person with a mood disorder. Now, I am a Christian who also experiences life with BD. I've not been fully truthful, fully transparent about how I manage because I haven't yet commented on that which is most fundamental to who I am, that is who I am in Christ.

Self-affirmations never worked for me. I do not believe that I am good, beautiful, wonderful, and powerful. I could lie about who I was, which never appealed to me. I could not, however, lie about who God was. God is all these things. Researched practices of modern psychology and the best counseling techniques were ineffective, for me, until I adopted my own bridge between worlds: biblical psychology.

In this chapter, I'll disclose the details of my journey walking with God before, during, and after BD diagnosis. Meanwhile, I'll examine common myths about mental illness in church culture, provide mutual ground for Christian leaders and mental health professionals moving forward, and outline a gospel-based biblical psychology approach to navigating life with BD. I aim to encourage those spiritually disillusioned with a renewed understanding of the role of grace in bipolar recovery.

Perhaps you or someone you know has been struggling with life on the mood disorder spectrum and tried combinations of medications, therapists, and other strategies, but like me, failed to find in them a vehicle for dealing with the feelings of guilt, shame, and remorse associated with our illness. Regardless of past experiences with the church, reformation breeds compassion. Biblical counseling bridges the abstract gap between brain and soul. If we've tried it all, but we're still struggling, it's worth considering for a few pages.

Running Toward God or Away from Him

I know without a doubt I was created to worship God. I was born to Christian parents who were raised by pastors in the Pentecostal church. Reading the Bible, praying daily, and attending church were normal routines. Words like "gospel" were introduced alongside identification of numbers and letters. After church one day when I was five, I told my mom I wanted to invite Jesus into my heart, something I had seen other people do at church, and she led me in the salvation prayer.

This prayer did not transform my life. I was five, no habitual sin to abandon, not so conscious of my consciousness. I'd been raised to follow the Ten Commandments. Praying this prayer meant being held accountable to the biblical standard undergirding my upbringing. I would keep learning scriptures, singing worship songs, becoming impassioned by who God was as I learned more about the world He created. No one forced religion on me. Faith came from within. I loved singing praises to the One who made me. I could feel God's presence when I sang psalms and hymns.

It is also important to define a few terms. If you're hearing about mental illness in the context of a sermon, for example, you might hear a pastor say depression is a "sin" issue or a "heart" issue. This can be a huge turn-off for someone who hasn't chosen a Christian way of life. As a child, I understood sin kept me from God. It was why I needed Jesus.

He was perfect, like God, but He was a man, like me. Jesus was my bridge to a holy God. When I lied or lost my temper, I felt terrible inside. In church, we learned to confess our sins to God, and He would always forgive us. Then, I wasn't supposed to feel guilty anymore.

So, when pastors say that mental illness is a sin or heart issue, what they're saying is that all humans mess up. None of us are perfect. A scripture from James often whispers to me: "To him who knows to do good and does it not, it is sin."[120] We've all made mistakes. Other times, we do things we know, deep down, are wrong. We break promises, make white lies, "borrow" paper clips from the office, or cancel at the last minute. We lose our temper, miss a deadline, or forget a birthday. Sometimes, it's hard to judge our own intention, so whether you call it a mistake or a sin, our missteps weigh on our subconscious. What pastors mean when they say mental illness is a heart issue might better be addressed as, "What do we do with the shame that accumulates inside?"

One pastor told me I experience bipolar-like symptoms because I'm running from God. What if I began experiencing bipolar-like symptoms while I was running toward God? In middle school, I started every morning with a devotional, reading the Bible and praying. I hummed worship songs all through the school day. I went to church for other activities throughout the week. I ended every night confessing and repenting my sins. As an adolescent, I wanted to be a good Christian. My sins grieved me. I wanted to please God. If God was pursuing me, I was chasing Him right back. He kept forgiving me, I just somehow kept my shame. I'm not sure why. It may have been an automatic mirror of childhood church culture.

It was, to some degree, a hyper-religiosity that fueled my racing thoughts, and to contextualize my earliest hypomanic endeavors, middle school was characterized by negative symptoms like heightened sexual curiosity, restlessness, and easily triggered temper tantrums. But more prevalent, more time-consuming, more frequent and repeated in my prayer journals and diaries, is an overlayed sense of being chosen by God, called, and set apart for holiness.

When I read the Bible, scriptures spoke to my life personally. Other features that characterize mania—having epiphanies, hearing God's voice, feeling a supernatural euphoria and peace—didn't raise any red flags. Those were the result of having an active, daily relationship with God. In Christian settings, intense emotional expressions are more common and accepted. This can make it challenging to distinguish between behavior considered fervent spirituality or the signs of mental illness.

Nevertheless, at thirteen, my mind raced when I should be sleeping, still convicted about confessed sins and convinced God was rightly punishing me when bad things happened. I'd memorized half the Bible; my nightly rumination script was curated from scriptures, selected out of context, mostly Old Testament themes. I knew God was so many things, but the One I imagined praying to was constantly disappointed by me, grieved by me, and so punitive, rightly standing in judgment of my inability to be without sin.

I still have thirty poems I wrote during middle school, and despite everyone's recollection of me being boy crazy and happy, only four of those poems are about love, and the rest are void of joy, reflecting a girl riddled with worry, shame, and grown-up existential crises of identity, purpose, and meaning. In many, I cry out to God. In some, I long to join Him in heaven. While we were learning to count to ten in Spanish class, I was obsessing over my awareness of the line between life and death, consciousness and unconsciousness, struggling to be a Christian kid in a secular world, fracturing under the pressure.

Starting in sixth grade, I maintained three written logs, which is why I can provide such a detailed account of my concurrent personal and spiritual development. One was a personal diary I typed on the computer and password protected. The second was a journal for daily prayers, devotionals, and sermon notes. The third was a little notebook of poetry, and I'd write in it during recess, on the bus, or in class if my work was finished. Had these been submitted for an English class assignment, my poetry might have been a teacher's cause for concern. I'll share with you my first poem, written at age twelve.

> *The Cliff*
> As the harsh winds blow,
> Against my cold, forlorn face,
> My tears of sorrow fall to the ground.
> The petals of my flower of love,
> Wilting at disappointment.
> The stresses build, forming a rigid cliff,
> Off which I plunge,
> Towards the raging seas below.
> I am swallowed in the deep waves,
> Blinded by the darkness,
> And all signs of light and hope,
> Are carried off with my tears,
> To linger above me,
> Until the moment that my breath of life ceases to exist.

This poem conveys a poignant sense of despair and emotional turmoil, no? Struggle and sorrow. Progresses to disappointment. Burdens

accumulate, emotions overwhelm, and I flirt with the cessation of life, a
haunting culmination. I loved God, and I had an overactive brain,
exhaustively processing the world through a spiritual lens. It did not
occur to me that these ruminations were uncharacteristic of other kids
my age. Rather, I was dubbed "deep" and "mature for her age".

Even Righteous Manic Ventures Yield Consequences

From twelve to thirty, I maintained a daily practice of devotionals,
self-reflection, and writing missives. I brought my concerns to God,
found inspiration in scripture, and wrote down my revelations first in
poems, then in song lyrics and a website. When I was fifteen, I wrote a
book I considered a teen's guide to purpose, Christian living, decision
making, and other controversial issues. It was normal to stay up late
writing these mini sermons. Eventually, I published these a chapter at a
time on website. I was an original blogger, circa 1997.

I led worship at church, was active in Young Life, and operated
from a default identity of: "I am a Christian." Yet, when I look back on
high school, I tend to only remember my sins. They tormented me. It's
easy to overlook the undercurrent of my faith and themes like hope or
resilience. My little brother credits me as inspiring his faith in Jesus, for
example, and I was always grateful God used me despite my weaknesses.
Even in college when I was put on an anti-depressant briefly, I didn't
want to take it and got off it quickly. As a Wheaton College student with
a foundational knowledge of biblical theology, I did not consider mental
illness as a possibility for what I experienced my sophomore year, as
described in chapter one.

In college, I'd stay up all night writing songs or papers during the week. I remember reading one of my professor's books in a single night, Dr. Sam Storms' *Singing God*, then wrote a song with a floormate called *Stupefied* about being entirely consumed by God. I could glorify God by singing to Him, an act of worship expressing my faith and awe, captivated by His goodness.[121] I'd sleep on the weekend.

And again, I made mistakes. I committed sins. I prayed and repented. I genuinely committed to not repeat those mistakes. I'd make it maybe a year between the events of habitual sin, which for me meant crossing lines of physical intimacy, and hit my knees in shame, devastated to have failed God again. I did not understand what grace was, not until much later. So, if someone argues there's a sin element to BD, I'd have to agree. It's impossible to divorce my illness from sin, times where I did something I had a right to feel bad about, something that could come between me and my Maker.

When I'm experiencing hypomania, it's easy to justify my behavior with a religious narrative, believing the heightened state divinely inspired, further veiling diagnosis. It was common to follow my creativity through the night until I was diagnosed and understood the need for a consistent sleep routine. Unable to sleep and inspired by God, I felt it was my duty to follow with action and sleep later, not suspecting a biological cause. Furthermore, what I considered righteous admonishment for my own sin, psychologists call self-harm.

Inspired by a story about Martin Luther, but perhaps under a paranoid delusion characteristic of BD, I believed I could cut my way to forgiveness, four hundred and ninety cuts, seventy times seven, an equation for forgiveness.[122]

Looking back, it sounds nutty, but at the time, I was attending a Four-Square Church, a charismatic setting. A woman prayed for God to heal me of my depression. She laid hands on me, rebuking the evil spirit. The depression did not loosen its grip on my sanity. For another decade to come, well-meaning churchgoers would tell me if I just prayed hard enough and had enough faith, the Lord would expel the demonic intervention that was a result of my sin. This over spiritualizing is a danger, too.

What's more, across high school and college, I read the entire *Left Behind* series by Tim LaHaye and Jerry B. Jenkins, detailing what happens after Jesus returns to take the saints with Him. Reading these books provided imagery for my nightmares and made me aware of a subconscious fear: I didn't feel saved. I wasn't sure I wouldn't be among those left behind. I was always struggling to be holy before a righteous God and failing, daily.

It's futile to draw a line to where sin ends and mental illness begins. The two are fundamentally interchangeable. We live in a fallen and broken world. Mental illness would not exist in paradise. That health conditions we experience today are products of man's impositions on God's original creation I do not question. There is something wrong with my sleep-wake cycle that requires medication. No amount of prayer, meditation, or attempt to live blamelessly changes the fact that, even after a few days, I won't need sleep. Does the sufficiency of Christ preclude me from taking medication? No, medication works in my body, making it possible to work on my spirit. Without medication, I lose touch with reality, unable to bring glory to God.

Edward T. Welch faces this topic head on in *Blame It on the Brain? Distinguishing Chemical Imbalances, Brain Disorders, and Disobedience.* He begins by laying a biblical foundation in part one: "We are created by God as a unity of at least two substances—spirit and body."[123] Welch explains this scripturally using Genesis 2:7. God made man from dust and spirit, these two separate substances to make spirit and body.[124] There is a symbiotic relationship between the two.

So, brain problems expose heart problems. Those busy pointing at one or the other are missing the bigger picture. "Our sins do not always lead to physical disability, and our faithfulness does not always lead to health," Welch writes.[125] Ultimately, BD symptoms did not distinguish between years of faithfulness or wandering. Being able to sleep and think clearly allows me to examine the heart problems. I journaled through manic and depressive episodes. I appear utterly incapable of accurately interpreting scripture in these times.

This struggle highlights the profound intertwined nature of mental and spiritual health; during bouts of depression, my faith clouds. I grapple with doubt. My prayers feel fragmented. I question the essence of my beliefs as I navigate the chaos in my mind. It's as though my connection to the divine is severed, albeit temporarily. I cannot feel God, not even when I sing to Him. It's only when the fog lifts that I can examine my heart issues—recognizing fears, regrets, and desires I might have overlooked in times of instability. For me, stability is best fostered by taking a low dose of a couple different medications. While the medication doesn't heal me, it keeps me from jumping off that cliff I wrote about in my first poem and joining God.

While Welch's book reflects a concern that people will over naturalize mental health issues and, subsequently, undermine the importance of spiritual health, it was my experience that over spiritualizing mental health problems can do just as much damage.

When Refusing to Blame it on the Brain Fails

There were times in my twenties when I can identify my sin and shame as contributing factors to mental instability, but such occasions for prioritizing immediate gratification and earthly pleasures were rare. My hypomania didn't manifest itself in self-serving, indulgent, worldly binges. I binged knowledge and scripture, directed that extra energy and creativity into videos and presentations for church and my classroom. I believed that my purpose was to glorify God by enjoying Him, so this larger-than-life passion simply made sense.

The problem remains: regardless of the object of my manic intentions, there are consequences to working the brain so hard for so long. I never strung together sleepless nights for pursuit of worldly passions; sleepless nights were reserved for righteous causes. I did so try to go sleep. I got in bed, turned out the light, and then the thoughts would race, worry or inspiration. I felt like I had to follow the thoughts in some sort of creative self-expression before I'd be able to sleep. I listened to worship songs and radio sermons, wrote lyrics and poems, and sat outside trying to find stillness.

Eventually, my primary care doctor put me on zolpidem, a sleep aid, and that worked for a couple of years. With regular sleep, I experienced mood stability. I was able to finish my college degree and start my teaching career with few significant mood episodes. I volunteered at the church all week long, and I did not think I had a mental illness. God created us to need sleep, and I was a better person if I slept.

This was my first mistake: taking a pill without examining the root cause. If I needed a pill to sleep, there was something more going on inside that needed to be addressed. Was it shame? Yes. Was it mental illness? Yes. In 2004, I'm not sure anyone was presenting a yes-and position. I did not ask these questions. Nor did my primary care physician. Dispensing was his job. Talk therapy was not. That I need to take medication is a fact I cannot escape. I have tried solely spiritual support, inspired by well-meaning church communities, going off my medication only to find myself amidst another string of sleepless night I wouldn't have gone seeking.

Busying myself in church service over the decades was an effective cover for my illness in its earliest stages. The elevated mood, increased energy, and impulsivity associated with hypomania was interpreted as spiritual zeal. Expressions of enthusiasm and inspiration were positive traits in these settings. When I was married in my twenties, I logged twenty-five hours of volunteer work each week at the church alongside fulltime teaching and taking graduate classes. I felt I could never say no to God.

I did not see the pattern when I was inside of it. I was hyperactive, capable of balancing this crazy load, but then winter blues came calling, and I felt unable to maintain the level of overactivity I had established as "normal". I did not realize my normal was abnormal, that I worked my way into the crash. Hypomania productivity. Depression recovery. I didn't connect my temper to insomnia to ruminations to depression.

They were separate spiritual issues, except for the insomnia, and I took a pill to alleviate that symptom.

My last winter in Nashville tarnishes my memories of the rest of my good life there. I desperately sought God, but I could not feel Him. In the months leading up to leaving my husband, I attended two church services on Sunday, my father-in-law's in the afternoon and Ray Ortlund's in the morning. I devoured worship music, increased my exposure to God's Word, and I believed my depression would lift by such measures, surely. Prompted by my husband, I'd quit teaching to save my marriage. I filled the time with three daily radio programs, a combination of R.C. Sproul, Allistaire Begg, and Ravi Zaccharias. I read six books from Christian scholars and theologians, most recommended by my mom. My depression did not lift.

Truthfully, like other times I'd experienced depression and sought so fervently for God and not experienced relief, I became so utterly spiritually minded that I was of no earthly good. Since I was working only part time as an adjunct professor at a career college, I had time to devote to my spiritual recovery. The six-week winter reprieve between semesters gave me so much time to disappear into spiritual matters that I was unable to make sense of any worldly pursuits when I rejoined society. Sitting at my in-laws watching them cheer for the Cowboys, it seemed suddenly bizarre and futile. Football, Barbie dolls, ice skating, laughter. Everyone unaware of the Creator, adding to Him. I wanted to disappear into an episode of *Dr. Quinn Medicine Woman* out on the pioneer before the comforts of modern technology.

When I was self-assured I had cut out all idols, my first husband's habitual sins shifted easily into focus. I became obsessed with changing him, starting with a change for us both. I suggested we relocate to Greenville, South Carolina or Hampton, Virginia where one of my brothers was raising his family. After all, his niece and nephew were grown, we'd spent a decade with his parents in town, sometimes down the street, and there were little Palmas we barely knew so far away. Though I threw scripture at him about leaving and cleaving[126], he was unwilling to leave his parents and their ministry.

One day at my morning church service, the pastor's wife Jani joined me in the pew after dismissal. She counseled me, reminded me depression was temporary, told me I needed a bigger support system, and assured me leaving my husband was not the answer. Had this been my church home instead of one stop on Sundays, maybe I would have developed my support network beyond relationships related to my in-laws to navigate this better.

My husband really wasn't the problem, though I made him the scapegoat. My mental illness impacted our marriage in profound ways I did not understand until after I accepted a diagnosis many years later. As is the case for most individuals with BDII, the people most aware of the negative symptoms are the ones closest to us. I accused him of imposing cultural limits, making me quit teaching to find a job that didn't consume me so I could be a good wife, focused on cooking and serving. Was it, perhaps, that over the course of our four-year marriage, my husband observed the decline of my mental state, suspected my workaholic teaching style was the cause, and wanted a better-quality life for both of us?

God's Intervention or a Bipolar Delusion

By January 2013, my psychiatrist was concerned about my familiarity with conversations about death. I assured him that I was a Christian, and I was not going to follow through on any actions to take my life. I also saw no harm in praying for an early exit. It's important to note that while I was unaware I had BD, Dr. Bogin received my diagnosis from this doctor. The last few years I lived in Nashville, I thought this psychiatrist was treating me for insomnia. In reality, I was mentally ill, I had BD, and I was prone to moods that would change.

My doctor ultimately added an antidepressant to my antipsychotic medication, convincing me that it couldn't hurt to try it, not unlike praying to die in my sleep, and that it would just be temporary. Had he been cataloguing my mood cycles? Up in the summer, down in the winter? It's a shame psychiatrists don't also do talk therapy. He might have said, "Laura Joy, do you notice this happens about this time every year? You say you don't feel God anymore. Let's unpack that." Medication was not the only support I needed, but until I accepted I had a mental illness and elicited the other measures of support, I was inclined to implode my life. It happened at thirty when I left my husband and again at thirty-five when Fenix arose, but they were two very different experiences.

My birthday in February was the turning point. I had a restless energy, unfamiliar during my depression. I was still on the fringe of society, observing people and wondering why we laugh and cry and feel, very fragmented. In essence, I think the antidepressant had mobilized me to some degree. I'd been praying every night at bedtime a reverse of the little children's prayer, for God to take me before I waked, and that prayer now concerned me. I wanted an answer to escape this desolation. It was not long after I temporarily separated from my husband, believing, for my sanity's sake, that I needed a change even if he was unwilling to join me.

It began as a three-week road trip to find the answer, the first change. I started at my brother's house in Greenville five hours east. I travelled south to Orlando to see my uncle and aunt. Then, I drove the coast west to Baton Rouge and attended a woman's weekend a few hours away with the wife of a childhood friend. Along the way, I asked questions about depression and divorce, faith and doubt, looking for a sign from God that would pull me out of the depths.

The last weekend of my search was the church retreat. I remember singing and being surprised that I felt something. Was God back? I could feel Him again, like as a little girl. The travel had been an adventure culminating in this supernatural experience. The veil lifted. I could see my depression like a demon in the form of my husband. During worship, scripture reading, and prayer, I frenzied. I believed, fiercely, that I was to ask God for permission to exit my marriage. And I did. I wrote it down on a piece of paper and threw it into a firepit symbolically the last night. It suddenly didn't matter if I had biblical grounds for divorce; I had looked into the fire and seen everything clearly.

We were back in Baton Rouge by Sunday. My friends volunteered to help with a homeless ministry that met beneath the overpass. We attended the open-air service that afternoon to help with refreshments, I think, but as is characteristic of manic haze, I can only clearly relay what I wrote in my journals. There were hundreds of people, or it seemed that way. I stood among them, listening to a street preacher moving from person to person, praying over them, ministering to their spiritual needs. That preacher found me in the crowd. He anointed my head and my feet with oil. He told me I could not go back where I came from. He said that door had been closed, but God would open new doors. God had already forgiven me, he said.

I'd prayed and searched so fervently for direction for the "big change" that I believed this was an answer from God, direction for my inner soul that it was time to leave Nashville, my husband, and the life I'd built for a decade. In 2017, I write about this experience in my blog as a time when God's intervention in my life was undeniable.[127] He spoke to me through that street preacher and gave me permission to leave my husband.

I'm sorry, God told me *what*? I believe God interacts with His creation, but would a personal message from God have undermined my marriage vow? Or was it a bipolar delusion?

The reason why I feel that it is best to get a diagnosis for our condition is that once we accept what we're working with, we know what to avoid. I set myself up for a manic episode, from the antidepressants to the three-week southern tour to the worship weekend.

I now question whether God spoke to me that day. It's tragic to cloud cherished memories, but it is also necessary. I'm still sifting through the past for clues to making better choices with the knowledge of my diagnosis in hand. I liked believing God personally intervened in my life, sent me signs, and gave me insights to share with others. I also felt I was a special case, entitled to be held to a standard other than His word. It is difficult to differentiate between times where God's intervention in my life was genuine—miracles, answered prayers, and signs of faith—or bipolar delusions of grandeur.

Discernment's an issue for every Christian, but especially for those of us living with mood disorder spectrum illnesses. Discernment forces me to confront uncomfortable truths about my faith and mental health. My experience has taught me to seek wisdom not just through spiritual experiences but also through the clarity that comes from grounding myself in reality. By relying more on scripture and the counsel of trusted friends, I've begun to redefine what it means to experience God's presence. While letting go of my previous beliefs may seem like a loss at first glance, it's paving the way for a healthier, more authentic relationship with Him—one that depends not on extraordinary experiences but instead on God's unchanging character and unconditional love.

I did not decide to leave my first husband overnight. It happened over the course of a month. One month. That's not much better. So yes, my problem was a heart issue. But it was also a delusional feature of bipolar affected brains. My BD did not make me leave my husband; it contributed, however, to the series of events that led me to believe I had God's permission to do so. I'd like to think knowing I'm inclined to blur the line between reality and imagination and call it divine intervention will help me avoid a situation like this from recurring. Since I can't know that for sure, I prioritize avoiding triggers that could cause me to start spiraling. When I'm not thinking clearly, I don't honor God well.

We Can't Run Away from God

The euphoria of my vision and divine revelation of God was quickly followed by my mother meeting me back in Nashville to pack up my life into a storage unit and drive to New York together with belongings enough for six months. I stopped taking the anti-depressant not long after I moved back into my childhood bedroom in Syracuse on March 17, 2013.

My dreams were colorful and vibrant, alive against the backdrop of a colorless life. I started seeing Dr. Bogin right away. I attended church with my parents, but I didn't feel God anymore, not since Baton Rouge. I applied for a job in Greenville near my oldest brother, didn't get it, and fixated obsessively on the role of prayer until the act itself seemed futile.

From March 2013 to March 2015, there are no poems. No song lyrics. No missives. No inspiration. I worked as a cog in the wheel at a nine to five job. I exercised daily. I fell in love with a guy that wasn't a Christian, met work friends at the bar for drinks, and was truly just a "Sunday morning Christian." I also experienced superior mood stability, perhaps as a direct result of being unplugged from my internal shame narrative. Dr. Bogin and I had deep theological discussions about my beliefs. He didn't need to be a Christian therapist to see the story I told myself didn't match with the young woman he met in his office. I was telling a different story by the time I left his care.

When I finally did move to Virginia, I really was myself again. There weren't signs of mental illness, even in the winter months. I was healthy, whole, happy, and at peace. Spring came and I felt inspired. It was one night in March after dinner with my brother's family. I had to the urge to write about the kinds of things I used to talk about with Dr. Bogin. That became the first entry in my blog, *Writer's Growth*. I broke up with my boyfriend soon after, started attending a church, and eventually did settle down with a Christian guy and Christian walk again. That walk was stable until I was diagnosed with ADHD, taken off my anti-psychotic, and put on a stimulant drug that caused the mixed episode featured in chapter seven.

During the year that followed my manic episode in 2018, I wasn't thinking clearly about anything. Taking the wrong medication protocol so severely impaired my cognitive functioning that I could not examine life. I was so busy facing the consequences of sin as defined by law enforcement in probation, drug education classes, and community service hours that getting up on Sunday for church stopped being a priority. I quit attending services for about nine months. It's the only period in my life I voluntarily opted not to join others for worship service.

I do not think it's a coincidence I was only able to see myself in the mental illness resources in the local library when I stopped interpreting every aspect of my life through a spiritual lens. My illness hid well inside supernatural ideations, but I was ill. One unique feature of antidepressant medications is their ability to confirm a biological element to BD. If you give an antidepressant to a person who is *not* on the bipolar spectrum, he or she will *not* have a manic episode. Only individuals genetically predisposed, those with BD, will experience a manic episode after being prescribed an antidepressant medication.

What I have is in me, this illness, and it can be treated. It skews my judgment. I was running from God, or at least I was trying to. My friend Van used to take me out on his unregistered motorcycle during this time. To say I loved it would be an understatement. It was the ultimate high, cruising down Chesapeake Avenue along the bay, holding tight to Van as he broke speed limits and avoided cops. Even when I was depressed, Van could cheer me up with a quick thrill ride through town.

After getting diagnosed correctly in February 2019, I tried a few medications before returning to quetiapine. A week later, Van took me out on his motorcycle. Only this time, I didn't enjoy it. I was suddenly aware how recklessly he was driving. The earth raced beneath our feet. Nothing was between my shoes and the pavement. I thought of what quick work the asphalt would make of my jeans. I squeezed Van's waist tightly, closing my eyes, only I wasn't holding onto him anymore. I was clinging to prayer. "God protect us both. Protect me. Bring me home alive." He did.

That was the last time I ever got on Van's motorcycle. I didn't know to pray for God's protection when I wasn't thinking clearly, but God had protected me, nevertheless. Now that I knew, I would never get on the back of Van's bike again. I may have tried to run from God, but God can't be left behind. God was always chasing after me, right or wrong brain, right or wrong heart, right or wrong guy, and that's the theme that matters. Van wrecked his motorcycle not once, but twice in the months that followed. And I went back to church.

Finding a Bipolar Sanctuary in Christ

What happened next? I'll save that for the last chapter. First, let me reiterate: the BD diagnosis isn't something to be kept under wraps save for fear of rejection. Conversations in the church needn't be kept hush-hush; let's not tiptoe around mental health issues or pacify outdated beliefs. The common thread through all of this is awareness. It's about owning our stories and refusing to let stigma dictate how we live or how we're seen. Instead of dwelling on whether our faith can coexist with our diagnosis, let's shift the focus to how we can embrace both fully. A person shouldn't need to try reconciling his or her BD with being fearfully and wonderfully made—both can be true, resoundingly so.

Our mood disorder spectrum journeys might be messy (mine certainly has been), but they're also rich with possibilities for connection and growth (and mine has been so, likewise). I suggest we stop playing hide-and-seek with our truths and instead be bold about our realities, inspiring those around us to do the same. True sanctuary is found in honesty, understanding, and compassion—qualities binding us far above any label, qualities born of a Heavenly Father full of grace and abounding in love.

This book is redefining what it means to live authentically and change the narrative surrounding my label one conversation at a time. Will others feel the need to share their own bipolar faith journeys in response? Have I inspired that yet? If not, give me one more chapter. Finding my sanctuary in Christ changed everything—not just for me, but for how I believe the church can respond to others like me.

Chapter Fourteen: How Can the Church Become a Sanctuary for the Bipolar Brain?

Once I found my own spiritual footing with BD, I began to see how the church could become a sanctuary for others struggling with mental illness. Going back to church wasn't, in itself, the answer to my mental health issues. In fact, it would take over a year to find a church community where I'd meet the people God appointed to facilitate spiritual healing in the wake of my BD diagnosis. During that time, I grappled with the challenging narratives I'd internalized—both from society and within the church—suggesting my struggles were a sign of weak faith or punishment for sin.

I was, however, unaware of the insidious narratives echoing in my psyche, so I could not have anticipated changing those inner narratives would be crucial for symbiotic spiritual and mental growth. In this chapter, I'll explore the significant impact reshaping our understanding of self, grounded in biblical truths, can have on our mental well-being. By embracing a narrative steeped in grace, acceptance, and the love of Christ, we can begin to heal the wounds of our past and welcome a new outlook on our present and future, by God's grace.

At least, that's the story God wrote to restore this shattered soul.

How Biblical Counseling Filled in the Gaps

At the time of that supernaturally declared last motorcycle ride with Van, I was attending a big church where it was easy to hide, and I decided to find a smaller community where I could find real fellowship and maybe even begin serving on the worship team again. After trying out seventeen different congregations recommended by Gospel Coalition[128], I found a reformed Baptist church in downtown Newport News, about ten minutes from where I lived.

I made friends with several young women around my age, joined the worship team, attended single's gatherings, and apart from operating under the delusion I'd one day marry one of our church elders, I began to see glimmers of hope: I could be a Christian with BD and be accepted there. It was the first setting in which I shared openly about my diagnosis and related struggles. That's when one of my new friends suggested we try biblical counseling together.

Another member of our congregation was pursuing a biblical counseling certification through the Association of Certified Biblical Counselors (ACBC). I'll call her Abigail, a name that means the source of joy, and she was that for me. Abigail met with my friend and I once a week to try out a counseling technique with us she called the "Strategy to Change Inner Narrative." It was a six-week study, which she developed one week at a time for us to try out.

Abigail said this study was designed for people who have relentless negative dialogues between themselves and God; who have thoughts and actions that don't glorify God that they don't know how to change; who've tried to change but keep responding in ways that bring guilt and shame; or who are struggling to forget sins they've committed. I felt like I fit all those categories.

The core message of Abigail's strategy was that by changing our thoughts, we change our hearts, and that ultimately changes our behavior. Abigail was challenging me to have a relationship with the God who *is*, not the God I'd created in my mind. Embedded within the Holy Bible are scriptures that characterize, accurately, the fullness of who God was, is, and will be. Abigail never encouraged me to go off my medication. She never told me I didn't have a mental illness. Neither did she tell me I could pray it away. No, she convinced me of this: I could honor God despite my illness, or perhaps because of it. My illness itself necessitated a reliance on grace that was new every morning.

If you are a Christian struggling with mood mismanagement problems, taking the opportunity to complete a biblical counseling program like this one might be among the first things you do after getting a BD diagnosis. Taking medications helped me be more stable, but they didn't touch the shame of not being "normal," falling short, and failing God. I needed grace through faith, not works or science.

Daily Grace: Put Off and Put On

One of our homework assignments for the first week in Abigail's counseling course was to memorize Colossians 3:17, but I misunderstood, instead committing to memory the first seventeen verses of this chapter. It was a fortunate error, as I now recall these scriptures at will and often. The passage encourages me to seek heavenly priorities and minimize earthly concerns because, as a Christian, my life is hidden with Christ.[129]

That doesn't mean I become perfect, become like Christ, instantly, as in the manner of justification. It means each day is a process of becoming more like Him. The all or nothing, black or white, critical framework of my mind during a depressive state overemphasizes the spiritual. In all things moderation, even religious study. I couldn't see the forest for the trees. By focusing on being sinless, I was missing the point of the gospel message. I'd never be sinless. I'd never stop needing forgiveness.

Instead, the author Paul calls for a renewal, advising I "put to death" sinful behaviors like sexual immorality, anger, and deceit, recognizing these as remnants of my old self. Instead, I must "put on" virtues like compassion, kindness, humility, forgiveness, and love, qualities reflecting Christ's character. The passage reminds me to let Christ's peace guide my heart, stay grounded in the Word, worship, give thanks, and do everything in Jesus' name.[130] This snapshot of renewal is a sanctuary for souls facing BD and other mood disorders.

Paul instructs us with an analogy in this passage. Put off and put on. Like clothing. Changing your clothes is something you do not once, but every day, sometimes twice or three times a day. When I was five and prayed the prayer to invite Jesus into my heart, the old self died and the new self was born, in that moment. I was justified, which I'd learned at AWANA meant "just as if I never sinned." It grieved me then, when my new self continued to lose her temper and accumulate more sins, after turning the course to follow Jesus.

In the context of Colossians 3, I made a most critical change to my internal narrative. The depictions of the old and new self were not established as before and after a salvation prayer. According to Paul, we put off anger, wrath, sexual immorality, and characteristics of the "old self with its practices" and "put on the new self which is being renewed in knowledge after the image of its creator."[131] We do it daily, sometimes twice or three times a day.

Telling myself a lie for decades fractured my self-worth. I was saved on the outside. I knew how to live, had memorized Bible verses about my deeds not being able to save me. I believed I could be a better Christian by doing good things, being in His word, and serving others. Despite knowing the Bible said that believing in Jesus was all that was necessary to save me, I still lived as though I had not been freely granted salvation when I asked as a girl. The fruit of my former life, things like being angry, worried, fearful, discontent, withdrawn, controlling, or self-centered—these didn't disappear the moment I placed my faith in God. Rather, I would need to put them off every day. I would never stop sinning, never be perfect, and never stop being in need of God's grace.

The gospel is a gift to all suffering in the brokenness of a fallen world. All of us have sinned and fallen short of the glory of God, so God the Father sent His son, Jesus Christ, to be the Savior of the world. He who was without sin took on flesh and was crucified, died, and was buried. On the third day He rose from the dead, defeating sin, and appeared to many to give the same message of hope He gives me: I am not a savior, but I have a Savior. I am a sinner, but by His grace, I am also a saint. I am redeemed, forgiven, and free from shame. That grace renews every morning. Sanctification, then, is a process. We don't become like Christ in one moment. It's a daily process of putting off the old and putting on the new, every day, until we take our last breath on this earth.[132]

When the Bipolar Brain Meets a Gentle Jesus

While doing biblical counseling, I also read *Gentle and Lowly*, recommended by friends at church. It was written by the son of the pastor's wife who counseled me in the pew before I left Nashville in 2013. In it, Dane Ortlund explores the heart of Jesus as revealed in the Gospels, emphasizing His compassion and humility towards sinners and suffering humanity. This read fundamentally transformed the way I conceived Jesus.

Gentle and Lowly emphasizes that Jesus is drawn to the broken and needy. Ortlund examines Christ's heart for the lost: He does not shy away from those who are sinful or struggling. The author articulates how grace is central to understanding Jesus' approach and emphasizes Christ offers mercy, forgiveness, and understanding rather than condemnation, helping readers like me grasp the depth of His love. Jesus walks alongside us in our pain, offering solace and hope. [133] The message I learned was, no matter my background or struggle, I can approach Jesus with confidence, knowing He welcomes me without judgment.

Where I had once viewed God in my own conception—punishing, punitive, righteous judge—I now understood I had an advocate before God, Jesus. His grace and mercy reframed my perception, revealing a loving Savior who intercedes on my behalf and understands my struggles. Instead of seeing God's righteousness as a threat to be feared, I could observe a protective boundary guiding me toward fullness of life. I understood I could bring my brokenness and imperfections to Him without shame. Through Jesus, I was not just accepted. I was cherished, redeemed, and beloved. [134] And I desperately wanted to grow closer to this Jesus.

If you are someone you know is struggling with BD or another mental health issue, getting to know the real Jesus is a gospel gift. Jesus is gentle and compassionate to those experiencing the extreme emotions associated with BD. He understands our struggles, meets us with kindness, and supplies solace. Jesus doesn't condemn those who suffer; rather, He offers us grace and acceptance, a place to alleviate the feelings of shame individuals with BD experience with regard to our condition or behaviors during mood episodes.

Even in our darkest moments, we're never alone. I recommend reading *Gentle and Lowly* if you want to understand this theological framework for processing emotions more fully. Understanding Jesus empathizes with our pain reframes our emotional experiences, prompting us to be honest before God rather than afraid. The daily practices Ortlund suggests like reading scripture and praying may serve as stabilizing forces for me, providing a sense of structure and spiritual connection across mood episodes.

If you'd prefer to see Jesus brought to life on the screen, Dallas Jenkins created a television drama series called *The Chosen.* I felt like I was meeting the same Jesus that Ortlund introduced me to. This drama tells the story of Jesus' life, starting with the calling of His first disciples. If you've got some stereotypes about the Lion and the Lamb, watching *The Chosen*, reading *Gentle and Lowly*, or doing a combination would be a great next step to find redemption exactly where you are. Once I met the real Jesus, I found a real sanctuary.

How the Church Might Respond to Bipolar Illness

And when you get to know Christ, you'll want to go to His house to worship. The people that attend church are not holy, righteous, or without sin. They are sinners made saints, like me, receiving daily outpourings of God's grace. Therefore, if you go to church expecting to find perfect people carrying out Jesus' mission to love and serve without flaw, you'll always be disappointed. Churches are sanctuaries for broken people like me. Even if it's just attending Sunday morning service, I need a place to go to that refreshes my perception of God and myself, week after week. In *Gentle and Lowly*, Ortlund discusses the importance of community in experiencing God's love, where churches become support systems.

Community is helpful, yes, but even if all I did was show up, sing, and listen, finding the right church means I get nourishment for my soul. I currently attend a reformed church in Williamsburg. While prepping this chapter, I told my husband, "Pastor Colin's going to give me insight for my book today, I just know it." He didn't have a chance to take the pulpit, and the worship leader transitioned to the last song in the opening set with a reminder that Jesus is gentle and lowly. I at once thought back to the section I'd just finished on Dane Ortlund's book; my heart was primed as the keyboardist played the familiar, waterfall chord progression of "Cornerstone." It's a worship song that draws from an old hymn about the sufficiency of Christ.

The word "sufficiency" might not mean much outside of Christian circles, just defined by word parts as the condition or quality of being adequate, enough. I listened to a two-part sermon delivered by John Street out of Grace Church called "The Sufficiency and Superiority of

Scripture in Addressing Bipolar Depression." I was looking for resources that would show how Christianity might be an answer for those struggling with the BD sin-shame cycle like I'd done before biblical counseling. Given that Street had just attended an ACBC conference in Memphis on self-harm and suicide prevention, the same organization through whom my friend Abigail was pursing her biblical counseling certification, I was hopeful.

Street's message boiled down to this: First, rely on God's sufficiency, His being all you need, by not taking medications to fix your life. Second, stop missing sleep to pursue sinful pleasures, and you won't have bipolar depression. Third, there are some physical diseases that can cause bipolar symptoms, but in the church, we don't recognize BD as a disease apart from that. This sermon essentially told people with BD that we caused our own illness through sin. Such a posture does not reassure anyone, believers or non-believers, that we'd find sanctuary in church or with his God. Hearing that after finding such healing through biblical counseling broke my heart—not for me, but for others who might hear that message and lose hope.

Ultimately, Street's stance opposes that of reformed thinkers and greatly oversimplifies the ACBC's nouthetic origins, whereby sin is the root of all post-fall problems. In *A Christian's Guide to Mental Illness*, authors David Murray and Tom Karel write, "While mental illness often has spiritual consequences, it is rarely only a spiritual problem that can be fixed simply with repentance and faith."[135] This is a better guiding principle. This is why I'm so passionate about sharing a different message. If someone with BD heard only Street's sermon, they might think God has no place for them. But I've found the opposite to be true.

I am not experiencing mood instability because I am not doing enough. I will never, ever be able to do enough. That's the wrong "sufficiency" to emphasize here. If you put your faith in Him as Savior, then Christ is enough, is doing enough in life. Even your bipolar life. He's enough when you're not enough. That's Someone I want to get to know.

The Sufficiency of Christ in Bipolar Storms

If I gave a sermon from a pulpit, it would be entitled "The Sufficiency of Christ in the Bipolar Storm." It would start like Pastor Colin did this week in Isaiah chapter six, where the prophet Isaiah has a vision in which he sees God. A person like me with BD might be able to relate first-hand to feeling tethered to a deeper connection, making the divine intervention in this scripture particularly powerful. I'm not a prophet, and God might not speak to me, but He appeared to Isaiah in this vision. Since it's in the Bible, not my personal experience, I can trust this was a real encounter.

Why is it significant that Isaiah sees God? Like Pastor Colin, I would explain the God I came to know in early childhood. He was before all things and would always be. He was holy, separate, cut off from me. I was created. He was not. I depend on God for this quality, this perfection, this constancy. God was and is and is to come. Where my BD moods change with the wind, God is steady and unchanging. I grasped, even at five, that I could not expect to face God someday in heaven without a mediator, an advocate, a sacrifice.[136]

All throughout the Old Testament, men and women made sacrifices to atone for their sins. There was nothing else standing between them and God. That's why it's so significant that Isaiah sees God in this vision. And when he does, Isaiah comes undone. He cries out that he's a man of unclean lips, fully aware of his humanity. God sends an angel with a burning coal to touch Isaiah's mouth and tells him, in verse seven, "Behold, this has touched your lips; your guilt is taken away, and your sin atoned for."[137] Atonement doesn't just mean being forgiven. To atone means to forgive and restore.

God didn't reveal Himself to Isaiah without making a means to forgive and restore. He gave us one, too, when an Old Testament prophesy was fulfilled. Jesus Christ came into the world to be the last sacrifice. He atoned for my sin on the cross. That means I'm forgiven and restored. I'm free to stand back up in the holy presence of God as I am today, not as the perfect self I hope to be someday. Like the burning coals on Isaiah's lips, having Christ as my Savior means my guilt is taken away and my sin is atoned for. I'm not condemned. Not forsaken. Psychiatrists call me bipolar. Jesus calls me redeemed.[138] We can be both and better for both labels.

There's a popular saying in church that we're either in a storm, headed toward one, or coming out of one. That's especially true for a person diagnosed with BD. By God's grace, I've experienced many seasons of stability and personal growth. I'm in one of those seasons now. But I've been in the throes of depression and the elation of mania, and both are confusing places. I've listened to podcasts of other Christians sharing about experiencing this illness, and I see the impact of emotional fluctuation on faith and daily life.

On one such podcast, a man named Tommy put it succinctly, "There very much could be something that is going on in someone's life that is rooted in their physical health, their emotional health, and stress plays a huge role in that." What did he suggest as an answer? "One of the best medicines for combatting and aiding recovery is honestly, not to sound oversimplistic, but I believe it's the gospel."[139] I agree with Tommy.

And like me, in the times Tommy felt alone, he could relate a lot to King David. And like me, in Tommy's manic episodes, he'd pick up the Psalms and start singing through them. "I feel like God's used the Psalms to be a guide and an encouragement to me and give me zeal for clinging to him in prayer," Tommy shared on the podcast episode. A loved one recently challenged me on this association, asking if I now thought King David had bipolar. Like Street, she's asking the wrong questions, but I'll play along. If we're assessing kings according to the DSM-5TR, David's predecessor Saul offers a better candidate, in my opinion.

In 1 Samuel, Saul exhibits intense mood swings—from deep depression and melancholia to periods of great anger and impulsiveness. We observe these shifts in his interactions with David, his jealousy and paranoia, as well as his moments of clarity and leadership. For instance, Saul experiences profound episodes of despair, particularly after being rejected by God, and he becomes increasingly isolated and unstable.[140] His erratic behavior, including sudden fits of rage and obsession with David, can be likened to the manic episodes associated with BD or perhaps even onset of dementia.

In biblical accounts, David expresses a wide range of emotions. He often shifts from profound joy and praise to deep sorrow. For example, in many Psalms, he writes about feelings of despair, abandonment, and distress, followed by assurances of hope and praise for God. These

emotional fluctuations can resemble the mood swings associated with
BD. Additionally, David's life was marked by periods of significant stress
and conflict, such as his flight from King Saul, which could exacerbate
his emotional struggles. His experiences with guilt, especially surrounding
his sin with Bathsheba, may have contributed to feelings of depression
and isolation at times.[141]

Nonetheless, it's crucial to approach these characterizations with
caution. The biblical narrative primarily portrays David's relationship
with God and his journey as a leader rather than functioning as a clinical
analysis of mental health. Likewise, the descriptions of Saul in 1 Samuel
reflect the narrative and theological context of Saul's story rather than an
accurate clinical diagnosis by contemporary standards. Thus, while there
may be moments in David's or Saul's lives that resonate with modern
understandings of mood disorders, these interpretations should be
considered within the broader context of their faith and personal
experiences.

I'm not a psychiatrist. I've studied my disorder for some time. I've
been a student of the Bible a lot longer. God is the original author of the
narratives developed in 1 Samuel and Psalms. What belongs in a sermon
about BD is that Saul and David are positioned side by side in scripture
for us. Both evidence emotional tumult. Ultimately, Saul serves as an
example of a man riddled with anxiety that maddened, consumed, and
destroyed him. David follows in Saul's footsteps, not just in taking the
crown, but in giving us an alternative example of what do with our grief.
David brings every thought captive before God, including his
ruminations. David channels his pain and confusion into heartfelt prayers

and songs, demonstrating vulnerability in trusting God's plan the way I need to do.

This contrast is essential; whereas Saul's struggles lead him to isolation and despair, David's response is to seek solace and strength through his relationship with God. The Psalms are a testament to this journey, revealing how David wrestles with his emotions yet ultimately finds hope in God's unwavering love and faithfulness.

This is a powerful lesson for anyone grappling with mental health challenges: the importance of bringing our struggles into the light, sharing our burdens with God, and allowing His truth to guide us through the turbulence. In being vulnerable, like David, we can experience the profound healing and grace found in a deep, honest relationship with the Creator.[142] In this way, David serves as a timeless example of faith-powered resilience amid life's storms.

Moreover, David—flaws and all—would be among those humans named in the lineage of Jesus Christ. When we sang "Cornerstone" in church this week, it struck me how perfectly it captures what I've been learning about finding solid ground when everything feels shaky. [143]

The first verse always gets me: "My hope is built on nothing less than Jesus' blood and righteousness. I dare not trust the sweetest frame, but wholly trust in Jesus' name." I used to think I could trust my own strength, my good days, my carefully managed routines. But "the sweetest frame," whether that means human strength or human thinking, crumbles when you have BD. My moods shift. My energy crashes. My thoughts spiral. But Jesus doesn't.

The chorus hits even deeper: "Christ alone, cornerstone. Weak made strong in the Savior's love. Through the storm, He is Lord, Lord of all." That line about being "weak made strong"? That's my story. I spent years ashamed of my weakness, trying to hide my diagnosis, pretending I had it all together. Now I'm learning that admitting I'm weak—that I need medication, Tony's perspective, that professional help—is not a failure. It's when God's strength shows up best. And "through the storm"? Yes, I know about storms. Manic episodes, depressive crashes, the whole bipolar weather system. But Jesus is Lord even when I'm in the red zone on Tony's color scale.

The second verse speaks to my depressive episodes: "When darkness seems to hide His face, I rest on His unchanging grace. In every high and stormy gale, my anchor holds within the veil." Depression feels exactly like God's face is hidden. I can't feel Him, can't sense His presence, wonder if He's forgotten me entirely. However, this verse reminds me the darkness is just hiding Him from view, like clouds covering the sunrise. He's still there, unchanging, sure as the dawn.

The final verse gives me hope for the future: "When He shall come with trumpet sound, oh may I then in Him be found, dressed in His righteousness alone, faultless stand before the throne." Standing "faultless"—not because I managed my bipolar perfectly, not because I never had an episode, but because Jesus covers all my brokenness. For someone who cycles through mood states and makes mistakes in every single one of them, knowing I can stand faultless before God? That's everything.

Embracing Grace: The Power of Transformed Narratives

The journey of transforming our inner narratives is a vital aspect of healing mentally and spiritually. By challenging the misconceptions and stigmas falsely branding mental health within Christian communities, it's possible to send a message of hope to shattered souls like me. No, not every church, pastor, biblical counselor, or Christian understands, accepts, and supports individuals on the mood disorder spectrum, but I don't doubt they'd like to if they just had a little more insight into the minds and hearts of people willing to be vulnerable like I am in this chapter.

I believe we're best served to embrace a new inner narrative rooted in biblical truths that help us consider struggles as integral parts of this human experiences instead of flaws to hide or loathe. Why? Because in the depths of the valley or the high and stormy gale when I'm burdened by my weakness and humanity, that's where God's grace abounds. Every time. This empowers me personally, of course, but this shift in perspective also calls for the church to be a true sanctuary for those grappling with mental health challenges. Ultimately, the transformation of our inner narratives leads to a deeper relationship with God, a renewed sense of purpose, and the ability to share our stories in ways that inspire hope and healing in others.

A Biblical Psychology: Sanctuary for the Bipolar Brain

Navigating the complexities of mental health, particularly for those living with BD, can often feel like an overwhelming journey through uncharted waters. Towering highs and daunting lows litter its landscape; hope and despair frequently intertwine. Our emotional experiences, however tumultuous, are inherently part of the human existence, intricately designed by God. He designed the church to be our spiritual sanctuary, a place of refuge and solace amidst turbulence. We can best provide that sanctuary for people on the mood disorder spectrum by unpacking complex emotions from a biblical perspective.

I started by picking up a copy of *Untangling Emotions* by J. Alasdair Groves and Winston T. Smith, a book that bridges the gap between science and faith. For those pursuing God alongside mental health challenges involving extreme moods, *Untangling Emotions* explores the complexities of emotions and how they impact our lives and relationships. Authors examine biblical perspectives on feelings, emphasizing that emotions are not inherently good or bad but are part of the human experience created by God.

Mama Sue recommended this book the night I came out about being a Christian with BD on my blog not long ago. Sue Fallin is my sister-in-law's mother. Essentially, I inherited a personal mentor in my brother's marriage to Cari's family. Before we met, Mama Sue battled for years with multiple autoimmune disorders at death's door. Like me, she had to take medication to manage her illness—until one day she didn't. Mama Sue received support from her church community and experienced a miraculous healing that's allowed me to get to know her over the past twenty-five years.[144]

Mama Sue rarely offers advice unless she's been prompted by God. Remember how I said I could trust Isaiah's vision of God was real because it was included in the Bible? I'm guided by a similar principle when it comes to Mama Sue because God intervened in a way even science had to recognize as intervention. She wrote about her journey through illness and healing in her book *Gathering Manna*. She's experienced times of great suffering, likewise been told to pray harder. She missed out on childhood memories with her daughters. Even a woman who's been healed by God of a physical illness sees the importance of untangling our emotions.

Untangling Emotions helped me understand and process emotions in a healthy way. It begins by defining key emotions like anger, fear, and sadness, examining how these feelings can be understood biblically and practically. Groves and Smith encourage readers to identify the root causes of their emotions and to respond to them in a way that aligns with God's truth. I learned to see my emotions as signals leading to deeper understanding of myself and a right relationship with God.

About half-way through my first read, I reached out to my father and recommended he check it out. My dad is a God-fearing man, firmly committed to upholding biblical truths as he encounters the world. He made incredible sacrifices and wise decisions to prioritize our wellness during childhood. I always had enough. Life was quite comfortable. But as I listened to the authors untangling emotions in a biblical way, my mind kept shooting back to exchanges with my father as a young girl and teen.

That my father loved me was never a question. That the depth of my emotions made him uncomfortable is most relevant here. It was a common scene in our family room, Dad on the couch, me standing there pleading for something. He'd entertain the exchange until I started to cry, then send me to my room with instructions to come back when I had control of my emotions. If I lost my temper in a car or a restaurant, Dad developed a private signal to silence me without drawing attention, reaching down and squeezing my thigh. While I was spanked on occasion and probably deserved it, this was a "spare the rod, spoil the child" minded household, and this thigh-squeezing method brought me swiftly back in line.

I had emotions, but when outward behavior reflected negative feelings, curtailing the behaviors was prioritized, sending a clear message in my formative years that such difficult emotions were to be avoided. It never occurred to my dad that sending me to my room or silencing undesirable behaviors in this way taught me to suppress those negative emotions. Unfortunately, as is often the case for little girls placing faith in God, I fashioned the Heavenly Father was after my earthly father. I got angry, and that was a sin; I certainly couldn't take my anger to God. What would be equivalent to a thigh squeeze from heaven?

My father taught me not to trust my emotions, and there is some wisdom in that. Experiencing life with BD, my emotions form an undercurrent foundational to my very personhood. *Untangling Emotions* helped me understand why it was so difficult for my dad and I to see eye-to-eye during conflict. I did see him try to connect over the years, but my intense moods came between us. My dad never appeared to have trouble regulating his emotions.

Authors present the way BD is characterized by people getting stuck in a single emotion. "It's as if in mania your body is blaring out the message that nothing can go wrong and no plan your mind alights on could fail," Groves and Smith write, explaining why people in manic episodes act in foolish and irresponsible ways. "Their mania leaves them feeling, even physically, so sure of the goodness of their every desire that they go crashing through barricades and warning signs till they fly off the cliff and crash into bleak depression."[145] There were times I sinned not intentionally, but as the result of false delusions about what I thought

God was telling me. Either way, we can do something with our emotions that honors God now.

I sent my dad the recommendation hoping he'd find a bridge to understand me better. Whether he read it or not, I finally understood why our relationship felt so complicated. It also gave me practical tools for navigating emotions, including how to communicate them in relationships and seek support from others. The book serves as a resource for people like Mama Sue, my father, and me—anyone seeking to grow in emotional awareness and cultivate healthier relationships, grounded in biblical wisdom. It made me better at understanding, processing, and integrating emotions into a life that honors God and makes much of Him in the highs and lows.

This book should be adopted as the central text for the next mental illness conference John Street and other pastors attend if inclined to mitigate the rising rates of mental illness and accompanied rise in suicides. A biblical psychology acknowledges mood disorders as an inseparable combination of both the body and the spirit, mind, and soul. Those diagnosed with mental conditions are in inherent need of freedom from sin and feelings of condemnation, myself included. I believe we all sin, experience shame, and need a guiding compass to navigate emotions.

Being diagnosed with BD should identify someone as primed for sanctuary in Christ. Mood disorder diagnosis is a mission opportunity to take the gospel to those without hope, yes. Equally, it's a mission to heal within the church by making real the daily grace promised us in scripture; we need to heal the inner narrative, the accumulation of lies we tell ourselves about who God is, about who we are, and about who we are to Him.

Untangling Emotions surveys a wide range of emotions including those we experience during different mood episodes, such as elevated moods, anxious ruminations, and depressive phases. This overview can help anyone, with or without a mood disorder, recognize and label feelings more clearly. I came to see my feelings as part of the human experience created by God, even my larger-than-life bipolar episodes.

Perhaps the most important takeaway for me was the necessity of acknowledging and working through emotions rather than suppressing them. Learning to process these feelings can lead to healthier coping mechanisms. I never stopped working through my emotions, but consider my outlets: creative writing by myself. When I was little, I had an audience of One. All the journaled prayers, poems, and diary entries—no person had access to my inner dialogue to understand or empathize with my struggle, just God, even when not addressed to Him.

Another premise, then, of biblical psychology, is the necessity for biblical counseling that intervenes in such cases as mine, to assist in right processing, presenting the Bible and characteristics of God through the framework of biblical counseling. The scriptures are divinely inspired, but not necessarily man's interpretation. My perpetual internal negative rumination cycle was, after all, cultivated by pulling disparate verses from scripture to support my creation of an other-God, one righteous but not gracious, judgmental but not compassionate. *Untangling Emotions* gave me practical strategies for managing emotions in everyday life, including grounding techniques beneficial for navigating the ups and downs of spiritual life with BD explored in the previous chapter.

Furthermore, this book reminded me of the importance of effective communication. I know from experience it's difficult to articulate feelings to loved ones, church leaders, and mental health professionals, but such communication leads to better support and understanding from friends, family, medical professionals, and my church community. Biblical psychology demands such an integrated support system, not separate measures to be pursued, by defining integrations the DSM does not outline. We want to send the message that it's okay to seek help and support when dealing with emotions, even the messy ones.

Ultimately, a biblical psychology emphasizes the vital intersection of faith, emotional processing, and mental health, particularly for individuals navigating the complexities of BD. By integrating principles from *Untangling Emotions*, we reposition the importance of understanding our emotions as part of God's creation, rather than viewing them as obstacles to our faith. Mama Sue's personal journey is proof of the transformative power of support, spiritual and communal, in times of deep suffering. Healing is about more than physical well-being; it's about finding the courage to embrace the spiritual and emotional depths of our illness.

I suppose I'm asking for a compassionate, multifaceted approach to mental health within the church, one with open dialogue and support systems that recognize mood disorders. I want to see stigma and suppression replaced by an honest dialogue about expressed emotions guided by biblical truths. I've learned profound healing comes from recognizing our struggles, leaning into our faith, and supporting one another as we navigate the intricate landscape of emotions shaped by bipolar, depression, and beyond. A diagnosis of BD is not a death sentence, certainly not for the Christian. We already have a savior.

And if you've faced life with a mood disorder without Jesus, I'm not sure what you do with the mistakes you've made. Maybe by this point,

I've shared the gospel for the first time in my life that wasn't trying to get it right like a good Wheaton College student should. I want everyone to have an advocate for life struggles, one who is sufficient in our storms, because Jesus never fails me, not even when I fail, and I do that so often. Like Jesus says in 2 Corinthians 12:9, "My grace is sufficient for you, for my power is made perfect in weakness." I have such profound weakness. What a relief to know Jesus' grace is enough for me, that He is at work in my highs and my lows. This has been my single, greatest comfort post-diagnosis.

The Convergence of Biblical Psychology and Mental Health Strategies

I've had other comforts, as well. I'd like to briefly revisit how mental health strategies from earlier chapters can work within a faith framework.

Consider CBT, introduced as a beyond talk therapy strategy that helps people identify and change negative thought patterns and behaviors. When I worked with Abigail in biblical counseling, she taught me to replace my negative self-talk not with generic affirmations, but with truths about God's character. Instead of "I'm such an idiot" becoming "I'm valuable," it became "God is wise and knows how to bring about the best results for my life." This shift changed everything for me—I stopped arguing with who God was, and the sin-shame rumination cycle was permanently disrupted. Essentially, Abigail used CBT to navigate mental health conditions by capitalizing on the power of changing my internal narrative.

Whether we're experiencing mania or hypomania or a weighing depression, our connection to God and the world is interpreted through the lens of a single emotion. Thus, we tend to reduce our God to qualities best evidenced by our current state of mind. In biblical counseling, Abigail gave me a list of ten characteristics of God to embrace when my emotions tried to reduce Him to whatever I was feeling in the moment: God is supreme, sovereign, sufficient, holy, loving, wise, gracious, merciful, forgiving, and faithful. He is all these things all the time, whether I'm manic, depressed, or stable.

I use this list when I'm the negative thoughts start. For example, I might think, "I'm ashamed to stand before God." I pivot by identifying the corresponding characteristic of God to embrace. In this case, God is forgiving, canceling the debt owed by us because of sin. God is gracious, never letting me experience the full consequence of my sin. If I think, "I can't feel God," I respond back that God is faithful, He will never leave me nor forsake me. He will always be there. Eventually, the substitution script began executing itself.

I've also adapted some of these learned techniques to include my faith. My thought-stopping method became "Mindful-S.T.O.P.5-Thanks"—when anxiety hits, I stop, breathe, observe what's happening inside, then name five things I can see, four I can touch, three I can hear, two I can smell, and one I can taste. But instead of just naming them, I thank God for them. I cannot look around at the world without being aware of the Creator of all things. Gratitude coaxes anxiety down.

Other tools I've applied in my healing journey include meditation and grounding exercises, replacing secular scripts with God's word. I start every morning journaling and talking to God then listen to a podcast reciting and reflecting on scripture. When I wake up in the middle of the night with racing thoughts, however, I don't read my Bible as it tends to energize me. Instead, I recite whole passages from memory, like Colossians 3:1-17 and Psalm 139:1-18. The recitation has an almost hypnotic quality; even if I can't get back to sleep, it soothes the distress of hypomania.

Psychoeducation has been foundational to my growth since diagnosis. My dream is to see more resources that thoughtfully address mental health through a biblical lens. Someone needs to write the next generation of books that bridge psychology and faith. By sharing our stories and growing this resource library, we can equip the Church to promote holistic healing and a deeper understanding of God's grace during life's challenges. That's true sanctuary.

Furthermore, God is the original author of the growth mindset. I like memorizing verses that speak to God's ability to transform me like 2 Corinthians 5:17 which says in Christ, we're new creations. He is the author of resilience. God is always doing a new thing. Beneath my growth mindset is the safety net of God's sovereignty. He's always working in my challenges, especially the bipolar ones.

Finally, I presented the BD self-management strategy of a voluntary, chosen dependence. This concept is not foreign to the Christian. Each of us commit to a voluntary, chosen dependence on God. Ultimately, I had to change my perception of my dependence on medications and other people and of my limitations to curtail the negative self-perception cultivated naturally by feeling perpetually dependent, out of control, and at the mercy of a disease. I do not believe God's sufficiency and chosen dependence on bipolar support measures are mutually exclusive. Rather, He's provided me the people and supports to help me live in a way that honors Him.

Calling for a Reformed Response to Bipolar Disorder and Christ

In this chapter, I've pushed for a renewed understanding of BD within Christian communities because I've lived on both sides—as someone who was hurt by the church's response and as someone who found healing through biblical counseling. We must recognize that mental health struggles are not personal failings or spiritual inadequacies, but complex experiences that need both medical care and spiritual support.

It's time to shift the dialogue focus from stigmatization to empathy. We must challenge the harmful notion that faith alone cures mental illness. Medication and therapy aren't signs of weak faith—they're vital tools God can effectively use in our healing journey. When we prioritize education and open conversation, we empower people with BD to live authentically and courageously, glorifying God through our unique stories.

Some will object to my intermingling of psychology and biblical principles, but the church has always adapted its methods while holding to core truths. We use acronyms like ACTS for prayer, small groups for fellowship, and contemporary music for worship—none of these are explicitly biblical, but they help us connect with God, and I'd come to learn a new acronym for prayer each decade.

Christians have core values, too, that support our central mission to bring others into the sanctuary of Christ's heart. What I'm asking for is simple: show the fruit of the Spirit to people with mental illness.[146] Demonstrate love by being present during difficult times. Share joy by celebrating small victories. Offer peace by creating safe spaces for honest conversation. Practice patience when our behaviors seem bizarre. Show kindness through practical help. Display goodness by refusing to judge. Be faithful by not abandoning us during episodes. Respond with gentleness when we share our struggles. Exercise self-control by not taking our mood swings personally.

Living with BD comes with unique challenges, and I know our behaviors can sometimes be frightening. But that's true of many things before they become familiar. If you want to support someone with BD, encourage healthy habits, offer gentle accountability, and celebrate forward progress. Check in during tough times, but be flexible if plans change. Most importantly, listen with sensitivity when we share our experiences, reserving judgment. Simple words are acts such as these show Christ's heart to those in need of Him.

The most faithful friends are those who meet us with Christ's love—unconditional, patient, and grace-filled. That's the sanctuary we're desperate to find.

The Source of Light: Our Sanctuary in Christ

My story isn't the first to marry BD and faith. In 2018, Micah and Bobbi Jo Yarborough published *My Anchor Holds Within the Veil: Bipolar Disorder and God's Providence*. Micah writes candidly about his lived experiences with BD, and Bobbi Jo interjects with her accounts of the same events from the perspective of a wife and partner. In about 130 pages, the duo effectively captures, illustrates, and navigates the signs and symptoms, triggers, and treatment options with a heavy reliance on Jesus Christ as their anchor in the storms. The title itself is a nod to the Hebrews scripture turned hymn turned worship song, "Cornerstone."

I stumbled upon the Yarboroughs' book in an eBay store while searching for another related title. I'd finished writing this chapter and was in the editing process when I devoured the book in one sitting. Micah and Bobbi Jo's mutual memoir is the first book I'd recommend to a Christian interested in getting a crash course in BD. It's good to see yourself in its pages, whether you have BD or love someone who's dealing with it.

In fact, the dual perspectives of husband-patient wife-caretaker riveted me. I could relate to Micah's depictions of adolescence—his obtrusive thoughts, his deepening mood states, his dependence on substances. I could identify with the lifetime cycle of winter blues and summer highs, alternating seasons of depression and hypomania. When I surveyed Bobbi Jo's accounts, however, I could see my husband. I found myself reading whole sections aloud to Tony simply to affirm he's not alone. I got to see inside another's hypomanic, depressive episodes and put myself in my spouse's shoes.

For example, at one point Micah's doctor asks him to surrender his keys and credit cards temporarily which made them both uncomfortable. Bobbi Jo admitted, "It is a very awkward situation to parent your adult partner and try to respect him at the same time."[147] Tony knows what she means. I've not had to surrender my cards or keys, but there are moments of mental illness where he's put in that position of partner and caretaker. Still, because our roles are reversed, it's even easier to compare Tony's love for me, his wife to Christ's love for His bride, the church. To love me well, I wonder if it requires you draw from Christ's well of sacrificial, pure, and unconditional love filled with the fruit of the Spirit and fitted in the armor of God.

The Yarboroughs' memoir is a living testament to God's providence. Throughout the unpredictable, changing phases of Micah's illness, he can recognize God as the sole constant, predictably unchanging. Moreover, Micah highlights the ways God used his illness to sanctify him. One manic episode laid Micah low. "My mind had been more broken before but not my heart, spirit, pride, rebelliousness, and selfishness," Micah writes. "He crushed those things in me, and I felt exposed and helpless. I had nothing to lean on but him."[148] This uncannily describes the process my manic episode initiated back in 2018. It's been years of sanctification, but ultimately, the only true sanctuary I have is in Christ.

I can expect everyone and everything to fail me save for the One who made me. Micah, like me, believed the right medication protocol was essential to be effective in living a God-honoring life and being the partner and parent he wanted to be, despite the side effects. Imperfect medications are part of my balancing act, too, but sovereign over all my transformation and maturation is God. "I had to acknowledge he would be the one to do this work inside of me," Micah admits. "I was failing, but he is a loving father who delights in reconciling and restoring relationships and making things new."[149] At the end of every day, my BD is not beyond God's scope. My mood disorder simply yields so many opportunities to cite His providence and grace. Like Micah, I fail so often, but I'm embraced, reconciled, and restored. That God delights in making things new is a recurring theme in both our lives.

When diagnosed with a mental illness like BD, the label itself can weigh you down: a pervasive new, negative self-concept; a flashing neon sign of abnormality; and a sickening fear in your gut because, let's face it, the easiest way to shatter stigma is to yourself be diagnosed as mentally ill. Those who haven't experienced life on the mood disorder spectrum often judge, dismiss, misunderstand, or offend us. My compassion for those suffering supersedes labels, bridging gender, race, and spiritual divides. I identify as a person with BD, but that is not my primary identity.

Nor was it Micah's. After his last manic episode, Micah saw God strip him of everything he'd placed his hopes in. "God was teaching me that putting my worth in anything other than my identity as a Christian would disappoint," Micah writes. "My idea of God was too small, my view of my sin was too small, and so my view of God's grace was too small."[150] I thought being diagnosed with BD was equal to being branded as permanently damaged. How misguided I was, how small my thinking. I am a Christian, a sinner saved by grace that's renewed daily. Am I not, then, fearfully and wonderfully made like King David?

I was always sinful, but I was so busy trying to be perfect before my manic episode I could not see the necessity to be humbled, laid low. Being human means being damaged; it's not unique to BD or mental health diagnoses. I've seen in my weakness, God's power abounds. Tears welled in my eyes on several occasions reading this book, but the confession most powerfully relatable was this. "Clearly, left to my own devices, I would continue on my way forever, selfish and immature," Micah writes. "God in his goodness and wisdom, however, gave me an illness that broke me down, stripped me of my pride, dignity, mental abilities, relationships, social gifts, and repeatedly took away my sanity."[151] Oh, Micah, thank you for articulating the unformed thoughts of my soul. Immediately, he praises God after the admission, the ever-present anchor in the storm.

Like Micah, I've discovered that BD—while challenging and sometimes overwhelming—has become an instrument in God's hands for my sanctification. What I once viewed as a curse, I now see as a complex gift. It's deepened my dependence on Christ and expanded my capacity for compassion. The mood swings that once felt like evidence of my brokenness have become reminders of my need for the One who remains constant when everything else fluctuates.

I think one of the major misconceptions we need to address is this: the sanctuary we find in Christ is not one that removes us from the storms of mental illness. If I woke up healed, I'd be giving Him the glory, of course, but true sanctuary provides an anchor within those storms. It's a place where our struggles are not spiritualized away but met with the full resources of heaven—grace sufficient for our weakness, strength perfected in our frailty, and a love that pursues us even in our darkest valleys. This sanctuary recognizes healing may look different for each of us. For some, like Mama Sue, it may be miraculous and complete. For others, like Micah and me, it may be a daily choosing to trust God's goodness while managing our condition with medication, therapy, and community support.

The church's response to BD (and mental illness, more broadly) must reflect this nuanced understanding of refuge. We need communities that can hold space for the reality of suffering and the hope of redemption, places where people can be honest about their struggles without fear of judgment or oversimplified solutions. When we create such sanctuaries, we mirror the heart of Christ, who came not for the healthy but for the sick, not for the perfect but for the broken.

As I conclude this chapter, it's my prayer that the framework of biblical psychology will continue to evolve, creating more bridges between the church and mental health communities. I hope to see more resources like *Untangling Emotions* and *My Anchor Holds Within the Veil* that honor the complexity of mental illness and the sufficiency of Christ simultaneously. May we raise up more counselors and pastors equipped to navigate these intersections with wisdom and grace.

Most importantly, may those of us who live with BD find in these pages not just understanding, but hope—hope that our stories matter, our struggles have purpose, and in Christ, we've found a sanctuary that can never be shaken. For in Him, we are not defined by our diagnoses but by our identity as beloved children of God. I praise God for being fearfully, wonderfully, and even bipolar-ly made, held secure in the grip of grace that will never let me go.

Concluding Remarks

It's July 2025. I've spent the last ten months of Friday evenings attending an online support group sponsored by the DBSA. When I finished the first draft of my manuscript and returned to teaching full time at my stepdaughter's middle school, I had just enough time to get home and set my computer up for that weekly Zoom line to sanity. Bad moods cannot dissuade me from logging in. There, I spend an hour with a dozen or so people who I can relate to for the shared purpose of giving and getting support. For one hour a week, I am reassured I am fearfully, wonderfully, and bipolar-ly made.

It's been seven months since I transitioned to a new post of shepherding sixth graders toward their reading and writing goals, editing my manuscript in stolen moments. Admittedly, there were times I doubted the book's core messages and themes, struggling so greatly to balance the new work-wife-mom existence while actively regulating my emotions on school and home fronts. Then, I attend a DBSA meeting and remember, one face and story like mine at a time, why this book must see the light of other's bedside tables.

In fifth grade, my mother took me on a little adventure to Atlantic City. We swam out together through a sea of hundreds of other summer waders and played in the waves, giggling and splashing, until suddenly there was only a sea of water, no waders within shouting distance. We'd been caught in a rip tide and an under tow, we'd be later told. My mother was strong enough to fight the current, but the ocean was pulling me out and away effortlessly. I remember Mom trying to carry me and being smacked back down, the Atlantic rejecting her efforts to swim us both to shore.

I tasted fear for the first time at ten. It was saltwater where there should be oxygen. Mom's cries for help muted under the roar. Treading water for dear life between waves that slapped me back under, reeling beneath swirling, fighting layers of seawater. Just when I'd break to the surface and gasp a breath, another wave came. The shore never got closer. *I'll drown*, I thought, *I'll die.*

I did not die, however, because there was quite suddenly a man in the water beside me where there had been none. My savior wore round, wire-rimmed eyeglasses and an open short-sleeve button down shirt; his hairy chest tickled me when he took me up in his arms. Hope smelled of sweat as he answered my mother's prayers and lifted me above the next wave. Arms outstretched above his head, he'd disappear beneath the swell. Wave after wave, that's how he saved my life, going under to hold me up, until he deposited me onto the shore. We thanked him, and he disappeared into the throng of Atlantic City beachgoers.

From the same crowd my saving angel disappeared into, an eager lifeguard emerged. "We were gonna send someone out for you," and he motioned with his hand, rotating his body back toward the ocean, out where I'd been drowning, "but it looked like you were getting in okay." Mom and I were still coughing, preventing her from expressing any opinions on that subject. With the same animated hand gestures to illustrate, the lifeguard explained how we'd been caught between that riptide and an undertow. We were fortunate to be alive.

Twenty minutes later, I found a beautiful shell and searched the shoreline for the man in the button-down shirt and eyeglasses, hoping to give him the pretty shell as a gift. I never found him. I believed he was my guardian angel who God dropped in the water just to save me, eyeglasses and all. Perhaps I still believe it. I kept the shell as a reminder of the miracle God had performed in saving me that day, and I wrote the story inside the shiny part of the shell. I was raising an Ebenezer, I just didn't know what that meant yet.

Mom said she knew I was resilient because I jumped right back into the water, only was that true? Did I jump? Or did I wade in up to my waist, never higher than my shoulders, for the rest of my life? I love frequenting lakes and oceans, boat rides and water activities, most of all sunbathing. Those who know me well realize Fort Monroe beach is my favorite place. I crave the scent and feel of the ocean. I savor painted landscapes over the Chesapeake Bay or York River at sunrise or sunset. I'm a seaside gal at my core; just after Atlantic City, I intentionally avoided putting my head under the water for nearly thirty years.

That was until one of my friends taught me to surf in Virginia Beach a few summers back. Our first few visits were calm, sunny days. I was learning by watching and experimenting. By the time I'd paddle out with the bright blue longboard far enough to pass the spot where the waves crashed, I was winded. I caught very few waves. When I did, I managed to hold on to the board at least until the shallow water. These first few visits, I thought surfing might be my new adult hobby.

One Saturday in August, my friend took me surfing just after a hurricane had hit further down the coast. The ocean was manic; her thrusting waves, choppy and crossing each other, made it difficult to swim out with that blue longboard past the breaking point. I was paddling out like the other surfers around me, but I couldn't seem to keep my body on my board. I gripped tight to its edges. My knuckles were white. My friend was still about ten yards beyond me when he disappeared behind the crest of a wave that would break on me.

It was a muted splash from my position under the sea. Forget Ariel's underwater sanctuary. Nothing was clear inside the spin. The water had weight. I kicked, but it occurred to me I did not know which way was up. Panicked arms and legs sprawled to find the ocean's surface. I fought until exhaustion. When my head finally found north and broke through, I choked on air. It took all the effort left to swim to my longboard and let the tide carry me back to shore where I collapsed in a heap, ripping off the strap on my ankle connecting me to that board.

All at once, I was ten again. Sitting there, breathing heavily, facing the raging ocean, coated in sand, I wept. I'd not tasted fear so profound in nearly three decades. My soul loved the sea—to gaze upon her, wade into her, boat atop her—but leave the underwater adventures to Ariel. I was recalling my angel with the eyeglasses from Atlantic City when a silhouette from Baywatch interrupted. "You're wasting all your energy out there fighting the waves," the off-duty surf instructor informed me. There was no judgment, just expert observation.

I listened briefly to her explanation of how to move with the water, to use its constant motion and save my energy. She reminded me my board was a tether to the surface; no matter how turned around I was below, I simply needed to follow my ankle tether up to oxygen. Where I saw unpredictability and threat, the surf instructor saw physics and logic. It was as though all at once, I understood what I'd been missing. The water was a force that could be understood and harnessed. It wasn't the enemy I'd made it to be in fifth grade on that adventure to Atlantic City.

I tasted fear for the first time at ten, about the same time I started exhibiting symptoms of BD. Rather than face my fear of the water, I simply avoided sticking my head under water for three decades. It's not much different from skirting diagnoses and navigating countless landmines of mood episodes more than twenty years before being put in a position to feel a similar fear, the fear that I had BD and would never be the same.

Life before diagnosis was like being caught in a rip tide and an under tow, Christian and psychological paradigms waging war in my ocean. I did not see my BD diagnosis as a guardian angel God had dropped in the water to save me, the lens through which I could come to understand and harness this powerful force of energy in me. At ten, I wrote on a beautiful seashell to remind me of God's faithfulness in saving me that day. He saved me again in the mental health section of the local library when I finally saw myself as I truly was, but instead of raising an Ebenezer, I hid in fear and shame.

I couldn't see the ocean for the waves. For so many years, I was wasting all my energy fighting my illness, loathing myself, and treading water for dear life. In writing this book, I learned how to move with my BD, not against it. I learned to respect its constant, cyclical motions. I didn't just dip my toe in, either. I fully immersed myself in the study of who I am now, and I told my story with no judgment, just amateur observation. The surf instructor reminded me my board was a tether to the surface. No matter how turned around I get when BD symptoms shake the seaboard, Jesus Christ is my anchor. I simply need to follow Him up and out of the eye of the storm.

I started this journey unable to write authentically because I was keeping secrets—the very thing that had made my blog Writer's Growth meaningful was impossible when I couldn't tell the truth about my bipolar diagnosis. How could I believe King David's words about being fearfully and wonderfully made when everything felt so broken? But like that surf instructor who helped me see physics and logic where I only saw chaos, understanding my BD has revealed the intricate, purposeful way God crafted my mind. The same intensity that creates my storms also fuels my empathy, my creativity, my passion for helping others.

Now, after diving deep into understanding who I am, I can finally write those thousand words, give or take eighty thousand, that make sense again. The secret once silencing me has become the story that might save someone else from drowning in shame. When I first read about others carrying the torch for bipolar awareness, I thought I was too broken to rep myself. But I've learned that the very experience of being caught in BD's riptide—and finding my way to shore—is what qualifies me to throw a lifeline to others.

Every person sitting in that DBSA meeting, every reader who might find this book on their bedside table, deserves to know they're not drowning alone. We who have tasted that saltwater fear and lived to tell about it become the guardian angels for those still fighting the waves, ready to lift them up until they reach solid ground. This book is my return to radical transparency, my Tuesday night brain dump that took ten months instead of two hours, but finally captures the whole truth of me.

Dr. Bogin was right, and mixing metaphors becomes necessary. I had to struggle lost in that dark wood, with all the hardships and tribulations, before I could come into the clearing and find myself: fearfully, wonderfully, and bipolar-ly made.

Epilogue

I found myself in that clearing. I did. I stood there, breathless and blinking in the light, and I believed I had arrived.

What I didn't know yet is that finding yourself and finding sanctuary are not the same thing. I thought they were. I thought if I could just name what was broken, the naming would fix it. And for a while, it felt like it did. I had a diagnosis I understood. I had medication that worked. I had faith I could articulate. I had a family forming around me like the life I'd been drafting since I was a little girl in Mrs. Feldman's class.

Nevertheless, the clearing wasn't the destination. It was just the place where I could finally see clearly enough to recognize what came next.

What came next was the worst storm of my life. Not the slow, disorienting fog of undiagnosed years. Not the manic waves I'd learned to ride. Something closer to the undertow that pulled me out at ten— except this time, the ocean had hands.

I will tell that story, but not here.

Here, I want to leave you with what the storm taught me because it's the thing I wish someone had told me in my darkest chapter: the sanctuary I'd been searching for… in a man, in a family, in a life that looked like the one I'd planned? That was never going to hold. Not because those things don't matter. They do. It's because I was asking them to be God, and they are not God.

The sanctuary held. It just wasn't where I thought I'd built it.

It was in the One who went under the waves to hold me up. It was always Him.

I am still fearfully, wonderfully, and bipolar-ly made, and the story God is authoring isn't over yet.

Acknowledgments

To the God who went under the waves to hold me up—every page of this book is Yours. You knew the story before I had the courage to tell it, and You gave me the courage anyway.

To my parents, who loved me fiercely even when my emotions filled every room in the house. Mom, you fought the current for me before I knew I was drowning. Dad, you taught me strength even when we didn't have the language for what I was carrying. This book is part of that language. I hope it builds a bridge.

To Mama Marci Welker, who answers every call. You have held me steady through storms I couldn't name and ones I could. Joshua's life— and his death—gave me the urgency to stop hiding and start writing. This book exists because he lived, and because losing him taught me that tomorrow is not promised to any of us. I carry him with me.

To Mama Sue Fallin, my God-voice. When I couldn't hear Him clearly, I heard Him through you. Your faith in the miraculous reminded me that God is not finished with any of us.

To Gabrielle and Cari Sue Palma, my first readers and my sisters by God's grace. You read these pages when they were raw and unwieldy and loved me through every draft. Your honesty made this book better. Your belief in it kept me going.

To Mary Beth Crawford, my walking companion. I dreamed up my book walking our dogs together at Sandy Bottom Nature Park. I read parts to you in the woods, and I was met with a kindred spirit and constant encouragement. Thank you for being vulnerable enough to process life's adversities out loud with me.

To Dr. Sam Storms, whose theological generosity gave this book wings I couldn't have built alone. Your endorsement told me this message belonged in the world.

To Lydia Brownback, whose writing showed me what it looks like when faith meets the page with honesty and beauty. You gave me permission I didn't know I needed.

To Dr. Dennis Bogin, who told me I had to struggle lost in the dark wood before I could find the clearing. You were right.

To Renee Reynolds, who met with me in Zoom from Florida during the years I was untangling everything in these chapters. So much of what I learned, I learned out processing with you first.

To Dr. Lindsey Henderson, who told me when I had to let go.

To Leslie Muhlhauser—thank you for seeing me when I couldn't see myself, having the courage to tell me I had bipolar disorder before I was ready to accept it, and graciously taking me back into your care when I was. You were my first advocate.

To Lex, Molly, and Penny—you will probably never know how much you shaped this book. Your trust, honesty, and courage showed me exactly why the next generation deserves better than what we were given. You are the reason Part Three exists. I'm forever your advocate.

To my nieces and nephews—I wrote this book for you, too. Someday, whether you need it to understand me or to understand yourselves, I pray these pages meet you exactly where you are and remind you that you are not broken.

To my DBSA community, every Friday face on that Zoom screen—you remind me weekly I'm not alone and this book needed to exist. One face and story like mine at a time, you kept me writing.

To my Monday night writer's group at Tabb Library—thank you for walking alongside me as my book grow and I did. You shaped it and me.

To my Writer's Growth readers who showed up on Tuesdays and stayed—you were the first people I practiced being brave with. This book grew because you did. You challenged me to be honest. I was.

To Calista—you made me believe the dream was real. Loving you has been one of the great privileges of my life, and nothing written in these pages or beyond them will ever change that. I hope you always know: you were never a chapter. You are the whole reason I wanted the story to be beautiful.

To Tony—you taught me more about sanctuary than you will ever know. Thank you for giving me the space to write this manuscript.

About the Author

Laura Joy Palma is a career English Language Arts teacher, mental health advocate, and the voice behind writersgrowth.com, where she has written openly about faith, mental illness, and the messy middle of healing since 2015. She holds a bachelor's degree in English Education with a concentration in writing from Belmont University, a master's degree in instructional technology from Wilke's University, and is completing her gifted education endorsement through Shenandoah University.

Diagnosed with bipolar disorder type II in her mid-thirties, Laura Joy spent over a decade navigating misdiagnosis, medication, and the silence that surrounds mood disorders in the church before finding the sanctuary she writes about in these pages.

She lives in Yorktown, Virginia, where she watches the sunrise every morning from the same stretch of beach. This is her first book.

Terms and Acronyms Glossary

Acetylcholine A neurotransmitter that works with other brain chemicals to stabilize moods.

Agoraphobia An anxiety disorder characterized by fear of leaving the house or being in situations where escape might be difficult.

Antipsychotics A class of medications used to treat bipolar disorder and other mental health conditions (e.g., quetiapine).

APA (American Psychology Association) The organization that publishes the DSM diagnostic manual.

Automatic negative thoughts Thinking patterns identified by Dr. Aaron Beck that include mind-reading, all-or-nothing thinking, and fortune-telling that happen without conscious awareness.

BD (Bipolar Disorder) A medical illness characterized by alternating periods of persistent abnormally elevated and depressed moods.

BDI (Bipolar Disorder type I) A form of bipolar disorder characterized by manic episodes, with or without depressive episodes.

BDII (Bipolar Disorder type II) A form of bipolar disorder characterized by periods of depression and hypomania (less severe than full mania).

BDNF (Brain-Derived Neurotrophic Factor) A protein related to neuroplasticity and nerve growth; decreased levels are present in both depressed and manic states.

Benzodiazepines A class of medications sometimes used in treating bipolar disorder and anxiety.

Bipolar spectrum A framework for understanding mood disorders as existing on a continuum rather than in separate categories.

CBT (Cognitive Behavioral Therapy) A form of therapy focusing on changing negative thought patterns and behaviors that perpetuate problems.

Cyclothymia A milder form of bipolar disorder where a person swings between mild depression and hypomania in a chronic mood pattern.

DBT (Dialectical Behavioral Therapy) A specialized form of CBT focusing on emotional regulation, particularly helpful for people with bipolar disorder who struggle with intense feelings.

DBSA (Depression and Bipolar Support Alliance) A support organization for people with mood disorders.

Delusions False beliefs that are characteristic of certain mental health conditions.

Dopamine A neurotransmitter involved in mood regulation; imbalances can contribute to bipolar disorder.

DSM (Diagnostic and Statistical Manual of Mental Disorders) The manual used by mental health professionals for diagnosis.

DSM-5 The fifth edition of the Diagnostic and Statistical Manual, published in 2013.

DSM-5-TR The text revision of the DSM-5, published in 2022.

DSM-III The third edition of the DSM from the 1980s that first used "bipolar disorder" instead of "manic depressive disorder."

Emotional temperature regulation malfunction An analogy describing how mood disorders affect the brain's ability to maintain emotional equilibrium.

GABA (gamma-aminobutyric acid) A neurotransmitter that works with other brain chemicals to stabilize moods.

Glutamate A neurotransmitter involved in mood stability that may be dysregulated in bipolar disorder.

Hallucinations Sensory experiences that aren't based in reality, sometimes present in severe mental health conditions.

Hypomania A milder form of mania with the same symptoms but shorter duration (days rather than weeks) and less severe impairment.

Latuda A brand name for lurasidone, an antipsychotic medication used to treat bipolar disorder.

Lithium A mood stabilizer considered the "gold standard" for bipolar disorder treatment, requiring regular blood work monitoring.

Major depressive episode A period of severe depression lasting at least two weeks, characterized by persistent sadness, loss of interest, and other symptoms that interfere with daily functioning.

Manic episode A period of abnormally elevated energy and mood lasting at least a week (or requiring hospitalization) that interferes with functioning.

MDD (Major Depressive Disorder) A mood disorder characterized by persistent depressed mood without the manic episodes seen in bipolar disorder; also called unipolar depression.

Mechanism of action The way a medication works at the cellular level in the body.

Mixed state/mixed episode A condition where a person experiences both manic and depressive symptoms simultaneously.

Mood episodes Distinct periods of abnormal mood (manic, hypomanic, or depressive) that provide data for bipolar disorder diagnosis.

Mood stabilizers A class of medications used to treat bipolar disorder (e.g., lithium, lurasidone).

NEC (Not Elsewhere Classified) A diagnostic label for bipolar cases that don't fit standard categories.

Neuroplasticity The brain's capacity to constantly remodel itself in response to environmental changes; enhanced by certain medications.

Neurons Brain cells that process information; described as "little processors" that can be reprogrammed.

Norepinephrine A neurotransmitter involved in mood regulation; imbalances can contribute to bipolar disorder.

NOS (Not Otherwise Specified) A diagnostic label for bipolar cases that don't meet full criteria for other types.

Nortriptyline A tricyclic antidepressant sometimes used for nerve pain and depression.

Quetiapine An antipsychotic medication commonly used to treat bipolar disorder, particularly effective for sleep and mood management.

Receptors Locations in the brain where neurochemicals are blocked or utilized, targeted by different medications.

Schizoaffective disorder A diagnosis given when bipolar disorder symptoms are accompanied by delusions and hallucinations.

Serotonin A neurotransmitter involved in mood regulation; imbalances can contribute to bipolar disorder.

"Soft" bipolar disorders A term challenging traditional mood disorder classifications, recognizing patients who fall on the bipolar spectrum without meeting strict diagnostic criteria.

Stimulants A class of medications sometimes used in treating ADHD, which may co-occur with bipolar disorder.

TCA (Tricyclic Antidepressant) A class of antidepressant medications that work by keeping more norepinephrine and serotonin available for use.

Telehealth Remote healthcare delivery through technology, preferred by some therapy patients.

Unipolar depression Depression without manic episodes; also called major depressive disorder.

ABC News. "Catherine Zeta-Jones Sheds Light on Bipolar II Disorder." *ABC News*, April 14, 2011. https://abcnews.go.com/Health/BipolarDisorder/catherine-zeta-jones-sheds-light-bipolar-disorder/story?id=13373202.

Angst, Jules, and Andreas Marneros. "Bipolarity from Ancient to Modern Times: Conception, Birth and Rebirth." *Journal of Affective Disorders* 67, no. 1-3 (December 1, 2001): 3–19. https://doi.org/10.1016/s0165-0327(01)00429-3.

Apple Podcasts. "I'm a Christian Who…Has Bipolar Disorder." October 16, 2023. https://podcasts.apple.com/us/podcast/im-a-christian-who-has-bipolar-disorder/id1708344645?i=1000631524424.

Behrman, Andy. *Electroboy: A Memoir of Mania*. New York: Random House Trade Paperbacks, 2003.

Brand, Russell. *Recovery: Freedom from Our Addictions*. New York: Picador, 2018.

Byrne, Suzy. "Yeah so I Cried My Way through Demi Lovato's Stay Strong TV Special." *Glamour*, March 7, 2012. https://www.glamour.com/story/yeah-so-i-cried-my-way-through.

Cagle, Jess. "Mariah Carey: My Battle with Bipolar Disorder." *People*, April 11, 2018. https://people.com/music/mariah-carey-bipolar-disorder-diagnosis-exclusive.

Cheney, Terri. *Manic*. New York: Harper Collins, 2009.

Erford, Bradley T. *40 Techniques Every Counselor Should Know*. 2nd ed. Boston: Pearson, 2020.

Fast, Julie A., and John Preston. *Take Charge of Bipolar Disorder*. New York: Balance, 2023.

Favor Hamilton, Suzy. *Fast Girl*. New York: HarperCollins, 2015.

Fink, Candida, and Joe Kraynak. *Bipolar Disorder for Dummies*. Hoboken, New Jersey: John Wiley And Sons Inc, 2016.

Fisher, Carrie. "I'm Bipolar – How Do You Feel at Peace with Mental Illness?" *The Guardian*, November 30, 2016. https://www.theguardian.com/lifeandstyle/2016/nov/30/carrie-fisher-advice-column-mental-illness-bipolar-disorder.

———. *Wishful Drinking*. New York: Simon and Schuster, 2008.

Fritz, Kristina, Alex M. T. Russell, Christine Allwang, Sandy Kuiper, Lisa Lampe, and Gin S. Malhi. "Is a Delay in the Diagnosis of Bipolar Disorder Inevitable?" *Bipolar Disorders* 19, no. 5 (May 22, 2017): 396–400. https://doi.org/10.1111/bdi.12499.

Gansa, Alex. "Homeland." TV Series. Showtime, 2011-2020.

Ghaemi, Nassir. *A First-Rate Madness: Uncovering the Links between Leadership and Mental Illness*. New York: Penguin Books, 2012.

Ghaemi, S. Nassir. *Mood Disorders: A Practical Guide*. Philadelphia: Lippincott Williams & Wilkins, 2008.

Groves, J. Alasdair, and Winston T. Smith. *Untangling Emotions*. Wheaton, Illinois: Crossway, 2019.

Guy-Evans, Olivia. "Grandiosity: How a Person with Bipolar Thinks." *Simply Psychology*, November 3, 2022. https://www.simplypsychology.org/grandiosity-in-bipolar-disorder.html#Grandiosity-Vs-Delusions-Of-Grandeur.

Herrman, C. S. "Learning to Live Responsibly with Bipolar Illness." *SSRN Electronic Journal*, January 11, 2011. https://doi.org/10.2139/ssrn.1737705.

Jamison, Kay Redfield. *An Unquiet Mind: A Memoir of Moods and Madness*. 1995. Reprint, New York: Vintage Books, 2011.

———. *Exuberance: The Passion for Life*. New York: Vintage Books, 2005.

———. *Touched with Fire: Manic-Depressive Illness and the Artistic Temperament*. New York: Free Press Paperbacks, 1994.

Keramatian, Kamyar, Jairo V. Pinto, Ayal Schaffer, Verinder Sharma, Serge Beaulieu, Sagar V. Parikh, and Lakshmi N. Yatham. "Clinical and Demographic Factors

Associated with Delayed Diagnosis of Bipolar Disorder: Data from Health Outcomes and Patient Evaluations in Bipolar Disorder (HOPE-BD) Study." *Journal of Affective Disorders* 296 (January 1, 2022): 506–13. https://doi.org/10.1016/j.jad.2021.09.094.

Lau, Paige. "Mental Illness, Normalization, and the Construction of the Abnormal Subject." *Furman Humanities Review* 34 (November 17, 2023): 63–82. https://scholarexchange.furman.edu/fhr/vol34/iss1/5.

Lohmann, Raychelle Cassada. *15-Minute Focus: Growth Mindset, Resilience, and Grit.* National Center for Youth Issues, 2022.

McElroy, Susan L., Renu Kotwal, Paul E. Keck, and Hagop S. Akiskal. "Comorbidity of Bipolar and Eating Disorders: Distinct or Related Disorders with Shared Dysregulations?" *Journal of Affective Disorders* 86, no. 2-3 (June 2005): 107–27. https://doi.org/10.1016/j.jad.2004.11.008.

McKidd, Kevin. "Grey's Anatomy." TV series episode. ABC Network, March 19, 2020.

Mondimore, Francis Mark. *Bipolar Disorder: A Guide for You & Your Loved Ones.* 4th ed. Baltimore: Johns Hopkins University Press, 2020.

Morgan, Reuben. *Cornerstone.* CD. Hillsong Worship, 2012.

Morton, Emma, Erin E. Michalak, Rachelle Hole, Simone Buzwell, and Greg Murray. "'Taking Back the Reins' – a Qualitative Study of the Meaning and Experience of Self-Management in Bipolar Disorder." *Journal of Affective Disorders* 228 (March 2018): 160–65. https://doi.org/10.1016/j.jad.2017.12.018.

Murray, David, and Tom Karel. *A Christian's Guide to Mental Illness.* Wheaton, Illinois: Crossway, 2023.

National Institute of Mental Health. "COVID-19 and Mental Health - National Institute of Mental Health (NIMH)." May 2024. https://www.nimh.nih.gov/health/topics/covid-19-and-mental-health.

One Flew over the Cuckoo's Nest. Film. United States: United Artists, 1975.

Ortlund, Dane. *Gentle and Lowly: The Heart of Christ for Sinners and Sufferers.* Wheaton, Illinois: Crossway, 2020.

Palma, Laura Joy. "I Used to Be." *Writer's Growth,* March 10, 2015. https://writersgrowth.com/2015/03/10/i-used-to-be.

———. "Like Grains of Sand." *Writer's Growth*, August 15, 2017.
https://writersgrowth.com/2017/08/15/like-grains-of-sand/.

———. "Maybe Half Full." *Writer's Growth*, October 9, 2018.
https://writersgrowth.com/2018/10/09/maybe-half-full/.

———. "Show Me a Sign: Lessons from an Alchemist." *Writer's Growth*, February 22,
2017. https://writersgrowth.com/2017/02/21/show-me-a-sign/.

———. "The Silver Lining in Suffering: A Dying Woman Believes for More Milestones
– REV." *MyRevApp*. REV, 2023. https://myrev.app/stories/the-silver-lining-in-
suffering-a-dying-woman-believes-for-more-milestones/.

———. "When Why's Lack Faith." *Writer's Growth*, April 7, 2015.
https://writersgrowth.com/2015/04/07/when-whys-lack-faith/.

Panchal, Nirmita, Heather Saunders, Robin Rudowitz, and Cynthia Cox. "The
Implications of COVID-19 for Mental Health and Substance Use." *KFF*, March
20, 2023. https://www.kff.org/mental-health/issue-brief/the-implications-of-
covid-19-for-mental-health-and-substance-use/.

Perales, Laura Joy. "Make Me See and Make Me Feel: Empathy and Meaning United."
Perception Educational Journal 1, no. 4 (August 7, 2010).

———. "Mania—Madness or Revelation." Unpublished manuscript, October 23, 2009.

Phang, Kar Cheng, Ling Shian Keng, and Chong Kai Chiang. "Mindful-S.T.O.P.:
Mindfulness Made Easy for Stress Reduction in Medical Students." *Education in
Medicine Journal* 6, no. 2 (June 1, 2014). https://doi.org/10.5959/eimj.v6i2.230.

Preuss, Ulrich W., Martin Schaefer, Christoph Born, and Heinz Grunze. "Bipolar
Disorder and Comorbid Use of Illicit Substances." *Medicina* 57, no. 11 (November
17, 2021): 1256. https://doi.org/10.3390/medicina57111256.

Rexha, Bebe (@BebeRexha). "I'm bipolar and I'm not ashamed anymore. That is all.
(Crying my eyes out.)." Twitter, April 15, 2019, 1:14 PM.
https://x.com/BebeRexha/status/1117838545538805761.

Riley, Cortney. "Demi Lovato Releases Powerful Mental Health Documentary." *Camber
Children's Mental Health*, March 1, 2017.
https://www.cambermentalhealth.org/2017/03/01/mental-health-documentary/.

Rusner, Marie, Gunilla Carlsson, David Brunt, and Maria Nyström. "A Dependence
That Empowers—the Meaning of the Conditions That Enable a Good Life with
Bipolar Disorder." *International Journal of Qualitative Studies on Health and Well-Being* 5,
no. 1 (January 2010): 4653. https://doi.org/10.3402/qhw.v5i1.4653.

Sink, Christopher A. *Mental Health Interventions for School Counselors*. Belmont, CA:
Brooks/Cole Cengage Learning, 2011.

Sit, Dorothy. "Women and Bipolar Disorder across the Life Span." *Journal of the American
Medical Women's Association* 59, no. 2 (2004): 91–100.
https://www.ncbi.nlm.nih.gov/pmc/articles/PMC3107596.

Storms, Sam. *Singing God*. Creation House, 1998.

Street, John. "The Sufficiency and Superiority of Scripture in Addressing Bipolar
Depression." Grace Community Church, 2019.
https://www.gracechurch.org/sermons/16065.

Walsh, John. "Being Ernest: John Walsh Unravels the Mystery behind Hemingway's
Suicide." *The Independent*, June 10, 2011.
https://www.independent.co.uk/news/people/profiles/being-ernest-john-walsh-
unravels-the-mystery-behind-hemingway-s-suicide-2294619.html.

Welch, Edward T. *Blame It on the Brain?: Distinguishing Chemical Imbalances, Brain Disorders,
and Disobedience*. Phillipsburg, N.J.: P & R Pub, 1998.

WilkesUVideo. "Spring Commencement 2012 - Laura Joy Speech." YouTube. Wilkes
University, May 31, 2012. https://www.youtube.com/watch?v=c7cZW80jLk4.

World Health Organization. "COVID-19 Pandemic Triggers 25% Increase in
Prevalence of Anxiety and Depression Worldwide." *World Health Organization*,
March 2, 2022. https://www.who.int/news/item/02-03-2022-covid-19-pandemic-
triggers-25-increase-in-prevalence-of-anxiety-and-depression-worldwide.

Yarborough, Micah, and Betty Jo Yarborough. *My Anchor Holds within the Veil*.
Createspace Independent Publishing Platform, 2018.

Notes

Chapter One

1 Laura Joy Palma, "Maybe Half Full," Writer's Growth, October 10, 2018, https://writersgrowth.com/2018/10/09/maybe-half-full/.

2 Kay Redfield Jamison, *An Unquiet Mind: A Memoir of Moods and Madness* (1995; repr., New York: Vintage Books, 2011), xi–xii.

3 Mariah Carey, quoted in Jess Cagle, "Mariah Carey: My Battle with Bipolar Disorder," *People*, April 11, 2018, https://people.com/music/mariah-carey-bipolar-disorder-diagnosis-exclusive.

4 Candida Fink and Joe Kraynak, *Bipolar Disorder for Dummies* (Hoboken, New Jersey: John Wiley And Sons Inc, 2016), 7–8.

5 Fink and Kraynak, Bipolar Disorder for Dummies, 9–10.

6 Fink and Kraynak, *Bipolar Disorder for Dummies*, 11–12.

7 Fink and Kraynak, *Bipolar Disorder for Dummies*, 13–15.

8 Francis Mark Mondimore, *Bipolar Disorder: A Guide for You & Your Loved Ones*, 4th ed. (Baltimore: Johns Hopkins University Press, 2020), 30-55.

9 Mondimore, *Bipolar Disorder*, 48-51.

10 Suzy Favor Hamilton, *Fast Girl* (New York: HarperCollins, 2015), 35.

11 Carrie Fisher, *Wishful Drinking* (Simon and Schuster, 2008), 11-13.

12 "Catherine Zeta-Jones Sheds Light on Bipolar II Disorder," *ABC News*, April 14, 2011, https://abcnews.go.com/Health/BipolarDisorder/catherine-zeta-jones-sheds-light-bipolar-disorder/story?id=13373202.

13 Russell Brand, *Recovery: Freedom from Our Addictions* (New York: Picador, 2018).

14 Suzy Byrne, "Yeah so I Cried My Way through Demi Lovato's Stay Strong TV
    Special," *Glamour*, March 7, 2012, https://www.glamour.com/story/yeah-
    so-i-cried-my-way-through.

15 Cortney Riley, "Demi Lovato Releases Powerful Mental Health
    Documentary," *Camber Children's Mental Health*, March 1, 2017,
    https://www.cambermentalhealth.org/2017/03/01/mental-health-
    documentary/.

Chapter Two

16 Carrie Fisher, "I'm Bipolar – How Do You Feel at Peace with Mental Illness?"
    The Guardian, November 30, 2016,
    https://www.theguardian.com/lifeandstyle/2016/nov/30/carrie-fisher-
    advice-column-mental-illness-bipolar-disorder.

17 Kamyar Keramatian et al., "Clinical and Demographic Factors Associated
    with Delayed Diagnosis of Bipolar Disorder: Data from Health Outcomes
    and Patient Evaluations in Bipolar Disorder (HOPE-BD) Study," *Journal of
    Affective Disorders* 296 (January 1, 2022): 506–13,
    https://doi.org/10.1016/j.jad.2021.09.094.

18 as described in Kristina Fritz et al. "Is a Delay in the Diagnosis of Bipolar
    Disorder Inevitable?" *Bipolar Disorders* 19, no. 5, (May 22, 2017): 396–400,
    https://doi.org/10.1111/bdi.12499.

19 Favor Hamilton, *Fast Girl*, 122–124.

20 Mondimore, Bipolar Disorder, 113.

21 Terri Cheney, *Manic* (New York: Harper Collins, 2009), 1–18.

22 Laura Joy Palma, "I Used to Be," *Writer's Growth*, March 10, 2015,
    https://writersgrowth.com/2015/03/10/i-used-to-be.

23 Olivia Guy-Evans. "Grandiosity: How a Person with Bipolar Thinks." Simply
    Psychology, 3 Nov. 2022, www.simplypsychology.org/grandiosity-in-
    bipolar-disorder.html#Grandiosity-Vs-Delusions-Of-Grandeur.

Chapter Three

24 Dorothy Sit, "Women and Bipolar Disorder Across the Life Span," *Journal of
    the American Medical Women's Association* 59, no. 2 (2004): 91–100,
    https://www.ncbi.nlm.nih.gov/pmc/articles/PMC3107596/.

25 Susan L. McElroy et al., "Comorbidity of Bipolar and Eating Disorders: Distinct or Related Disorders with Shared Dysregulations?" *Journal of Affective Disorders* 86, no. 2-3 (June 2005): 107–27, https://doi.org/10.1016/j.jad.2004.11.008.

26 Ulrich W. Preuss et al., "Bipolar Disorder and Comorbid Use of Illicit Substances," *Medicina* 57, no. 11 (November 17, 2021): 1256, https://doi.org/10.3390/medicina57111256.

Chapter Four

27 World Health Organization, "COVID-19 Pandemic Triggers 25% Increase in Prevalence of Anxiety and Depression Worldwide," *World Health Organization*, March 2, 2022, https://www.who.int/news/item/02-03-2022-covid-19-pandemic-triggers-25-increase-in-prevalence-of-anxiety-and-depression-worldwide.

28 Nirmita Panchal et al., "The Implications of COVID-19 for Mental Health and Substance Use," *KFF*, March 20, 2023, https://www.kff.org/mental-health/issue-brief/the-implications-of-covid-19-for-mental-health-and-substance-use/.

29 National Institute of Mental Health, "COVID-19 and Mental Health - National Institute of Mental Health (NIMH)," May 2024, https://www.nimh.nih.gov/health/topics/covid-19-and-mental-health.

Chapter Five

30 Laura Joy Perales. "Mania—Madness or Revelation," unpublished manuscript, October 23 2009.

31 Mondimore, *Bipolar Disorder*, 3.

32 Mondimore, *Bipolar Disorder*, 3.

33 Mondimore, *Bipolar Disorder*, 3.

34 Jules Angst and Andreas Marneros, "Bipolarity from Ancient to Modern Times: Conception, Birth and Rebirth," *Journal of Affective Disorders* 67, no. 1-3 (December 1, 2001): 3–19, https://doi.org/10.1016/s0165-0327(01)00429-3.

35 Angst and Marneros, "Bipolarity from Ancient to Modern Times."

36 Jean-Pierre Falret, *De la folie circulaire ou forme de maladie mentale caracterise´e par l'alternative re´gulie´re de la manie et de la me´lancolie*, Bull. Acad. Natl. Med. (Paris), 1851, quoted in Angst and Marneros, "Bipolarity from Ancient to Modern Times."

37 Angst and Marneros, "Bipolarity from Ancient to Modern Times."

38 Nassir Ghaemi, A First-Rate Madness: Uncovering the Links between Leadership and Mental Illness (New York: Penguin Books, 2012), 3.

39 Ghaemi, A First-Rate Madness,3-4.

40 Ghaemi, A First-Rate Madness, 26.

41 Mondimore, *Bipolar Disorder*, 257.

42 Kay Redfield Jamison, *Touched with Fire: Manic-Depressive Illness and the Artistic Temperament* (New York: Free Press Paperbacks, 1994), 203–5, cited in Mondimore, *Bipolar Disorder*, 257.

43 Kay Redfield Jamison, *Exuberance: The Passion for Life* (New York: Vintage Books, 2005), 150–51.

44 Ghaemi, A First-Rate Madness, 26.

45 Cheney, *Manic*, 15.

Chapter Six

46 Joshua Wolf Shenk, *Lincoln's Melancholy* (Boston: Houghton Mifflin, 2005), quoted in Ghaemi, *A First-Rate Madness*, 70.

47 Ghaemi, A First-Rate Madness,70-71.

48 Fisher, *Wishful Drinking*, 116-121.

49 Jamison, *An Unquiet Mind*, 63.

50 Hamilton, *Fast Girl*, 101-124.

51 Cheney, *Manic*, 5-21.

52 Cheney, *Manic*, 21.

53 Laura Joy Palma, "Like Grains of Sand," *Writer's Growth*, August 15, 2017, https://writersgrowth.com/2017/08/15/like-grains-of-sand/.

54 Cheney, *Manic*, 1.

Chapter Eight

55 Jamison, *An Unquiet Mind*, 81.

56 Mondimore, *Bipolar Disorder*, 191.

57 Mondimore, *Bipolar Disorder*, 195-196.

58 Fast and Preston, Take Charge of Bipolar Disorder, 47.

Chapter Nine

59 Mondimore, *Bipolar Disorder*, 156.

60 Fast and Preston, Take Charge of Bipolar Disorder, 18.

61 Fink and Kraynak, Bipolar Disorder for Dummies, 228.

62 Mondimore, *Bipolar Disorder*, 292.

63 Fink and Kraynak, Bipolar Disorder for Dummies, 230.

64 Mondimore, *Bipolar Disorder*, 291.

65 Fast and Preston, *Take Charge of Bipolar Disorder*, 19, 131-132.

66 Fink and Kraynak, Bipolar Disorder for Dummies, 228.

67 Janine Crowley Haynes, quoted in Fink and Kraynak, *Bipolar Disorder for Dummies*, 235.

68 Mondimore, *Bipolar Disorder*, 210.

69 Fink and Kraynak, *Bipolar Disorder for Dummies*, 242-243.

70 Fink and Kraynak, *Bipolar Disorder for Dummies*, 241-242.

71 Fast and Preston, Take Charge of Bipolar Disorder, 87-91.

72 Fast and Preston, Take Charge of Bipolar Disorder, 87.

73 Mondimore, *Bipolar Disorder*, 160.

74 Mondimore, *Bipolar Disorder*, 168.

75 Mondimore, *Bipolar Disorder*, 160.

76 Mondimore, *Bipolar Disorder*, 162-165.

77 Mondimore, *Bipolar Disorder*, 165.

78 Mondimore, *Bipolar Disorder*, 161.

79 Matthew 19:26 ESV.

Chapter Ten

80 Ghaemi, A First-Rate Madness,10-11.

81 Ghaemi, A First-Rate Madness,7.

82 Mondimore, *Bipolar Disorder*, 30-55.

83 Mondimore, *Bipolar Disorder*, 51.

84 Mondimore, *Bipolar Disorder*, 196.

85 Mondimore, *Bipolar Disorder*, 218-224.

86 Fast and Preston, Take Charge of Bipolar Disorder, 48-49; Mondimore, Bipolar Disorder, 198.

87 Mondimore, *Bipolar Disorder*, 198.

88 Fink and Kraynak, Bipolar Disorder for Dummies, 240.

89 Fisher, *Wishful Drinking*, 121.

90 Ghaemi, A First-Rate Madness, 58-61.

91 David Owen, In Sickness and in Power: Illness in Heads of Government During the Last 100 Years (Westport, CT: Praeger, 2008), 41 as quoted in Ghaemi, A First-Rate Madness, 60.

Chapter Eleven

92 Cheney, *Manic*, 162.

93 C. S. Herrman, "Learning to Live Responsibly with Bipolar Illness," SSRN Electronic Journal, January 11, 2011, https://doi.org/10.2139/ssrn.1737705.

94 Herrman, "Learning to Live Responsibly with Bipolar Illness."

95 Emma Morton et al., "'Taking Back the Reins' – a Qualitative Study of the Meaning and Experience of Self-Management in Bipolar Disorder," *Journal of Affective Disorders* 228 (March 2018): 160–65, https://doi.org/10.1016/j.jad.2017.12.018.

96 Marie Rusner et al., "A Dependence That Empowers—the Meaning of the Conditions That Enable a Good Life with Bipolar Disorder," *International Journal of Qualitative Studies on Health and Well-Being* 5, no. 1 (January 2010): 4653, https://doi.org/10.3402/qhw.v5i1.4653.

97 Rusner et al., "A Dependence That Empowers."

98 Five steps outlined in Rusner et al., "A Dependence That Empowers." 1) Turning the course; 2)Protecting ourselves from running out of energy; 3) Being oneself through reliable others; 4) Being needed by others; and 5) Using personal landmarks to navigate life.

99 One Flew over the Cuckoo's Nest, film (United States: United Artists, 1975).

100 Alex Gansa, "Homeland," TV series (Showtime, 2011-2020).

101 Kevin McKidd, "Grey's Anatomy," TV series episode (ABC Network, March 19, 2020).

102 Cheney, *Manic*, 13.

103 Bebe Rexha (@BebeRexha), "I'm bipolar and I'm not ashamed anymore. That is all. (Crying my eyes out.)," Twitter, April 15, 2019, 1:14 PM, https://x.com/BebeRexha/status/1117838545538805761.

104 Genesis 50:20 ESV.

Chapter Twelve

105 WilkesUVideo, "Spring Commencement 2012 - Laura Joy Speech," YouTube, Wilkes University, May 31, 2012, https://www.youtube.com/watch?v=c7cZW80jLk4.

106 Laura Joy Perales, "Make Me See and Make Me Feel: Empathy and Meaning United," *Perception Educational Journal* 1, no. 4 (August 7, 2010).

107 Raychelle Cassada Lohmann, *15-Minute Focus: Growth Mindset, Resilience, and Grit* (National Center for Youth Issues, 2022), 17.

108 Sink, Mental Health Interventions for School Counselors, 41-42.

109 Sink, Mental Health Interventions for School Counselors, 44.

110 Paige Lau, "Mental Illness, Normalization, and the Construction of the Abnormal Subject," *Furman Humanities Review* 34 (November 17, 2023): 63–82, https://scholarexchange.furman.edu/fhr/vol34/iss1/5.

111 Lau, "Mental Illness, Normalization, and the Construction."

112 Bradley T. Erford, *40 Techniques Every Counselor Should Know*, 2nd ed. (Boston: Pearson, 2020), 3-4.

113 Erford, 40 Techniques Every Counselor Should Know, 4-8.

114 Erford, 40 Techniques Every Counselor Should Know, 93-94.

115 S. Nassir Ghaemi, *Mood Disorders: A Practical Guide* (Philadelphia: Lippincott Williams & Wilkins, 2008), 12-14.

116 2 Corinthians 1:3-4 ESV.

117 Erford, 40 Techniques Every Counselor Should Know, 127.

118 Erford, 40 Techniques Every Counselor Should Know, 130.

119 Kar Cheng Phang, Ling Shian Keng, and Chong Kai Chiang, "Mindful-S.T.O.P.: Mindfulness Made Easy for Stress Reduction in Medical Students," *Education in Medicine Journal* 6, no. 2 (June 1, 2014), https://doi.org/10.5959/eimj.v6i2.230.

Chapter Thirteen

[120] James 4:17 ESV.

[121] Sam Storms, *Singing God* (Creation House, 1998).

[122] Inspired by Jesus' words in the parable in Matthew 18:21-22 ESV.

[123] Edward T. Welch, Blame It on the Brain?: Distinguishing Chemical Imbalances, Brain Disorders, and Disobedience (Phillipsburg, N.J.: P & R Pub, 1998), 15.

[124] Welch, Blame It on the Brain?, 28-33.

[125] Welch, Blame It on the Brain?, 60.

[126] Genesis 2:24 ESV.

[127] Laura Joy Palma, "Show Me a Sign," *Writer's Growth*, February 22, 2017, https://writersgrowth.com/2017/02/21/show-me-a-sign/.

Chapter Fourteen

[128] The Gospel Coalition is a Reformed evangelical ministry founded by D. A. Carson and Tim Keller and revolved around a shared commitment to the gospel of Jesus Christ. They offer resources for Christians and local churches.

[129] Colossians 3:1-3 ESV.

[130] Colossians 3:15-17 ESV.

[131] Colossians 3:5, 3:8; quoted from Colossians 3:9-10 ESV.

[132] The Gospel as paraphrased from Romans 3:23, 6:4; John 3:16, 4:14; Hebrews 4:15; 1 Corinthians 15:3-4; Ephesians 2:8-9; Colossians 3:9-10 ESV.

[133] Dane Ortlund, Gentle and Lowly: The Heart of Christ for Sinners and Sufferers (Wheaton, Illinois: Crossway, 2020).

[134] Paraphrased from 1 John 2:1; Hebrews 4:16, 7:25; Ephesians 2:8-9 ESV.

[135] David Murray and Tom Karel, *A Christian's Guide to Mental Illness* (Crossway, 2023), 5.

[136] Paraphrased from Colossians 1:17; Revelation 1:8; Isaiah 57:15; Habakkuk 1:13; Malachi 3:6; 1 Timothy 2:5; Hebrews 9:26 ESV.

[137] Paraphrased from Isaiah 6:1-5; quoted from Isaiah 6:6-7 ESV.

[138] Drawn from Isaiah 6:6-7, 53:5; John 3:16; Ephesians 1:7; Romans 8:1.

139 "I'm a Christian Who…Has Bipolar Disorder," *Apple Podcasts*, October 16, 2023, https://podcasts.apple.com/us/podcast/im-a-christian-who-has-bipolar-disorder/id1708344645?i=1000631524424.

140 Depicted in 1 Samuel 16:14, 18:8-9, 19:9-10, 20:30, 22:1, 28:15 ESV.

141 Depicted in Psalm 32:3-4, 34:18, 42:5; 51:1-3, 57:1-3; 1 Samuel 19:18-24 ESV.

142 Drawn from Psalm 42:11, 46:1, 62:8, 73:26, 91:2, 147:3 ESV.

143 Reuben Morgan, *Cornerstone*, CD (Hillsong Worship, 2012).

144 Laura Joy Palma, "The Silver Lining in Suffering: A Dying Woman Believes for More Milestones – REV" *MyRevApp*, REV, 2023, https://myrev.app/stories/the-silver-lining-in-suffering-a-dying-woman-believes-for-more-milestones/.

145 J. Alasdair Groves and Winston T. Smith, *Untangling Emotions* (Wheaton, Illinois: Crossway, 2019), 60-61.

146 Gal. 5:22-23a ESV.

147 Micah T. Yarborough and Betty Jo H. Yarborough, *My Anchor Holds within the Veil* (Createspace Independent Publishing Platform, 2018), 46-47.

148 Micah and Betty Jo Yarborough, *My Anchor Holds within the Veil*, 78.

149 Micah and Betty Jo Yarborough, *My Anchor Holds within the Veil*, 79.

150 Micah and Betty Jo Yarborough, *My Anchor Holds within the Veil*, 97.

151 Micah and Betty Jo Yarborough, *My Anchor Holds within the Veil*, 115.